**IT'S NEVER DONE
THAT BEFORE!**

IT'S NEVER DONE THAT BEFORE!

A Guide to Troubleshooting Windows XP

by John Ross

NO STARCH
PRESS

San Francisco

IT'S NEVER DONE THAT BEFORE! Copyright © 2006 by John Ross.

 Printed on recycled paper in the United States of America

1 2 3 4 5 6 7 8 9 10 – 09 08 07 06

No Starch Press and the No Starch Press logo are registered trademarks of No Starch Press, Inc. Other product and company names mentioned herein may be the trademarks of their respective owners. Rather than use a trademark symbol with every occurrence of a trademarked name, we are using the names only in an editorial fashion and to the benefit of the trademark owner, with no intention of infringement of the trademark.

Publisher: William Pollock
Managing Editor: Elizabeth Campbell
Cover and Interior Design: Octopod Studios
Developmental Editor: Peter Spear
Copyeditors: Judy Flynn and Publication Services, Inc.
Compositor: Riley Hoffman
Proofreader: Stephanie Provines
Indexer: Publication Services, Inc.

For information on book distributors or translations, please contact No Starch Press, Inc. directly:

No Starch Press, Inc.
555 De Haro Street, Suite 250, San Francisco, CA 94107
phone: 415.863.9900; fax: 415.863.9950; info@nostarch.com; www.nostarch.com

Library of Congress Cataloging-in-Publication Data

```
Ross, John, 1947-
  It's never done that before! : a guide to troubleshooting Windows XP / John Ross.
      p. cm.
  Includes index.
  ISBN 1-59327-139-5
  1.  Microsoft Windows (Computer file) 2.  Operating systems (Computers)  I. Title.
  QA76.76.O63R682 2006
  005.4'46--dc22
                                                         2005028821
```

BRIEF CONTENTS

CONTENTS IN DETAIL

3
WHAT TO DO WHEN WINDOWS WON'T START   39

4
BLACK SCREENS AND BLUE SCREENS   55

5
SOLVING DEVICE DRIVER PROBLEMS   65

6
USING THE MICROSOFT KNOWLEDGE BASE AND OTHER ONLINE RESOURCES 75

7
USING SYSTEM RESTORE AND OTHER ROLLBACK TECHNIQUES 89

8
UNDERNEATH IT ALL: THE BIOS 97

9
THE WINDOWS REGISTRY: HERE BE DEMONS 107

14
LOCAL NETWORK PROBLEMS 157

15
DEALING WITH HARDWARE PROBLEMS 165

16
TROUBLESHOOTING AND REPLACING HARD DRIVES 175

17
TROUBLESHOOTING AND REPLACING
OTHER HARDWARE   193

18
IF ALL ELSE FAILS . . . CALL TECH SUPPORT   209

ACKNOWLEDGMENTS

This book carries my name as author, but it has been improved through the efforts of many other people. In particular, thanks to Bill Pollock for his guidance in moving from concept to finished book, and to Peter Spear for his editorial attention and advice. The editorial and production staff at No Starch Press, including Riley Hoffman and Elizabeth Campbell, have made the book far better than it might otherwise have been. As always, their professionalism and enthusiasm make working with them a pleasure.

INTRODUCTION

This book was inspired by the cover of a *Datamation* magazine that appeared about 20 years ago. It shows a man in an office with what used to be a desktop computer on the table in front of him. The poor guy has his hands poised over the keyboard, but the rest of the machine is in tiny pieces all over the room. His eyebrows have been burned off, his hair is blown straight back, and his coffee cup has tipped over. There's a huge cloud of black smoke over his head. It's obvious that the computer exploded about five seconds earlier. He's thinking, "It's never done that before."

Most computer problems aren't that violent or that dramatic, but the immediate result is often the same: you sit there in a state of shock, staring at the computer, saying to yourself, "What happened? What should I do now? It's never done *that* before!" This book will tell you how to understand and fix most personal computer failures, whether they were caused by the computer hardware, by the Windows operating system, or by some other program running on the computer.

There's not much you can do when your computer explodes except to sweep up the remains and open a window to let the smoke out of the room. But if Windows won't start, or your hard drive breaks down, or you get a cryptic Blue Screen error message, or any of a jillion other things go wrong, you can almost always restore the machine to useful operation and recover most of your data if you take an organized approach to troubleshooting. The tools for understanding most computer problems are out there on the Internet, in manuals and user guides, and through both on- and offline communities of people who use similar equipment and programs. But they won't do you any good unless you know where to find them. That's what this book is for.

This is a book for people who use their computers all the time but who don't always know how to deal with the major and minor problems that eventually seem to attack most computers. It will tell you how to apply troubleshooting techniques and methods to evaluate and solve computer problems, with an emphasis on computers running Windows XP. It won't tell you exactly what to do for *every possible* problem that might appear, but it will tell you where to find detailed explanations of most problems and instructions for fixing them. I will also show you how to recognize specific symptoms and how to understand and use error messages, beep codes, and other diagnostic tools that aren't always clear on first inspection. I'll also show you where to find help from Microsoft, from other manufacturers and users, and from the Combined Wisdom of the Internet. And finally, I will tell you how to decide if the time and cost of a repair just isn't worth the effort.

Equally important, as the book's author, I've made every effort to reassure you. Your computer isn't haunted (although it might be infected by a virus); computers don't break without leaving hints about the cause of the failure; and you're not the first person to have a particular problem. Don't panic; there are information resources and a huge community of support people and other users out there who are anxious to help you. One way or another, you'll get your computer working again.

Remind me again; weren't computers supposed to make our lives easier? Why should using a computer be more complicated than driving a car? The difference between using Windows and driving is that to drive, you have to take a test and convince an examiner from the Department of Motor Vehicles that you know how to operate a car first. But the only thing you have to do to start using a computer is to turn on the power switch. Computer manufacturers don't tell you where to find the power switch (let alone any of the hidden controls you might need to keep the computer going). And Microsoft doesn't tell you how to fix Windows when it breaks. You have to know where to look or you might never find that essential but elusive piece of information. Consider this book to be your guide.

If you change the wrong combination of Windows features and functions by accident, you may end up with a very broken system and the feeling that you'll never get it fixed again. When something goes wrong, you might see a message that provides no useful information and, even worse, no hint at all about how to recover. Again, don't give up. The text of the error message might not tell you anything, but those cryptic code numbers underneath the text can often lead you to a document buried in a knowledge base or some other website that reveals everything. This book can help you find that document.

I don't expect you to read this book from cover to cover, but it won't hurt to skim the chapter titles and main headings *before* you encounter a problem. With luck, you will remember that the book includes a section on understanding error messages, or restoring Windows settings, or whatever other information you need to fix your computer, and you'll come back to find specific advice and information when you need it. I do encourage you to take a close look at the final chapter on preventive maintenance right now and to do what you can to reduce the likelihood of some avoidable problems.

I hope the troubleshooting tools and methods in this book make your life as a Windows user more pleasant and less stressful. Over time, some of the basic techniques—try restarting the computer, look for the cheap fixes first, isolate the problem, and so forth—will become second nature to you and you'll solve many problems almost without thinking about them. But be warned: When you gain a reputation as somebody who's good at fixing computers, some of your relatives and friends will start calling and visiting more often. If they're good friends or close relatives, go ahead and help them; blood and friendship are thicker than silicon and software. But when you start hearing from complete strangers and fifth cousins twice removed, why don't you suggest that they get their own copies of this book? My publisher and I will both appreciate it.

1

TROUBLESHOOTING METHODS AND TOOLS

Windows is pretty good at finding and diagnosing problems, but it does a lousy job of explaining how to fix them and what has gone wrong. The error messages and other information that appear on your screen when a problem occurs often make things more confusing rather than providing clear instructions for solving the problem.

In spite of appearances, there *is* some kind of logic to the way Windows XP reports problems. And there's usually some kind of detailed explanation available if you know where to look.

However, there's a whole other category of problems that don't count as "failures." These are the times when some feature of the computer's behavior has changed and you don't know how to return to the original configuration. That's the "it's never done that before" part of this book. This is usually the product of somebody or something changing one or more of the settings or options that control the computer's performance and the Windows XP user interface. This could be something as simple as the function of the middle button on a three-button mouse or as complex as a completely different screen layout or an unexpected response to a command. If you (or somebody else using your computer) change a setting, or a new program or component makes the change automatically, you'll often have to find and reset some hidden option, setting, or menu item to change it back to the original configuration.

Troubleshooting Basics

The first step in troubleshooting Windows is to find as much information as possible about the problem. If an error message appears on the monitor screen, read the whole message; it won't always tell you exactly how to fix the problem, but it's usually a good starting point. And even if the message itself doesn't contain any useful advice, you can often look up the text in Microsoft's Knowledge Base or in some other online source of information that will offer a better and more detailed explanation.

Troubleshooting Windows is a lot easier when you have access to the Internet because many of the sources of helpful information are websites. If you can't go online with the computer that has the problem and you don't have access to a second computer, you might have reached a temporary dead end; you'll have to either borrow another computer or go someplace where you can use one—such as the home or office of a friend or colleague, an Internet café, or the public library.

Even better, try to borrow a laptop or other portable and set it up near the one you're trying to fix. You will save a lot of time and aggravation if you can read instructions for possible repairs on the screen of the second computer and immediately try them without the need to copy or print them and carry them back to your own home or office or from one room to another.

What May Have Gone Wrong?

Windows does not suffer from completely random failures. There's always a cause or a combination of causes when Windows goes haywire. If your computer has been operating more or less correctly and then it fails, something has changed: it might be a new piece of software, two different programs fighting for the same segment of memory, or a hardware component that has failed. That's why many problems occur just after you load a new program (or a new version of an existing program) or install a new piece of hardware: the thing that you tried to add doesn't work properly with all the stuff that was already running. This is why Microsoft has included a "restore" function in Windows XP that returns the computer to an earlier configuration.

What Has Changed?

If the fix for a problem is not immediately obvious, it's always useful to ask, What has changed? The change that caused the problem won't always be apparent, but it's usually there. Have you installed a new driver for your network interface or loaded the newest update to your antivirus program? Did you connect a new sound card or mouse to the computer? Has some kind of software loaded itself through the Internet without your knowledge? Has somebody turned off the power switch on the printer? If you can find the thing that has changed, you can almost always fix the problem. The general rule is to look for as much information about the problem's symptoms as possible.

Here's a real-world example: One of my computers would crash without warning after it had been running for an hour or more. Windows displayed a Blue Screen error message that identified the problem as a hardware failure, but none of the usual sources of information—Microsoft tech support, the hardware manufacturers' websites, and the combined wisdom of the Internet—could tell me exactly what was going wrong. I hadn't added or removed anything, so I didn't think the computer's configuration had changed. None of the usual tests came up with anything. The best anybody could tell me was that the Stop codes indicated that it had something to do with hardware rather than Windows and maybe something was warmer than usual.

After several weeks of pain, I figured out what had changed: the computer began to fail shortly after the floor in another room of the house had been sanded and refinished. When I opened up the computer, I discovered that the cooler that was supposed to keep the central processor from overheating was full of sawdust. Because the heat could not escape, the processor would fail when the temperature increased. Five minutes with an air hose and a soft brush was all it took to solve the problem. Yup, it was the dreaded "Floor Sanding Screen of Death."

Record Your Steps

As you try to repair a problem and restore your computer to normal operation, keep track of what you're doing. Even if something doesn't work, you will want to tell a help desk person (or your neighbor's daughter the computer expert) that you tried it and how the computer responded. Sometimes a failed fix might contain the seeds of success for somebody with more experience. And if you stumble onto something that does solve the problem, you might want to know exactly what you did in order to fix it again later.

Is This a New Problem? Has It Ever Done This Before?

It's always useful to ask whether you're dealing with a new problem or one that has appeared before or existed for a long time. It's often easier to just restart a program or reboot the computer and get back to work rather than to take the time to find the source of the underlying problem, but that does nothing toward preventing the problem from occurring again.

Anytime your computer fails, you should have two goals: the first is to restore the computer to proper operation, and the second is to identify and eliminate the source of the problem so it doesn't happen again. These objectives are not always on the same track—sometimes it's possible to fix the problem without knowing the cause. But when that happens, there's always the danger that the same problem will come back at the most inconvenient time. So it's a good idea to spend some time looking for the cause rather than simply working around it.

Start with a Plan

A formal troubleshooting plan may itself seem like a lot of trouble, but it's almost always the most effective way to move from a problem to a solution. A typical troubleshooting plan might include the steps presented here.

1. Identify the Symptoms

Any unexpected behavior can be considered a "problem," even if the computer does not actually fail. The troubleshooting methods are the same for minor irritations and catastrophic failures.

First, define the problem. Does an error message appear on the screen? Has some hardware component stopped working? Is some element of the computer's behavior different from what you're expecting? Just exactly what is wrong?

Changes in Performance

The most obvious problems are the ones that cause the computer to crash. If the keyboard or mouse stops working, if the monitor screen goes dark, or if Windows won't start, you have a pretty clear indication that something has gone wrong. Other problems are more subtle: A program takes forever to start, or a network link that worked yesterday won't work today. Or maybe your web browser is taking you to a site that you didn't request.

When you discover that something isn't working the way you expect it to work, try to describe the problem to yourself in detail. If the problem seems connected to a particular program, identify the program by name and release number. If you're seeing a strange website, note the web address and anything else that might identify the site. If the computer crashed, try to remember exactly what you did and what the computer was doing before it stopped working.

The point of this exercise is to provide as much information as possible to the people and other resources that will help you to solve the problem. Whether it's a human tech support representative (or your brother-in-law) or an online list of problems and solutions, you will have to describe the problem before you can find a way to fix it.

Error Messages

If an error message appears, make a complete copy of the text. If it's a brief message, you can make a handwritten copy or use another computer to copy it into a text editor, but it's often easier to use the Print Screen function to take a picture of the error message window. Either way, make sure you include the exact language of the error message in your notes, including all the cryptic codes. We'll talk more about Windows error messages and screens in Chapter 4.

NOTE *Unfortunately, the Print Screen function won't work when Windows produces a Blue Screen error following a catastrophic failure. In that case, you'll have to copy the text by hand.*

Follow these steps to capture an error message window:

1. Make the window that contains the error message the active window.
2. Hold down the ALT key and press the PRINT SCREEN key to the right of the regular keyboard.
3. Open the Windows Paint program (in the **Start ▸ Programs ▸ Accessories** or **Start ▸ Programs ▸ All Programs ▸ Accessories** menu) or some other graphics program.
4. Choose **Edit ▸ Paste** to display an image of the window.
5. Print the image.

Don't forget the digital readout or the LED indicators on your printer and some other external devices. There are generally more and better diagnostic displays on more expensive printers than on low-end units, but even a flashing LED can sometimes provide some kind of useful information. If an error message or some other unfamiliar display appears anywhere in the system, make a note of it. For network problems, look at the lights on the interface card's back panel and on the router or data switch; some network devices identify problems with specific displays.

Event Logs

Windows and other programs often use log files to store lists of specific events. Most of the entries in the Event Viewer are routine actions, but the Viewer also lists some types of errors that can be useful as troubleshooting tools.

To open the Event Viewer, use the **Start ▸ Run** command and type **eventvwr.msc**. Figure 1-1 shows the Event Viewer.

For details about a log entry, double-click the listing for that entry. The Event Properties window, shown in Figure 1-2, contains information about the event, including a description that can be useful for troubleshooting.

When you find an entry that corresponds to the problem you're trying to fix, make a note of the codes and other information in the Event Properties window.

Power-on Self Test Errors

Other error messages appear during the startup routine before Windows starts. These are usually caused by hardware problems detected by the computer's power-on self test (POST), which is generated by the basic input/output system (BIOS) software that runs when you turn on the computer. (For more information about these startup errors, see Chapter 3.)

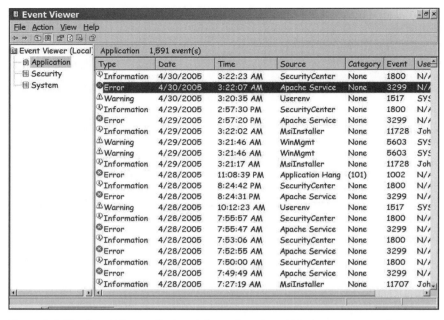

Figure 1-1: The Event Viewer displays information about Windows events and errors.

Other Log Files

If Windows or an application program creates a log, the data in the log file may be helpful for troubleshooting. Look for entries that correspond to the approximate time that the problem or failure occurred. Most log files are located in the root directory of your primary hard drive; in other words, they're generally in the top-level directory on the C: drive.

Figure 1-2: The Event Properties window can include a description that might identify the source of a problem.

What Else Was Happening?

Look for other elements that might be related to the problem. For example:

- If other users have their own accounts on this computer, do they see the same problem?

- If the computer is connected to a network, do other computers on the same network have the same problem?

- Have you recently installed an update to Windows or to one of the other programs installed on your computer? How about a new driver?

Is the problem related to a particular activity? Does it occur every time you try to run a specific program or when you enter a specific command? Does it happen at startup or at shutdown? When you try to print or use some other peripheral device? Make a note of all the symptoms that appear to be related to the problem and anything else that seems to be different from the performance you're expecting. The more information you can provide, the easier it will be to find a way to solve the problem.

2. Try Restarting the Computer

Before you try anything else, try shutting down the computer and all the external components, and then turn them back on. Sometimes that's all that it takes to fix a problem. This might happen when a badly designed program has grabbed a chunk of the computer's memory and not released it or when some internal software switch or setting has latched itself in the wrong position. When that occurs, returning the computer and its peripheral devices to their startup configuration can be all it takes to get back to normal operation.

NOTE   *Don't dive for the power switch or the reset button until you have copied the text of the error message or noted the other symptoms of the problem. Sometimes a problem will produce a different message or another symptom the next time it appears, and knowing that can be another valuable troubleshooting tool.*

When you restart the computer, don't just use the Restart option in the Turn Off Computer window; try the Turn Off or Shutdown option, and then either disconnect the power cable or use the power switch on the back of the computer to turn off the power supply. Count to 10, and then reconnect the power plug or turn the power switch back on. The idea is to completely remove power from all of the computer's internal circuits for long enough to remove any residual charge and return to the startup condition.

If it seems relevant to your problem, you can also shut down and restart one or more of the external devices that are connected to the computer, or even disconnect them. These include the video display monitor, the modem, the router or switch that controls your local network and your connection to the Internet, and anything else that takes power from a wall outlet. If the device has a power switch, turn it off, count to 10, and turn it back on; if there's no switch, disconnect and reconnect the power cable where it plugs into the device or the wall outlet.

Restarting doesn't always work, but it's a common enough fix that you should try it before moving on to other possible methods. If it's a one-time glitch (or it occurs very rarely), that might be all you ever need to do; but if the problem returns frequently, you will want to continue with the trouble-shooting process to fix the underlying problem.

3. Look for an Explanation

Eliminate the simple reasons for a failure first. For example, if the printer won't print, make sure the power cable and the signal cable are still connected, the ink or toner supply hasn't dried up, the power switch is turned on, and the printer is On Line before you start running diagnostics. When power to the computer disappears, make sure your cat hasn't walked across the power outlet strip and turned it off or the person polishing your floor didn't cut the power cord. If no sound comes out of the speakers, open the Volume Control window and the control for your audio program and make sure none of the Mute options are active, and check the physical cables and volume control on the speaker box.

NOTE *In general, look for the quick fixes before you spend a lot of time searching for something more complicated. Problems like that are quick and easy to check, and even easier to repair, so you should get them out of the way before you waste a lot of time looking for something more serious and complex.*

Sometimes an apparent problem can occur because somebody else on your network is running tests or installing new software or hardware or some program is running a scheduled event such as a virus scan or it's downloading and installing an automatic software upgrade. If you can't connect to the Internet from your office computer, call the system administrator to make sure the whole network isn't down before you tear into your own computer; if there's some kind of unknown activity on your own computer, open the Task Manager to see if a scheduled program is running. Even if you're using a stand-alone computer, it's possible that some program is running in the background.

When the simple answers don't solve the problem, it's time to perform a more systematic search.

Examine the System

If a hardware component appears to have failed, look for some obvious reason for the failure. In particular, check these possibilities:

- Make sure that all the cables and plugs are securely connected at both ends.
- Confirm that all the power switches are turned on and any other controls (such as an On Line switch on a printer or the Brightness and Contrast controls on a monitor) are set correctly.
- Check the status of any consumable supplies. Is the printer out of ink or toner?

- Look for a configuration window or menu. Make sure all the settings and options are set correctly.

- Turn off the computer, unplug the power cable, and remove the cover. Make sure all the expansion cards and both ends of all the internal cables are firmly seated in their sockets. If you've just installed a device, confirm that the ribbon cables are not upside down: the red stripe on the ribbon cable should be closest to the No. 1 pin on the sockets at both the motherboard and the drive or other devices. If you have a copy of the user manual for the motherboard, confirm that all of the switches and jumpers are in the right positions.

- If the computer produced beep codes or other error messages related to system memory (according to your user manual or your BIOS manufacturer's help), make sure that all of the memory modules are firmly seated in their sockets.

- While the computer is open, use an air hose, a vacuum cleaner, or a soft brush to remove any dust that may have settled inside. Pay particular attention to the motherboard and other circuit boards, the heat sinks on the central processor chip, and all of the grilles and ventilation holes in the computer's case that are supposed to allow air to move through the box. Get that floor dust out of there.

- Before you replace the cover, plug in the power cable and any other external cables that you may have disconnected, turn on the computer, and confirm that all of the fans and blowers are operating. In particular, look at the fan mounted over the central processor on the motherboard and the exhaust fan on the power supply.

- Plug a cable from the computer's internal power supply into an inexpensive power supply tester (available from a computer supply retailer like Fry's or CompUSA) to confirm that all of the necessary voltages are present. Figure 1-3 shows a power supply tester.

Figure 1-3: A simple power supply tester makes it easy to check power supply voltages.

- If the computer or any other components run on batteries, make sure the battery has not run down. Try replacing the battery with a new one, or use a voltmeter to measure the voltage at the battery's terminals. If there's a power socket that allows you to use the computer on house current, see if it will run with external power.

USING A VOLTMETER

An inexpensive voltmeter is often helpful for testing the outputs of power supplies and batteries. You can spend hundreds of dollars for a durable, high-precision test instrument, but that's more than you will need for computer troubleshooting. If you have a meter and you know how to use it, you can use it to measure the voltages. If you're not comfortable using a voltmeter, let a qualified technician do it for you.

Most voltmeters are actually volt-ohm-millimeters that can measure electrical potential (volts), impedance (ohms), and current (amperes or amps). The selector switch at the front of the meter chooses the type of measurement.

Voltmeters are either digital (with numbers in the display) or analog (with a needle that moves to show the measured value); either type is fine for our purposes. Your meter should come with two test cables that plug into the meter and have metal probes at the other end.

Follow these steps to measure voltage:

1. If your meter has a power switch, turn the meter on.

2. Set the selector switch to one of the DC Volts settings. Use the range that is the next setting higher than the voltage you're measuring; to measure the +5 VDC and +12 VDC voltages from a computer power supply on the meter shown in Figure 1-4, set the switch to the 60 DC V range. To measure the power from a battery or external power supply, look at the label on the power supply to find the voltage.

3. Insert the test cables into the + and – sockets (or the COM and VDC sockets) on the front of the meter.

4. If you're measuring a power supply, turn it on.

5. Touch one of the test probes to the + terminal or connector on the device you want to measure; touch the other probe to the – terminal or connector. Figure 1-5 shows the correct voltage on each pin in the cable connector.

6. Look at the meter's display. The needle or the digital display should show the voltage of the device. If the needle on your analog meter moves to the left, reverse the two test leads.

Figure 1-4: Set the meter to one of the DC V ranges.

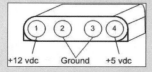

Figure 1-5: Measure the voltages on the power connector.

- Sometimes a laptop computer will work with external power only when there's no internal battery in place. This may mean that the battery is completely drained or that the external power supply isn't strong enough to run the computer and charge the battery at the same time. Compare the power requirement (in volts and amps) specified for your computer (in the user manual or at the manufacturer's website) with the capacity marked on the power unit. If the computer needs more amps than the power supply can provide, find a different power unit.

- If the computer's clock or calendar doesn't display the current time and date, replace the coin-size battery on the computer's motherboard. You will have to reset the computer's BIOS settings after you remove and replace the battery.

- Try running a complete virus scan and a scan for spyware. If you don't already have antivirus and antispyware programs installed on your computer, see Chapter 11 for more information.

For problems with Windows or other software, look for a configuration setting that might be the source of the problem. There is no universal standard for finding settings and options in Windows programs, but the Tools menu in the toolbar at the top of most program windows is a good place to start. Many programs include a menu item called Options, while others offer one or more separate settings. Look in each configuration window and dialog box to see if there's a setting that might be causing the problem.

Anytime you change either hardware or software, note what you have done and test the system to see if you have solved the problem before you move on to something else. If the attempted fix didn't work, return the setting to its original state before you move on to something else. Obviously, that doesn't mean that you should replace the dust that you removed from inside the computer or loosen the plugs and circuit boards that you inserted firmly into their sockets, but when you change a configuration setting or a software option, change it back if it doesn't solve the problem. Otherwise, you run the risk of creating new problems before you solve the original one.

Isolate the Problem: Hardware

For hardware problems, it can often be helpful to isolate the problem by replacing individual components and cables one at a time until the problem disappears. If you don't have your own set of spares, ask your friends and colleagues if they have a junk box full of cables, video cards, modems, network interface cards, and other parts to try. If there's another computer nearby, try swapping major components like the video monitor, keyboard, or printer.

If the problem disappears when you install a replacement, you can be pretty certain that the original device is the source of the problem. If the offending piece is an inexpensive item like a cable, either leave the working spare in place or buy and install a new one.

If the bad component is something more expensive, such as a printer, you might want to either try to repair it yourself or take it to a service center. But don't be surprised if it costs more to repair the original unit than to buy a new one. Technicians' time is often a lot more expensive than hardware, and the price of many computer components is dropping, so it's often not worth the time and trouble to spend an hour or more fixing something like a $15 network interface or a $25 keyboard.

Monitors are especially notorious for costing more to repair than to replace. The price of old-fashioned video displays with cathode ray tubes (CRTs) has dropped through the floor as the newer flat-panel displays have taken over the market. You can find new high-quality brand-name 17-inch CRT monitors for less than $150; it could cost that much or more to repair an old one, if your technician can find the parts. I've also seen decent used 15-inch units for as little as $5. At that kind of price, you're ahead of the game if the thing lasts more than three or four months.

NOTE   *Don't try to repair a monitor yourself unless you know exactly what you're doing. Unlike the low voltages inside a computer, a video display can contain high-voltage capacitors that can kill, even if the power is disconnected.*

Isolate the Problem: Software

Similar techniques can also work with software. When a problem appears, try closing each active program, one at a time. If the problem disappears once a particular program has been shut down, that program could be the source of the problem.

If you recently installed a new device driver, a software patch, or a completely new program, try uninstalling the new software and reinstalling the original version.

Software problems can occur when there's a conflict between two programs that try to use the same portion of the computer's memory at the same time. To identify the program that is causing trouble, use the Services tool to disable the active background software services, one at a time. Follow these steps to use the Services tool:

1.   From the Start menu, open **Run** and enter **services.msc**.
2.   The line for each active service includes the word *Started* in the Status column. To turn it off, right-click the name of a service, and select **Stop** from the pop-up menu.

If the problem goes away when you shut down a service, that service could be related the problem. If stopping a service makes no difference, turn it back on and try the next one.

Use Safe Mode to Simplify the System

If the problem persists, try restarting the computer in Safe Mode, which loads a bare-bones version of Windows XP without any extra programs or services. If the problem still occurs when you boot into Safe Mode, and you've eliminated hardware issues, you can pretty well assume that there's some problem with your Windows installation. If the problem is gone in Safe Mode, you can assume that it's caused by some other program or service that loads when Windows boots normally.

To start Windows in Safe Mode, follow these steps:

1. Shut down and restart Windows.

2. When the computer restarts, press F8 a few times. A list of startup options will appear on your screen.

3. Choose one of the Safe Mode options and press ENTER. The computer will open Windows in Safe Mode.

NOTE *Don't be alarmed if the screen doesn't look the same as it did before. One of the "extra" services that Safe Mode ignores is the display setting. It will return to normal when you leave Safe Mode.*

Retrace Your Steps

Even if a computer problem seems to appear without warning, it was probably caused by something that has changed within the hardware or software. Therefore, trying to reproduce the problem by repeating your steps can often help identify and solve it.

Your troubleshooting routine should include asking these questions:

• What programs were running when the problem occurred?

• Have you recently installed or removed a program, device driver, or other software?

• Have you recently tried to update or upgrade Windows or some other program?

• Have you changed any settings or options?

• Have you added or removed any hardware devices?

• Is anybody else using this computer? Have they made any changes?

• Did the computer receive a command or message through its network connection?

Don't forget about external events that might have caused a computer problem. For example, has there been a change to your power source (are you using a different power outlet?), or have you moved the computer to a new location?

Check for Updates

The problem you're facing could be due to a known bug in Windows, in a driver or other software, or in the firmware supplied with the computer's motherboard or other hardware. Sometimes replacing the software or firmware with a new version is enough to solve the problem, so check the various manufacturers' websites to make sure that you are using the most recent releases. And read their message boards to see if anyone is having a problem similar to yours.

4. Places to Look for Help

Whenever you encounter a problem with Windows, remember this: It's extremely likely that somebody else has had to deal with exactly the same problem that you're trying to fix. Somebody someplace has almost certainly come up against the same kind of failure or unexpected behavior before. And there's probably a description of the problem someplace on the Internet, in the Microsoft Knowledge Base or elsewhere. If you're lucky, you may even find an online forum where several people who have suffered from the same problem shared their experience trying to solve it.

NOTE *Working with a second computer will make troubleshooting a lot easier, even if the broken machine does have access to the Internet. With a single screen, you'll find yourself constantly switching between the web page or help screen that contains a procedure and the program or dialog box where you must enter commands, select options, or read text. And when the troubleshooting procedure tells you to restart the computer, your information page will disappear. If you can't move a second computer next to the one you're trying to fix, the next best approach is to print the web pages and other information sources that contain the possible fix before you start to step through the procedure and work from a paper copy.*

Describe the Problem

If you can describe the specific symptoms of your problem, you can probably find help fixing it. But before you go online or pick up the telephone in search of help, make a list of specific facts related to the problem, including the names and version numbers of the software that was running when it occurred, a complete description of the symptoms, and the things you have already tried. The more useful the information you can offer to the people trying to help you, the better the chances that they'll know how to solve the problem.

- To identify the version of Windows XP currently running on your computer, choose **Start ▸ Control Panel ▸ Performance And Maintenance System** (in the Windows XP menu), or **Start ▸ Settings ▸ Control Panel ▸ System** (in the Classic Start menu) and look at the General tab. The version of Windows XP is listed under the System heading.

- To identify the version of most Windows programs, open the Help menu (at the right end of the program's menu bar), and choose **About** *Name Of Program*.

- To identify the firmware versions of your computer's motherboard and other devices, use the **Start ▸ Run** command and enter **msinfo32** in the Open field. The System Information window shown in Figure 1-6 will appear. Click **System Summary** and look in the right pane for the BIOS Version/Date entry, and click each item under Components to see its release number and the date of the driver associated with it.

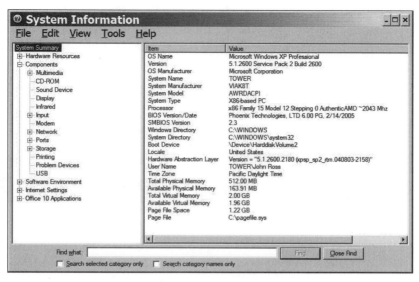

Figure 1-6: Use the System Information tool to identify the BIOS version and date.

NOTE   *If you're using an external device connected to the computer through a USB, SATA, FireWire, or other port, or a network adapter, you may have to consult the device manual or the manufacturer's website to identify the firmware version.*

Look for a Solution

Once you have defined the problem in detail, you're ready to look for an explanation of its cause and a way to fix it. Many of the best sources of problem-solving information are literally at your fingertips—they include the Help and Support Center built into Windows, the printed manuals and text files supplied with your computer's hardware and software, formal computer help desks and support services that you can reach with a telephone call or an e-mail message, and a variety of resources that you can find on the Internet.

As that old TV show kept telling us, "The truth is out there." An explanation of your problem is indeed out there someplace; it's just a matter of knowing where to look.

Here are some places to find information that can help identify and solve the source of a problem.

Open the Built-in Help Screens

Windows XP and most programs that run under Windows include a set of help screens that often contain information about using and trouble-shooting that software. Unfortunately, the quality of online help screens varies widely, even within Windows XP—some programs include everything a user will ever need, while others tell you next to nothing. Help screens might not do you much good if the computer has broken down completely (unless you can check them on another machine), but if you can get to the help screens, they're often a good place to start.

NOTE *Some programs use an interactive help system with links to the manufacturer through the Internet. This can be a great way to provide the latest information about new features, functions, and fixes.*

To open the Help and Support Center in Windows XP, choose the **Help And Support** option in the Start menu. When the window shown in Figure 1-7 appears, type a keyword that describes your problem in the Search field, or open the Index window from the toolbar and look for a keyword in the pane on the left side of the window.

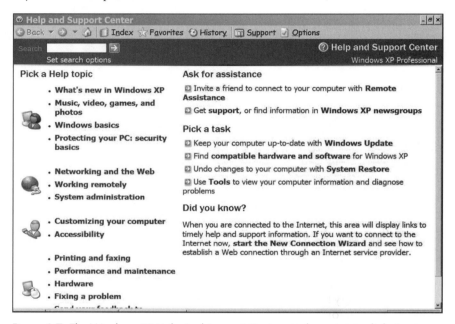

Figure 1-7: The Windows XP Help And Support Center window contains links to many troubleshooting resources.

In most other programs, you should find a Help menu in the toolbar at the top of the program window. When the Help window opens, type a one- or two-word description of the problem into the Index or Search tool. If that doesn't produce anything useful, try scrolling through the list of keywords until you find something close to the problem you're trying to solve.

Open the Windows Help and Support Center

The Help and Support Center in Windows XP includes both the local help screens and other tools, such as System Restore and several diagnostic screens, as well as links to Microsoft's online support center and Windows newsgroups. The help screens in Windows XP are the closest thing to a user manual supplied with the software. When you're looking for instructions for finding and changing any of the settings and options, start here.

Because Microsoft has thrown so many things into the Help and Support Center, it's not always easy to find the route to the information you need.

To go to the help screens, choose the **Index** button in the toolbar at the top of the window. Type a keyword or use the list of keywords in the Index pane to find the specific information you need.

Most of the time, your initial keyword search will open a page that contains a lot of text but not the specific information that you want. It's often quite astonishing how well and how often Microsoft's help writers can avoid answering the most obvious questions at the top layer of a help hierarchy. But don't give up yet. If the initial help screen linked to a keyword doesn't tell you what you want to know, scroll to the bottom of the text and click the **Related Topics** link. You may well find that the pop-up menu that lists other topics often includes more useful information than the original page.

Look for README Files

README files are text files that contain last-minute information, such as descriptions of compatibility problems with other hardware or software, changes since the manual was published, and workaround instructions for bugs. It's always worth the time to look for a README file on the CD or floppy disk or in the download directory that contains new software or updates to an existing product.

Unfortunately, there's no standard format for README files. They can be text files, formatted documents, web pages, or PDFs. Sometimes, the Install or Setup routine will place a link to the README file on the Windows desktop or the Programs menu. Rarely, they are printed pages inserted in the box along with the software, or they are links to an online site. The file might be called readme.txt (or .doc or .pdf or .htm), or read.me, or something else entirely.

Regardless of their exact name and format, a README file is often the very last thing that a manufacturer or software developer adds to the product before releasing the package to manufacture or posting it on the Internet. So it's the last opportunity to tell you about problems that appeared late in the development and testing process. For example, the README file on the Windows XP Service Pack 2 CD is called README SP.HTM (shown in Figure 1-8). It's a document formatted as a web page, with links to other files on the CD and additional information on Microsoft's website. The file includes a list of the updates supplied in the service pack, instructions for installing and removing the new software, and links to online resources that can be updated more easily than the CD itself.

Many software products that are distributed on CDs include a README file that does not show up on the autostart menu that appears when you insert the disk into a CD drive. To find and open one of these files, follow these steps:

1. From the Windows desktop, open My Computer.
2. Right-click the icon for the CD drive. A pop-up menu will appear.
3. Choose the **Open** or **Explore** item from the menu to view the contents of the CD.

4. Look for a file called readme.txt or something similar. If there's nothing in the main directory, try looking in each subdirectory. When you find a README file, double-click the filename to open it. It should display in an appropriate program.

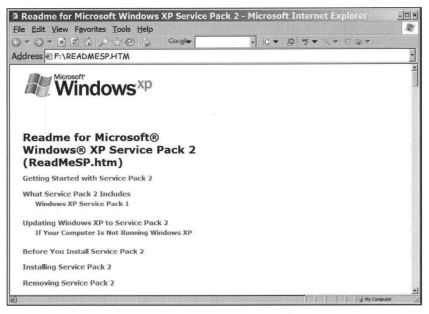

Figure 1-8: The README file on the Windows XP Service Pack 2 CD is an HTML document.

Read the User Manuals and Other Printed Matter

In the early days of computing, the manuals that came with a computer and its associated software would fill an entire bookcase. Of course, the computer itself filled a whole room, and probably cost several hundred thousand dollars or more, so the cost of the documentation was a relatively small part of the total package.

Today, the typical software product comes in an "air box" that contains nothing but a CD and maybe a single sheet of paper with installation instructions and half a dozen advertisements for other products. A hardware package often includes some cables and a little package of screws and jumpers along with the CD and the product itself.

If there's a complete user manual in the package at all, it's often in digital form, in a file on the CD. Printed manuals are still the easiest format to use, but they're expensive to print and ship, so many hardware and software providers reduce their manufacturing costs by replacing their hardcopy manuals with books encoded as PDF (Adobe Acrobat) files or as straight text or word-processor files. Considering that a 100-page manual could add $10 or more to the price of a product that retails for less than $100, that's a significant savings.

Look on the CD for .pdf, .txt, or .doc files in the main directory or in a folder called Manual, Documents, or something similar. If there's more than one program on the CD, look for manuals in the folders or directories for each program.

NOTE   *While you can, of course, read a manual on-screen, it's not always easy to do so, especially when you have to flip back and forth between two or more pages. To reduce the pain, print copies of each page or chapter that applies to the problem you are trying to solve. If the manual contains less than a couple of dozen pages, consider printing the whole thing and placing the pages in a loose-leaf binder.*

The quality of the manuals supplied with modern computer hardware and software varies. Some manuals are excellent, with full details about how the product works and instructions for installing, using, and troubleshooting every feature. But many others seem to have been an afterthought, assembled at the last minute by an outside contractor who may or may not have ever used the product. And some products, including Windows XP itself, don't include any manuals at all.

NOTE   *Some manufacturers might offer a complete printed manual as an extra-cost add-on item. If you use a program or device a lot, try calling its tech support line and asking about obtaining a printed manual. Don't bother asking Microsoft for a Windows manual; they'll point you to the books about Windows published by Microsoft Press and other publishers.*

If you do have manuals for any of the programs or hardware related to a problem, read them. Look for descriptions of the configuration settings and explanations of specific features that might be the source of the trouble. If there's a troubleshooting section, there's a good chance that you might find a fix for your problem. Don't forget to look in the back of the book for appendixes that contain lists of error messages, settings for switches and jumpers, and other essential information.

Find Your Symptoms Online

The alternative to reading the manual is to consult the Collective Wisdom of the Internet. This is where the specific description of the problem (discussed earlier in this chapter) becomes important. Use Google or some other Internet search tool to look for specific answers to your questions and solutions to your problems. Include the name of the program in the search field, along with one or more keywords that describe the problem (such as "XP can't find USB scanner" or "Whizz-com 643A smoke").

Ask Your Help Desk for . . . um, Help

A help desk is a technical support center that exists to answer questions and help employees or customers use their computers and network services. If you have access to a help desk, a quick telephone call or a walk across the office can often be an easy way to solve a problem and get back to work. The people who work at help centers are there to make your job easier by keeping your computer running properly.

If you can't find the solution to a problem on your own, your help desk is the first place to call for assistance. The people who work there are probably familiar with the specific combination of hardware and software that you're using, and they will know how to fix common problems for you. If there's a virus or other intruder going around your network or workgroup, they will know about it, and they'll be able to cut through a lot of the usual diagnostic methods to focus in on the current local plague.

Different help desks offer different levels of support. Some work entirely by telephone or e-mail, while others will send a live expert to your site. If it's possible to solve the problem by talking you through the fix, that's often the fastest way to get your computer up and running again, but when the computer is suffering from a hardware failure, or if you're in the same building as the help desk, it might be easier for a technician to come to you.

Some help desks may want to use the Remote Assistance feature in Windows XP or a similar third-party program that allows a technician to take control of your computer through the network. If your technician or help desk advisor wants to use Remote Assistance, they will tell you exactly how to make the feature active on your computer.

Ask the Family Expert

If you don't have access to a formal help desk, a knowledgeable friend or relative can sometimes be the next best thing. If your daughter or brother-in-law or a family friend is a computer expert, it might be possible to call them for help when your computer breaks down. This kind of unofficial technical support can be a great resource, but it's important to remember that you're asking for a personal favor. Depending on the other demands on their time, they might not always be able to drop whatever they're doing when you call and take the time to help you.

When you call a help desk, or a helpful friend or relative, try to give them as much information as possible about the problem, including all of the things described in the first part of this chapter. The symptoms, the text of any error messages that you have received, and the things you were doing when the problem occurred are all important hints that will help an advisor identify the problem and tell you how to solve it.

NOTE *If you call a particular help desk or informal advisor often, consider some kind of lightweight bribery after they take your fourth call in one week or when they spend two hours talking you through a particularly nasty problem—a pot of flowers from your garden or a batch of fresh-baked cookies can do wonders in convincing someone that they should continue taking your calls. They might even move your next request for assistance to the top of the stack.*

Consult the Microsoft Knowledge Base

The Microsoft Knowledge Base is a huge collection of articles that describe problems and answer questions about many Microsoft products. They include error codes and other messages that were written into the software code and descriptions of potential problems that were discovered during prerelease testing. When a user tells Microsoft about a new and previously unknown problem, that problem gets added to the Knowledge Base, so the next person who calls with the same problem doesn't have to start from scratch. There are full-time groups of people at Microsoft who spend their time keeping the Knowledge Bases for various products up to date.

When you call or e-mail Microsoft's technical support center or your local help desk, the technician who takes your request for help uses the Knowledge Base to find and help solve your problem. However, it's not necessary to go through a technician to get to the information in the Knowledge Base; you can read most Knowledge Base articles on Microsoft's website at www.microsoft.com. Chapter 6 of this book explains how to use the Knowledge Base and other Microsoft resources.

Try a Manufacturer's Tech Support Center

Microsoft is not the only company that offers technical support for its products. Most major hardware and software manufacturers will answer questions from users who are having trouble installing or using their products. Some companies prefer to take technical support questions by telephone, but others will accept them only via e-mail or though an interactive website.

Unfortunately, requesting tech support is not always particularly effective. Too often, it involves spending a lot of time waiting for somebody to answer the telephone or reply to an e-mail, only to receive nonspecific answers that don't help solve the problem. Worse, many companies now charge for access to their support services. Therefore, alternative source of information are often a better choice.

Chapter 18 of this book contains more information about finding and using manufacturers' technical support services.

Join an Online Newsgroup

The tradition of sharing information among computer users is older than the Internet. Starting back when online computer discussions used store-and-forward bulletin board systems that sometimes took days or weeks to move messages from one location to another, people who were looking for help would post their questions to online conferences and complete strangers would respond with detailed advice.

Today, there are thousands of newsgroups, forums, and mailing lists distributed through the Internet devoted to just about every imaginable computer-related subject. Some are sponsored by hardware and software manufacturers, and others are operated by independent user groups. Still others are part of the worldwide Usenet newsgroup system.

Asking a question or describing a problem in an appropriate newsgroup can often be the most effective way to find a solution. Chapter 6 of this book explains how to find newsgroups and similar online sources of help from other users.

NOTE *And of course, the generosity of Internet users isn't limited to help with computer problems. Newsgroups and e-mail lists devoted to other technical subjects can be equally valuable when you're trying to restore an antique radio or find a part for your 1959 DeSoto.*

Look for Other Websites

In addition to the official sites maintained by hardware and software suppliers, the Internet also offers a wealth of sites created by user groups and self-appointed experts, and a web search using a search tool like Google can frequently produce useful results. If you see an error message, try searching for the exact text of the message, the first few words of the text, the error code number, or anything in the message that seems to make it unique. If that doesn't work, try searching for one or two keywords that describe the product and the problem. Some of the hits will be more valuable than others, but keep looking through the first hundred or more search hits.

Again, Chapter 6 contains more information about searching for symptoms online.

5. Try a Fix

When you find a possible solution to your problem, go ahead and try it. Follow the instructions as closely as possible, and keep careful notes that describe exactly what you have done. If the first things you try don't solve the problem, remember to undo any changes before you move on to another possible approach.

6. Check the Result

Once you have applied whatever fix your research has told you will solve your problem, take a close look at your system to confirm that the problem has in fact gone away. This might be as simple as observing that the computer is no longer frozen, but it's often more subtle than that. If the problem occurred after you entered a particular set of keystrokes or when you turned on an external device, try to reproduce the failure by repeating the same actions.

Of course, the first repair you try, or even the first six things you try, may not produce the results you want. In some cases, they might even make matters worse than they were before you started. That's the reason to keep track of each attempted fix: Before moving on to the next possible solution, do what you can to restore the computer to the condition it was in before you tried to fix it. Otherwise, the negative effect of a failed solution might get in the way of solving the original problem.

7. Keep a Record of the Fix

Eventually, you will probably find a way to solve the problem. It might require major surgery on your computer, but most often, it's a lot easier than that. The most time-consuming part of the whole process isn't loading the new driver or changing the configuration setting or whatever it might be; it's finding the right solution. Slogging through help screens, websites, and the Microsoft Knowledge Base can take up the better part of a whole day. On the other hand, when a friend or colleague comes up against the same problem that you have already fixed, you can become the hero of the day by knowing exactly what to do.

The last thing you want to do is to waste another day trying to remember exactly where the @#$%! you found the specific information that solved the problem. If the same problem happens again, you should know what to do about it. It's easy to tell yourself, "I'll remember how to fix this," but it's not always true. Six months from now, will you know where to find that obscure setting that's buried under three layers of configuration windows? Or which website has the downloadable patch that repairs the bug in the original software or deletes a particular type of spyware? Don't count on it.

The best way to deal with this is to keep a simple log or notebook that describes each problem and how you fixed it, complete with web addresses, configuration settings, and everything else that will help you go directly to a solution without any of the dead ends that waste so much time. You can create and store the log as a text file in your computer, but remember that the computer might not be accessible when you're trying to solve the problem. So it's a better idea to print each description and store them in a file folder or a loose-leaf binder near the computer. Or stick your notes between the covers of this book to keep everything in one place.

NOTE *If you consulted an online forum or newsgroup to find help solving the problem, remember to post a message to let the other readers of the same thread know that you have found a solution. Even a simple message like, "Hey guys! It worked! I tried x, y, and z, and now my hard drive works again. Thanks for all your help," will tell the next person facing the problem that somebody was able to fix it.*

8. Prevent a Repeat

Remember the old joke about the man who goes to see his doctor? The guy holds up his left arm and says, "It hurts when I do this with my arm." The doctor tells him, "So stop doing that."

That's not always possible with a computer problem. A cure may not be the same thing as preventing its return. For example, a virus or spyware program could reappear after you've deleted it, or some other person using your computer might change the configuration settings without your knowledge. So just because you stopped doing whatever caused the problem doesn't mean you won't see the same problem again.

Therefore, as the final step of your troubleshooting routine, take the necessary steps to avoid a repeat of the same problem. This might mean installing an antivirus or antispyware utility or adding password control to the startup routine. Or it might require some other very specific actions that are described in the Microsoft Knowledge Base or some other online document or manual. Every problem and solution is different, but the general rule is to read through all of the documents, web pages, and other sources of information; don't just look for the part about performing a quick fix.

2

TYPES OF WINDOWS PROBLEMS AND FAILURES

The range of things that can go wrong with Windows XP is truly amazing. Some problems are more serious than others, but they all can interfere with your ability to do the work you want to do on your computer. Each type of problem demands a different set of solutions, so recognizing what type of failure you're experiencing is the essential first step toward fixing it and getting on with your work.

This chapter contains brief descriptions of some common Windows problems and some common computer problems that don't involve the Windows operating system. If there's a simple fix, the description includes the steps for solving the problem; if it's more complicated, the description provides a pointer to another chapter of this book with more detailed information.

No Power

If absolutely nothing happens when you turn on the computer—no sound, no lights, nothing on the display—the source of the problem is almost certainly related to the computer's electric power. Either the power to the computer has failed, something has been turned off, or a cable is not connected.

Checking Power on a Desktop Computer

On a desktop computer (or a tower computer that normally sits on the floor), there are some things you can do to identify possible problems:

- Confirm that the power cable from the computer to the AC outlet is plugged in at both ends.
- Confirm that the monitor's power cable is also plugged in and the monitor is turned on.
- If the computer is plugged into a power strip, a surge protector, or an uninterruptible power supply (UPS), confirm that the power switch on the power unit is turned on and that the power unit's own power cord is plugged into an AC outlet.
- Confirm that the AC power from the wall outlet has not failed. Try plugging a lamp or a radio into the socket that normally powers the computer; if there's no power, check for a blown fuse or circuit breaker.
- Look for an on/off switch on the computer's power supply at the back of the processor unit, separate from the power switch you normally use to turn on the computer (not all power supplies have separate on/off switches). If there is a power switch, make sure that it's turned on.
- Try a different power cord. If all of the external cables are connected properly and there's AC power reaching the computer, disconnect the power cable, open the case, and confirm that the cables from the power supply are plugged into the motherboard and each hard disk drive, floppy disk drive, and CD drive and any other devices. Also, confirm that the cable from the front-panel power switch is plugged into the correct pins on the motherboard; on many boards, it's easy to plug that cable into the wrong place, and even a one- or two-pin offset could be enough to cause a problem.
- If your computer uses SCSI devices, make sure that all the SCSI devices are properly terminated and that each SCSI device has a unique ID number.
- Make sure all of the jumpers and DIP (dual in-line package) switches on the motherboard and all expansion cards are in the right position. Consult the manuals or online technical support web pages for each component to find the correct configuration for each switch or jumper.
- If you're still having power problems, confirm that the computer's power supply is working. If you have a voltmeter or a power supply tester and you know how to use it, turn on the computer and check the voltages on

one of the spare connectors that normally supply power to the disk drives. If you don't have a meter, turn on the computer and confirm that the fans on the motherboard are spinning. If there is no power present, it may be necessary to replace the power supply.

Checking a Laptop Computer

A laptop or other portable computer can run on either external power or an internal battery, so you should look for several additional sources of trouble:

- If you're trying to run a laptop on battery power and you get no response, confirm that a battery is in the battery compartment.

- If the battery is in place, try connecting the external power supply. If that solves the problem, recharge or replace the battery.

- Make sure the external power unit is securely plugged into the computer and the power unit's own power cable is plugged into a wall outlet, a power strip, uninterruptible power supply, or some other source of AC power.

- If the computer doesn't work or the battery doesn't charge when the external power unit is connected, use a voltmeter (I showed you how in Chapter 1) or other test instrument to make sure the power unit is providing the proper output voltage.

- Try removing the battery and connecting the external power supply. If the power supply does not provide adequate current (measured in amps), there may not be enough power to charge the battery and run the computer at the same time. This doesn't happen often because the manufacturer normally provides a power unit designed to match the computer's power requirements, but if you buy a used or refurbished machine, or if you're using a replacement power unit, it is possible.

The maximum current of a power unit is almost always imprinted onto the device's case. For example, the power adapter shown in Figure 2-1 provides a maximum output of 2.2 amps at 16V.

Errors During Startup

Between the time you turn on your computer and the point at which Windows is ready to accept commands, there are many opportunities for failure. If you understand what's supposed to happen before Windows starts, you can usually identify the cause of a startup problem and find a way to fix it. The startup routine is both complex and important, so all of Chapter 3 is devoted to describing it in detail and explaining how to respond to error messages and other symptoms of startup problems.

However, many of the things that happen during startup (and especially during a restart after a problem occurs) can help you understand what's happening inside your computer's tiny little mind, so it's useful to run through them briefly as part of this discussion of Windows failures.

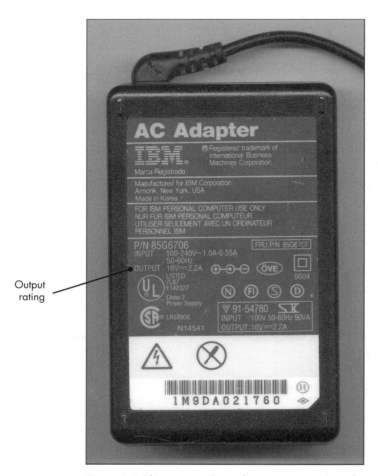

Output rating

Figure 2-1: This power adapter has an output rating of 2.2 amps at 16V.

Here's what happens after you turn on your computer's power switch: First, the central processor tests the computer's memory and some other components to confirm that the hardware is working properly. This is the *power-on self test (POST).*

Next, the processor runs a simple program called the *basic input/output system (BIOS)* that identifies the hard drives and other storage media, the keyboard and mouse, and various other inputs and outputs that allow the computer to run more complex software and exchange information with the rest of the world. It also sets the time and date. After the BIOS completes its configuration settings, it runs another program called the boot loader from a hard drive.

The boot loader is the first of a series of programs that leads to Windows running on your computer. Each program depends on the ones that precede it to provide essential information and controls, and each supplies guidance to the next one in line. When the whole sequence is complete, there's a graphic display on the screen, device drivers are sending and receiving commands and data through each of the computer's input and output devices, and Windows XP controls the computer.

When one of the programs in the startup sequence fails, it produces a distinctive error message of some kind. If there's a failure during POST, the computer sounds a series of beeps that identify the type of problem; after the central processor begins to communicate with the video display, error messages appear on the screen. Chapter 3 offers a guide to finding and understanding error messages during startup.

Not every message that appears before Windows loads is an error message. Depending on the specific BIOS settings, you will probably see a series of other messages scroll down your screen, maybe telling you about IDE and video settings, hard drive configuration, or some other results of individual POST tests. As a general rule, if Windows starts normally and you don't hear an unusual beep code, you can assume that the POST didn't detect any problems.

Troubleshooting Windows Failures

After startup is complete and Windows is in control, error messages and other failures generally follow a consistent pattern. If there's enough life left in the system to display a message, Windows will try to tell you what has gone wrong. If the problem is truly catastrophic, you might see nothing but a Black Screen of Death.

Black Screens

A Black Screen is exactly what the name suggests: the monitor goes completely dark, with absolutely no information or images in the display, and there's no response from the keyboard, the mouse, or any other input device. You've probably heard of the Blue Screen of Death. A black screen is often called the *Black Screen of Death*. For all practical purposes, the computer has frozen up. If a Black Screen error does occur, you will probably lose whatever work you were doing when the computer failed.

Fortunately, Black Screens are not common in Windows XP. But when they do occur, the only thing you can do is to turn off the computer and turn it back on again. First, try pressing the CTRL, ALT, and DELETE keys at the same time to enter a restart command. CTRL-ALT-DELETE probably won't do anything, but it's the gentlest way to restart. Next, if there's a Reset button on the computer's front panel, this is the time to use it. If you're lucky, the Black Screen was caused by some kind of temporary problem and restarting Windows will allow you to get back to whatever you were doing before it appeared.

Rumor has it that there's an entire department at Microsoft headquarters in Redmond in charge of generating these random unrepeatable errors. But, as with most rumors, we're sure it isn't true. Aren't we?

If restarting the computer doesn't work, or if the Black Screen appears again, you will have to figure out what has gone wrong. See Chapter 4 for more detailed information about recovering from a Black Screen of Death.

If a Black Screen appears before Windows starts, it's possible that one of the startup files is seriously corrupted. Use the Recovery Console (described in Chapter 3) to replace the Master Boot Record (MBR), the boot sector, and the ntldr and Ntdetect.com files.

NOTE *Don't confuse a Black Screen failure with a power failure. If somebody pulls out the computer's power cord, or if the AC power in the building goes out, the screen will go to black and the LED indicators on the front panel of a desktop or tower computer will also go dark. Also, your computer will suddenly become very quiet because the fan and the hard drive will have stopped spinning and making noise. And if the power to the building goes out, the lights in your room will probably go dark at the same time.*

Blue Screens

A Blue Screen error is also a fatal error, but the display on the computer's monitor will show a screen full of text on a solid blue background. The text contains specific details about the cause of the failure. Microsoft calls Blue Screens *Stop messages.*

Blue Screens are not as bad as Black Screens, but they're still fatal errors. Obviously, the "fatal error" metaphor has broken down here—both Black Screens and Blue Screens inform you that Windows has suffered a fatal error, but a Blue Screen isn't as fatal as a Black Screen. It seems like a failure is either fatal or it isn't, but a Blue Screen appears when the computer still has enough life to tell you what has gone wrong, whereas a Black Screen indicates a more complete failure and doesn't give you any hints about its cause.

Blue Screens always follow a standard format. In most cases, a Blue Screen will provide enough information to identify and solve the problem if you know how to interpret the cryptic text. Sometimes, they even include specific instructions for dealing with the failure. But more often, you will need an explanation of the data on your screen from another source. (See Chapter 4 for an explanation of each element in a Blue Screen, where to find more details, and how to use that information.)

Everything Is Frozen in Place

Another form of system failure is similar to a Blue or Black Screen error: the display remains visible on the monitor, but the computer fails to respond to instructions from the keyboard, the mouse, or any other input device. For all practical purposes, the computer has frozen.

As with a Black Screen, there's not much you can do about this except restart the computer. If it happens again, look for a pattern that might help identify the cause: Does the computer freeze when you are running a particular program or performing a specific action? What other programs were active at the time? Was some automatic activity running in background? If you can duplicate the lockup by repeating the combination of commands and active programs, you are part way to fixing the problem.

One possible cause of a system freeze is a conflict between the computer's video display controller and some other component. To search for conflicts, open the System Information window (**Start ▸ Run** and type **msinfo32**) and select the **Conflicts/Sharing** display under Hardware Resources, as shown in Figure 2-2.

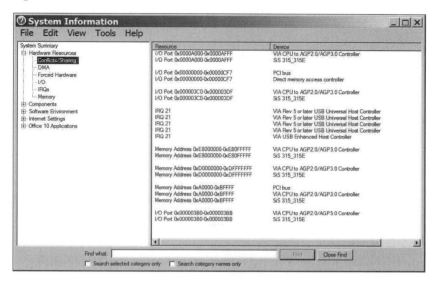

Figure 2-2: The System Information window can identify hardware conflicts. In this example, there appears to be a possible conflict between the VIA CPU to AGP controller and the SiS 315 video adapter because they're both using the same memory addresses.

If a spare is available, replacing the video card to eliminate the conflict would be the best solution; if the system does not freeze again, the conflict was the source of the problem. But the computer might lock up again because the actual cause may be something else entirely. Like most trouble-shooting efforts, this one involves an element of trial and error.

Nonfatal Error Messages

Fortunately, not every Windows problem produces a fatal error. Many other problems are less serious, so they don't force the entire computer to shut down. Some of these errors might cause a single program to close, but Windows itself will keep running. Others will simply interrupt a program without closing it completely.

Responding to Nonfatal Error Messages

Nonfatal error messages can come from Windows and from applications and utility programs. These error messages usually show up in pop-up windows.

When an error message does appear, read the text. That seems obvious, but it's often tempting to just close the thing and get on with your work. This is like ignoring the Check Engine light in your car and hoping that it will go away; it's a bad idea. It's always better to fix a minor problem now than to wait for it to turn into something more serious later on.

Sometimes the text contains instructions for fixing the problem, but often the most useful part of the message is some odd string of letters and numbers at the top or bottom of the window, such as Stop 0X000000024. Either way, the first thing to do when any error message appears is to copy the complete text, including any ID numbers and other strange codes.

The program or other software that produces an error message almost always identifies itself someplace in the error message window. For the name of the offending software, check the title bar of the window that contains the message if you can't find it anywhere inside the window. If the name of the program that produced the message does not appear anywhere in the error window, look in the toolbar at the bottom of your screen to see which programs are active.

Error Messages: Finding Translations from the Cryptic

The most important thing to remember about any error message is this: They don't appear out of thin air. And, unlikely as it sometimes seems, somebody, someplace knows what it means. When an error message appears on your screen, it is there because a piece of code inside the software told Windows or some other program to display it when some specific event or combination of events occurred.

Therefore, you can assume two things about that message: First, your computer is probably not the first one that has ever had this problem; and second, there's an explanation out there someplace. So you should take the time to search for a set of specific instructions for solving the problem rather than wasting time reinventing a procedure on your own.

If the solution to the problem that produced the error message is not immediately obvious, talk to your local help desk, ask a knowledgeable friend, or look for the text (or the ID code) in the user manual, the software provider's support website, or the online Microsoft Knowledge Base. If (when) you can't find anything helpful, either because you don't have the manual, you can't find a website, or the Microsoft Knowledge Base doesn't tell you anything useful, it's time to put yourself at the mercy of the Collective Knowledge of the Internet. Use Google or your favorite web search tool to search for the exact text of the error message, or if it's a long message, try searching for the first five or six words. If the message has an ID code, try searching for the name of the product and the complete ID code.

Don't forget to include Internet newsgroups in your search. Among others, try searching in the archive of Usenet newsgroups at http://groups .google.com. It contains something like 20 years of past entries in several thousand groups. You can also access the separate Microsoft Product Support newsgroups at http://support.microsoft.com/newsgroups/default.aspx.

Many other Internet sites contain forums and bulletin boards devoted to individual products and systems. Some are maintained by the product manufacturers, and others are independent. So it's sometimes productive to look at the web pages operated by your computer manufacturer and the manufacturers of individual components inside the box, including motherboards, video adapters, sound cards, and networking devices.

If your computer contains an AMD processor, you might also find help at the AMD Processor Support Forum (http://forums.amd.com). Unfortunately, Intel does not offer a similar forum for its processors, but its website does include an extensive list of Frequently Asked Questions (http://search2.intel.com/support).

And even if the problem appears to be with some other company's products, try a general search at http://support.microsoft.com. The Microsoft Windows XP Knowledge Base includes a lot of information about Windows problems caused by non-Microsoft products.

For more about searching for help, see Chapter 6.

What to Do When Windows Is Acting Oddly

Over time, the "look and feel" of Windows becomes part of your working environment. You know what the screen is supposed to look like and how the keyboard, the mouse, and the other devices connected to the main processor respond to your instructions. But when one or more of those elements changes, the whole computer no longer feels right and your productivity goes straight out the window (that's the proverbial window, not one of the windows on your screen). It could be a different background color or type face, or the way the on-screen cursor responds when you move your mouse, or any of a long list of other things that you didn't think about until they went wrong—if it's never done that before, changing a minor setting can be just as distracting as a total failure.

It's easy to think about Windows as a well-integrated package, but it's really a large collection of separate elements that all contribute to the look and feel of the computer (sort of like a helicopter, which has been defined as a set of spare parts moving though the air in close formation). There are dozens of settings and options that affect the appearance of windows, text, data, icons, backgrounds, sounds, keyboard response, and just about every other element of the interface between you and the computer. When one or more of those settings changes, something—on your screen, or your speakers, or your printer—may be completely different from what you expected. In fact, as many have experienced repeatedly, if enough settings and options change, it's possible to mess up Windows beyond all recognition.

Unfortunately, most of those settings are buried under two or three layers of dialog boxes, menus, and configuration windows. Even if you do find the one you need to make an adjustment, it's easy to forget where a particular setting is hidden when you want to change things back to normal. Even worse, some hidden settings change without a specific action by a user; for example, you might hear some unexpected sounds coming from your speakers after changing the visual theme.

Microsoft does not give you a printed instruction manual with Windows, and there's often no obvious logic behind the location of certain options and settings, so it can be difficult to learn where to find the settings you need to change some particular element of the user interface. You can probably find specific information about the element you want to change through online help or a web search, or you can look at all of the buried configuration options until you find the one that you want. That's often tedious, but Microsoft hasn't given us much choice.

Just about all of the windows and dialog boxes that control parts of the Windows user interface are accessible from the Control Panel, so that's the best place to start. Chapter 10 includes a more detailed guide to all of the options and settings that control elements of the Windows XP user interface.

Pop-up Ads and Redirected Web Pages: Your Desktop Under Attack

Unwanted windows that contain advertisements and bogus information, messages that appear on your screen without warning, and unwanted web pages that show up in your browser are all symptoms of some kind of interference with Windows. Either a virus, a hijack program, or some other type of *malware* (software that deliberately does uninvited, unwanted, and often harmful, nasty, or annoying things to your computer) has probably introduced itself into your system.

Malware can take several forms:

- *Adware* is software that displays advertisements when your computer is connected to the Internet and a specific program is running.

- *Spyware* is software that gathers information from your computer without your permission and sends it to somebody else through the Internet. Spyware often tracks the websites you have visited, reads your data files, or captures your keystrokes.

- *Hijacking* software changes the settings for your web browser (most often by changing your home page), your Windows desktop, or other parts of the computer to display advertisements in the browser or in pop-up windows.

- *Viruses* are programs, often hidden inside other software, that duplicate themselves and often perform other damage—some might reformat a hard drive, delete or change files, or run malicious programs during startup.

These things are *everywhere*. If you're connected to the Internet or you share programs on disks or CDs and you don't take positive action to shield your computer, it will almost certainly become infected, if it hasn't happened already.

Here are some of the symptoms of malware infections:

- The computer seems to be operating more slowly than it did when you first started using it.

- It takes a long time for Windows to start up.

- You see advertisements or other messages during startup.

- Advertisements appear in pop-up windows without warning.

- Strange programs run at random times.

- Your web browser opens at a strange home page that you didn't request.

- The browser won't let you change the home page.

- When you run a search, the browser takes you to a site you did not request.

- Your browser takes you to web pages other than the ones you requested.

- Nothing happens when you click a link to a website.

- Web links from programs (such as a word processor) don't work.

- You see extra toolbars on your browser or other programs.

- Links that you never requested appear in your desktop or your Favorites list.

- Certain programs or Windows utilities won't start.

- The LED indicators on your modem or broadband Internet router appear to be flashing a lot when you haven't entered any Internet commands.

Obviously, this stuff can make it a lot more difficult and unpleasant to use your computer. Some spyware, such as the programs that can steal your credit card information when you type it into the computer, can complicate your whole life.

It's absolutely essential to remove any malware that has infected your computer and to protect yourself from new attacks. For now, try running a complete antivirus and antispyware scan (see a list of recommended programs in Appendix B) of your computer's memory and hard drive, and install programs that will keep new infections out of your system. With luck, that will be enough to find and remove any problem. If not, try the detailed instructions I give you in Chapter 13. Finally, don't overlook the possibility that your browser took you to the wrong web page because you mistyped the address in the Address field. Check your spelling and try again.

Not all pop-up windows are malware. Some pop-ups can contain status messages from legitimate programs that are running in the background, such as firewall, antivirus, and antispyware utilities, and communication through instant messaging programs.

For example, the Microsoft AntiSpyware utility (which you can download free from www.microsoft.com/athome/security/spyware/software) displays a pop-up message like the one shown in Figure 2-3 when a program adds itself to the list of programs that run automatically during startup. Other antimalware applications and utilities do the same. This is useful and important information that you will want to know about.

Unfortunately, many other programs also foist pop-ups onto your screen, whether you want them or not. Instant messaging, system utilities, and even some entirely harmless websites all produce pop-up windows. Except for the ones where the pop-up message is an essential feature (such as nonfatal Windows error messages), most programs that use pop-ups include some kind of option for turning them off.

Figure 2-3: Some pop-up windows do provide useful and timely information.

Many pop-up windows are nothing more than visual clutter on your screen. If you never use instant messaging, use the Add/Remove Programs tool in the Control Panel to delete the messaging programs that Windows, America Online, Internet service providers, and "helpful" software packages have installed on your computer.

Service Pack 2 (SP2) for Windows XP includes a Pop-up Blocker tool for Internet Explorer. To turn the tool on or off, or to change its settings, open the Tools menu and choose the Pop-up Blocker option. The Google Toolbar (download it from www.google.com/downloads) also includes a blocking tool. Both of these utilities allow you to bypass the blocker when you want to view a specific window. You can test the effectiveness of your pop-up blocker by using the tools at www.popuptest.com.

Hardware Problems

Sometimes Windows is working fine but one of the hardware components—the central processor, a memory module, or some other part of the physical machine—is not working properly.

Hardware problems can occur in several forms:

- A physical component (such as a cable, a capacitor, or an integrated circuit) within a hardware device can fail, or it might have a manufacturing defect.

- A component or connector might have come loose from the socket in which it was mounted.

- A connector might have been installed incorrectly.

- The software embedded in a memory chip inside a component (the firmware) can contain bad or damaged code.

- The software interface between the device and the central processor can conflict with some other device.

- The device driver (the software that exchanges commands and data between the device and the central processor) may be damaged, it may contain bad code, or it may be completely absent.

When any of these problems occur, the component affected by the problem won't work properly, if it works at all. If an essential major component such as the power supply, the central processor, or a memory module fails, the computer won't start at all, or if it does, it will fail the POST. If it's a hard drive, the computer will start but Windows will not load. And if the problem occurs in some other input or output device, Windows might load but that device won't work.

Chapter 5 contains a more detailed explanation of device drivers, including instructions for finding and installing them. In Chapter 16, I offer more general information about hardware troubleshooting.

Memory Problems

Memory problems can present an entirely different set of issues. If one or more of the memory modules inside your computer is defective, or if the computer contains two or more incompatible modules (for who knows what reason), the computer can display Blue Screen error messages, freeze up, or simply fail to run. If your research suggests that a memory problem is possible, the first line of memory troubleshooting includes these techniques:

- Run the free Memtest86+ memory test utility from a boot disk or CD. You can download Memtest86+ from www.memtest.org.

- If the computer contains more than one memory module, try removing a module and running the machine with the remaining modules to see if the one that you removed is bad. Do this for each module, one at a time. Consult the motherboard manual to learn how to arrange the remaining modules. If the manual specifies that the system requires memory modules in pairs, test the modules two at a time.

For more about finding and fixing memory problems, read the section "Memory Problems" on page 193.

Internet Connection Problems

Whether your computer connects to the Internet through a dial-up telephone line, a high-speed DSL or cable TV connection, or a local area network, it ought to be easy to make the connection. You might have to log on to an account through your Internet service provider, but after that the link between your computer and the one that provides a web page, e-mail, or some other service should be completely transparent—you shouldn't have to worry about any of the Internet's internal plumbing.

But before you can make an Internet connection, you must configure your own computer and the router or modem (or both) that moves data between your computer and the Internet. If any of the configuration settings are wrong, your connection may not work. Those settings should not change at random, but the configuration screens are the first place to look when a connection fails.

Other possible but less common sources of connection problems include trouble with the telephone line or cable TV connection, problems with the proprietary software supplied by the Internet service provider, and failures at the Internet service provider or someplace else along the way. (See Chapter 14 for more detailed information on troubleshooting your Internet connection.)

Local Network Problems

When your computer is connected to a network, you should be able to exchange files and messages with other computers connected to the same network and, often, to connect through the network to the Internet. If you can't, and you used to be able to, look for the most common causes of network problems:

- Incorrect or missing configuration settings on your computer, such as the numeric address assigned to the computer by the local network or your Internet service provider or the address of your domain name service (DNS) server
- Configuration settings on your computer that don't match the settings on the network hub or gateway that controls the local area network
- Missing or damaged cables
- Failure of some other network component (such as a hub, router, switch, or destination computer) that is improperly configured or broken
- A firewall blocking access

Finding and fixing a network problem can be particularly frustrating because the source of the problem can just as easily be located on another computer or in the equipment that connects the network together within your own system. If you can't find the problem on your own machine, look at the configuration settings for other computers, switches, and routers connected to the same network. See Chapter 15 for more detail on solving network problems.

Where Do We Go from Here?

Up to this point, I've really just given you a detailed overview of the whys and wherefores of things that can and do go wrong on Windows-based computers. And, of course, they're the first things to look for when you discover that It's Never Done That Before!

The remaining chapters of this book describe Windows failures, error messages, and less-traumatic problems in more detail. If you can't find information about the specific problem you're facing, try reading the chapter with a title that comes closest to describing it. Even if you don't find instructions for fixing a specific problem, you will probably be able to use the methods described to deal with a problem in the same general category or follow a pointer to another source of information.

3

WHAT TO DO WHEN WINDOWS WON'T START

You know the routine: Turn on the computer, a bunch of text scrolls past as the monitor warms up, you see a sequence of "Windows is loading . . ." screens, and then Windows starts. You have to wait a couple of minutes for everything to load, but eventually your familiar desktop fills the screen, and you're ready to get to work. After the third or fourth time, you don't even notice that it's happening.

But one day, for no obvious reason, Windows won't load. Either the screen goes dark or one of the "Windows is loading . . ." screens stays there forever. Or worse, you get a Blue Screen error. Yikes! What happened?

This chapter explains what normally happens when Windows starts and how to use several tools and techniques for troubleshooting when it just won't start.

The Windows Startup Sequence

Every time you turn on your computer, the machine and Windows XP perform a series of actions, always in the same order: First, the read-only memory basic input/output system (ROM BIOS) performs a series of diagnostic tests to confirm that the processor and memory are working properly. Then it tests some of the computer's other components, including the hard drive and the video display. When those tests are complete, the BIOS runs the first of a series of programs that lead to starting the full Windows operating system. In other words, the whole startup process uses a relatively simple program located on a memory chip to start other, more complex software in several stages.

Power-on Self Test (POST)

The power-on self test (POST) is the first thing that happens when you turn on the computer. During the POST, the central processor uses instructions in the BIOS firmware (software located in a memory chip on the computer's motherboard) to confirm that the power supply is working properly, run some memory and hardware tests, find operating system software on a hard drive or some other storage media, and set the configuration options specified in the BIOS.

When the computer detects a problem during the POST, it either displays a text message that describes the error, or it sounds a series of beeps (actually, *beep codes*). If the problem is so serious that it will not allow the computer to work properly (such as a massive memory failure), the system will either lock up or turn off the computer completely.

Some of these error messages halt the POST, so the message remains visible on your monitor screen, but others might scroll past before you can read them. To stop the text from disappearing, press the PAUSE BREAK key on the right of the normal keyboard. To resume the startup routine, hold down the CTRL key and press PAUSE BREAK again.

Beep Codes

If the POST detects a memory problem or some other condition that keeps the video display from showing error messages, a beep code will sound within the first 30 seconds after you turn on the computer. If you hear a beep code, note the number of long and short beeps and the order in which they sound. See Appendix A for a list of common beep codes.

Each type of BIOS uses a distinct beep code pattern, so it's relatively easy to identify the problem that produced the code, even if you don't know the brand of BIOS your computer is using.

For example, if you hear one long beep followed by three short beeps, the computer has an AwardBIOS, and the POST has detected a memory problem; a 1-2-2-1 code (one beep, pause, two beeps, pause, two beeps, pause, one beep) indicates a keyboard problem on a PhoenixBIOS.

Some computer motherboards also display POST codes on an LED readout mounted on the board. You'll have to remove the cover from the computer case to see this display. If your computer has such a display, you can find a list of codes in the manual or on the motherboard maker's website.

Initial Startup: What Happens When You Push the Button

After the computer completes the POST built into the motherboard, it may run additional tests on some of the other components, including the hard drive and the video adapter. Each of these tests can produce its own set of error messages.

When the POST is complete, the computer tries to load the operating system software stored on the hard drive (in this case, Windows XP), a floppy disk, a CD, or some other storage device.

A problem can occur during initial startup for several reasons:

- There's a disk in the floppy drive or the CD drive, but it does not contain the essential startup files.
- The designated startup disk is damaged, whether it be a floppy, CD, or hard drive.
- The hard drive has not been formatted.
- The hard drive has been damaged, or the startup data is corrupt.

If the BIOS does not discover any problems, it locates the boot sector on the startup drive and runs a Windows boot loader program called ntldr (NT Loader or boot loader). Ntldr takes over control of the computer from the BIOS. (The filename ntldr is left over from the earlier version of Windows called Windows NT; hey, whatever works.)

Run the Boot Loader

The boot loader program loads a series of startup programs, instructs the central processor to handle 32 data bits at one time, and starts the file system that Windows will use to exchange data with the hard drive.

Finally, the boot loader reads the boot.ini file that identifies the location of the operating system files and runs the ntdetect.com program to detect and configure the hardware connected to your computer.

Detect and Configure Hardware

Windows uses the information gathered by ntdetect.com to identify and configure the various hardware devices that it uses to send, receive, and store data. This includes the keyboard and mouse; disk drives and other data storage devices; the video adapter that controls the monitor display; the I/O (input and output) ports, including the serial, parallel, Ethernet, and USB ports; and any other input or output devices installed in the expansion slots on the motherboard. Ntdectect.com also reads certain information from the BIOS firmware, including the time and date.

Load the Windows Kernel

The file ntoskrnl.exe in your Windows installation is the Windows kernel; it contains the core of the Windows XP operating system. The ntldr program loads the kernel into memory, along with a file that contains information about the specific hardware installed on this computer. Once these two files (ntoskrnl.exe and the hardware file) load successfully, Windows starts a series of programs called the "Windows executive" that reads configuration information from the Windows Registry and starts the secondary programs and background services that have been set to load during startup.

Once the kernel finishes running the startup instructions in the Registry, it runs the Session Manager program (smss.exe), which, among several other important functions, shifts Windows from text mode to graphics mode. In other words, this is the point at which you begin to see graphic images on your screen.

Logon

At this point, Windows XP is in control of your computer. The logon routine requests the current user's username and password (if any). Once that user logs in, Windows loads any additional startup programs specified in the Registry for that user's account.

NOTE   *It's possible to set Windows to load the username and password automatically, in which case you might not see the logon screen, but Windows always runs a logon sequence.*

The Registry specifies a set of logon scripts, startup programs, and services for each user. These might include enhancements to the core Windows operating system, security (such as antivirus or antispyware) programs, and other utility programs that run in the background. Once Windows finishes running those scripts and all specified programs and services have started, the Windows startup sequence is finished, your Windows desktop is visible, and the computer is ready to use. Well, that's the idea anyway.

So What Can Go Wrong?

When everything is working properly, all of this takes longer to describe than it takes to complete. The whole startup process should take no more than two or three minutes, unless there's some time-consuming program (such as a complete antivirus scan) included among the list of programs that run automatically after logon.

Obviously, there are a lot of separate processes involved in starting Windows. Each of the phases described in this section depends on the ones that precede it; if something goes wrong in any of them, the whole sequence will probably stop. So the key to troubleshooting a startup failure is to identify the particular startup phase that failed and the individual process that failed within that phase.

When startup fails, one of the following things will happen:

- A POST beep code will sound, and the computer will either freeze or shut down.
- The scrolling text display will freeze.
- The computer will display an error message as it scrolls the startup text.
- The monitor will go dark.
- The "Windows is loading . . ." graphic image will remain on the screen permanently.
- A Blue Screen error will appear.
- An error window will appear.

Yes, there are quite a few possibilities. Fortunately, the type of failure should give you a good idea of where in the sequence the failure occurred:

- If you see an error message, in text mode, in a Blue Screen, or a in pop-up error window, you can use the text of the message to identify the source of the problem.
- If the computer freezes in text mode, the last line or two of text should identify the last part of the startup routine that worked properly.
- If the screen goes dark, or if the "Windows is loading . . ." graphic remains on the screen, the first thing to do is nothing: wait a couple of minutes to allow Windows to try to recover from the problem. This doesn't always work, but it's worth a try. If there's no change after about five minutes, try pressing the ESC key two or three times. If *that* doesn't help, use the Reset button on the front of the computer case and see if the computer starts properly this time; if the same error appears again, try booting the computer into Safe Mode.
- If an arrow or other mouse cursor is visible on the screen but nothing seems to be happening, try moving the mouse. If the cursor follows the mouse, you can assume that the rest of Windows is still loading; if there's no response on the screen when you move the mouse, the computer has probably frozen.

Making Sense of Startup Error Messages

An error message is often cryptic, requiring a more detailed explanation before you can correct the problem that produced it. The easiest way to find such an explanation is to use a second, working computer to conduct an Internet search for the exact text of the message or some of its keywords. If you don't find what you're looking for on the Web, try searching newsgroups. You'll probably find it.

Non-System Disk Error

One of the most common startup error messages looks like this:

```
Non-system disk or disk error
Replace and press any key when ready
```

This message appears when the first disk drive or other storage device that the processor tries to read does not contain a copy of Windows or some other operating system. The startup routine ignores drives with no media in them, but if there's a floppy disk or a CD in the startup drive, or if the processor can't find a copy of Windows on the hard drive configured as the C: drive, the computer will display a "Non-system disk" message. (Just because it can't find Windows doesn't mean that it's not there—it may simply be missing one or more key startup files.)

The error message is very badly written; it doesn't really want you to "replace and press any key," but to replace a disk and then press a key. To solve this problem, make sure there are no disks in the floppy disk drive or the CD drive, and then press the space bar or some other key on your keyboard. This will instruct the computer to try reading the startup drive again.

If the same error message appears again, the problem is in your hard drive: the hard drive does not contain the Windows startup files, the startup files are on the drive but they are damaged, or the computer is having trouble reading the drive because the drive has been damaged or the cables to the drive are not connected. (See Chapter 16 for information about how to troubleshoot hard drive problems and recover data from damaged drives.)

NOTE *You might also see a "Non-system disk" message after you install a new primary hard drive because the processor won't find a copy of Windows on that drive until you install Windows from the CD.*

Master Boot Record Problems: The Root of Everything

Microsoft describes the Master Boot Record (MBR) as "the most important data structure on the disk." If the computer's processor can't read the MBR, it won't make sense of anything else on the same drive or floppy disk. Without the MBR, the rest of the drive is useless.

The MBR is stored in the first sector of each hard drive. When the POST is complete, the computer loads the MBR from the drive that contains the operating system software into memory and the MBR runs the ntldr startup program that loads Windows.

If the computer can't read the MBR—due to a corrupt file, a virus, or other damage to the hard drive—one of these messages might appear:

```
Invalid partition table.
Error loading operating system.
Missing operating system.
```

```
A disk read error occurred.
NTLDR is missing.
NTLDR is compressed.
```

The first thing to do when you see one of these messages is to place an antivirus boot disk in your computer's floppy drive or CD drive (whichever drive the computer tries to read first) and run an antivirus scan. Most commercial antivirus programs include an emergency boot disk that can perform a startup scan. If the scan does not detect a virus, use the Recovery Console (see "Bypassing Windows with the Recovery Console" on page 46) to restore the MBR, the ntldr file, or a corrupted boot sector. I'd suggest considering first any changes that you've recently made. Sometimes I think even running the recovery tools can mess up your system. If it's not a virus, it will be a damaged file. Undoing changes is unlikely to repair the damage.

Other Startup Error Messages

After the ntldr runs the boot loader, it starts the Ntdetect.com program, which gathers information about additional devices installed in your computer. These devices include the time and date set in firmware and the video adapter, keyboard, mouse, communication ports, disk drives, and other devices on plug-in expansion cards.

If ntldr detects a problem with any of these devices, it will display an error message during startup. Each device produces different messages, so there's no universal standard message text. To find more information about a message, run a web search on the exact text of the message. In most cases, a search on the first three or four words is enough to find an explanation of a message. (Place quotation marks at the beginning and end of the phrase to restrict your search to the exact phrase rather than the individual words.)

Returning to the Last Known Good Configuration

If Windows won't start after you install a new program or device driver or an update or patch to existing software, the Last Known Good Configuration tool can often solve the problem by returning the computer to the state it was in before the new software was installed and any other recent configuration changes took place.

Every time Windows starts successfully, it stores a copy of the current configuration in the CurrentControlSet section of the Registry. The copy is called LastKnownGood. As the name suggests, the Last Known Good Configuration tool returns the computer to that configuration and ignores any changes that might have occurred since then. By returning to the last known good configuration, you can sometimes fix Windows so that it will start; this is kind of like turning back time.

To return to the last known good configuration, follow these steps:

1. With no disks in the CD drive or the floppy disk drive, restart the computer.

2. When the results of the POST appear on your screen, press the F8 key until the Windows Advanced Options menu appears.

3. Use the up and down arrow keys to highlight the Last Known Good Configuration option, and press the ENTER key. Windows should restart using the LastKnownGood control set.

If the LastKnownGood control set can load Windows, the computer should restart, and Windows should start with the old configuration settings. If the restart is unsuccessful, you should see another text screen with a menu of startup options; try the Last Known Good Configuration option again, and if that doesn't work (again), try starting Windows in Safe Mode.

If neither Last Known Good Configuration nor Safe Mode works, you might have to use the Recovery Console to remove one or more damaged system files or the Windows CD to completely reinstall Windows.

Bypassing Windows with the Recovery Console

The Recovery Console is a simple text-based tool for changing the file structure that controls Windows and repairing or replacing damaged files. The Recovery Console is a command-line interface that accepts a limited set of troubleshooting and maintenance commands. It's similar to the old DOS shell that we used before Windows and other graphical interfaces were introduced. When Windows will not start in either Normal Mode or Safe Mode, you can often use the Recovery Console to disable a driver or service that is causing a problem, restore a damaged file or a corrupt Master Boot Record (MBR) on your hard drive, or fix a host of other potential problems.

NOTE *The Recovery Console can be a powerful tool for finding and fixing certain types of startup problems, but if you don't know exactly what you're doing, it can also allow you to create new problems that will complicate the ones that are already on your computer or even completely trash Windows' ability to start. Therefore, it's best to use the Recovery Console only when you have detailed instructions for performing a specific task from a reliable source such as the Microsoft Knowledge Base or your local help desk (the procedures later in this chapter count as a "reliable source").*

The best way to load and use the Recovery Console is to run it directly from the Windows XP CD. To do so, follow these steps:

1. Place the Windows XP CD into the drive.

2. Restart the computer from the CD.

3. At the Welcome to Setup screen, press the R key. The Recovery Console starts and shows a list of Windows installations on your computer. In most cases, there will be just one item in the list.

4. Enter the number of the version you want to use, and press the ENTER key. The Recovery Console will ask for the administrator password.

Type the same password you would normally use to log into Windows as an administrator, and press ENTER. If there is no administrator password, just press the ENTER key. When the Recovery Console accepts the password, it will display a C:\WINDOWS> prompt.

To close the Recovery Console, type **Exit** at the C:\ prompt.

Solving Startup Problems with the Recovery Console

As I explained earlier in this chapter, the BIOS built into your computer's motherboard uses ntldr to begin the process of installing and running Windows. It uses NTDETECT.COM to find and configure input and output devices. If the BIOS can't process either of these program files, Windows cannot load.

You can use the Recovery Console to restore a missing or damaged copy of ntldr or the NTDETECT.COM startup file and to replace the Master Boot Record and the boot sector.

To enter a command into the Recovery Console, type the command at the C:\WINDOWS> prompt. Press the ENTER key at the end of each command to send it to the computer.

To replace ntldr, enter

```
copy drive:i386\ntldr
```

In place of *drive*, use the drive letter for the CD drive.

To replace NTDETECT.COM, enter

```
copy drive:i386\ntdetect.com
```

In place of *drive*, use the drive letter for the CD drive.

To replace the Master Boot Record, enter

```
fixmbr
```

To replace the boot sector, enter

```
fixboot
```

The Recovery Console will ask, Overwrite system? (Yes/No/All). Enter **Y** for yes each time the question appears.

NOTE *When the ntldr and NTDETECT.COM files have been damaged, you may also have other damaged system files at the same time. Using the Recovery Console to restore those files alone might not be enough to get Windows up and running, but it's a good start.*

Safe Mode

Safe Mode is a special startup sequence that loads only the files and drivers needed to run Windows and nothing else. It's a valuable troubleshooting tool because it starts the core Windows services without any of the additional programs or services that normally start with Windows. If Windows won't start normally but it will start in Safe Mode, the cause of the problem is not in the Windows kernel.

Even though Safe Mode loads a limited version of Windows, it may be enough because it will often let you bypass whatever is keeping you from running Windows normally (such as a device or software conflict) and let you use troubleshooting tools and techniques to identify and solve a problem.

NOTE *If Windows will run in Safe Mode but it won't start normally, you can usually isolate the problem to one of the add-in drivers or services that normally start with Windows.*

To enter Safe Mode, follow these steps:

1. Turn the computer off and then on again, and immediately press F8 a few times. A text screen that contains the Windows Advanced Options menu should appear.
2. Use the up and down arrow keys to choose **Safe Mode** or **Safe Mode With Networking**. A window appears and asks you to confirm that you want to work in Safe Mode.
3. Press ENTER or use your mouse to select **Yes**.

Safe Mode is a troubleshooting tool. Your desktop in Safe Mode will probably look quite different than it usually looks (different resolution, larger text and icons, no background image), because Safe Mode does not load the configuration file that controls its appearance. Because Safe Mode supports only essential devices and services, including the mouse, the keyboard, the hard drives and the CD drive, and most VGA display controllers, when Windows is running in Safe Mode, you won't be able to use audio devices, printers, or most other peripheral devices.

Safe Mode is also useful because it can sometimes allow you to bypass the problem that was interfering with startup and run Windows with enough power to support many applications. If you don't have time to fix your computer until after you complete your current project, you might be able to use Safe Mode after Windows crashes to make a copy of your work that you can then use on another computer. When that kind of disaster happens, a computer at the public library or a 24-hour copy shop can be a lifesaver.

The System Configuration Utility

As I explained earlier in this chapter, Windows often loads additional programs and background services after the core Windows software starts. Because the commands that load these programs can be located in at least half a dozen different places in the Windows Registry, it can be confusing (to say the least) to find and control all of these startup commands. The System Configuration Utility gathers all the startup programs into a single list and makes it possible to disable each program.

As a troubleshooting tool, the Configuration Utility can instruct Windows to skip one startup program at a time during startup; if Windows starts successfully without one of the programs, that one is probably the source of the problem.

Follow these steps to run the System Configuration Utility:

1. Choose **Start ▸ Run**.

2. Enter **msconfig** in the Open field as shown in Figure 3-1, and click **OK**.

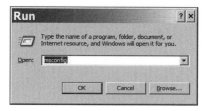

Figure 3-1: Running the System Configuration Utility

In Windows XP, the System Configuration Utility window (see Figure 3-2) has six tabs. In earlier versions of Windows, you may see fewer tabs. All but the General tab contain a list of individual commands, programs, and services that normally start as part of the Windows startup sequence.

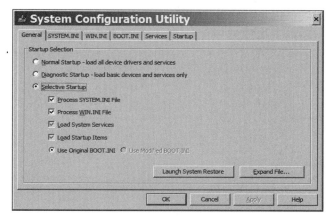

Figure 3-2: The System Configuration Utility offers startup options under six separate tabs.

The two tabs at the extreme right, Services and Startup, open pages that list the programs and services that load during the final startup phase. Figure 3-3 shows the Startup page. If the Windows desktop appears on your screen but the computer never completes the startup sequence, the source of the problem is probably one or more of the items listed on these pages.

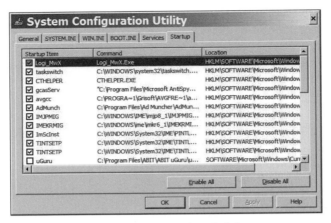

Figure 3-3: The Startup tab opens a list of all the programs that run when Windows starts.

To identify the specific program or service that is causing the problem, follow these steps:

1. Open Windows in Safe Mode.

2. Open the System Configuration Utility (**Start ▸ Run ▸ msconfig**).

3. Select the **Services** tab or the **Startup** tab.

4. At the left side of the list of Services or Startup Items, click one of the check boxes to remove the check mark. The next time you restart Windows, the program or service on the same line as the unchecked box will not start.

5. Click the **OK** button at the bottom of the window.

6. The Configuration program will ask if you want to restart your computer now. Click the **Restart** button.

7. Watch the screen as Windows restarts. If Windows starts normally, the program or service you unchecked was the source of your startup problem.

8. If Windows continues to hang, use the Reset button on the front of the computer to restart the computer, and press the F8 key to start in Safe Mode.

9. Open the System Configuration Utility again.

10. Select the **Services** tab or the **Startup** tab, and restore the check mark that you removed in Step 4.

11. Uncheck the next item in the list and repeat the restart process.

Continue to disable one program or service at a time; then restart the computer after each modification until you isolate the program or service that is causing the startup problem. This can be a tedious and time-consuming process, but it really is the best way to isolate the program that is keeping Windows from starting properly.

Every time you restart the computer after changing the list of startup items, the Configuration Utility adds itself to the list of startup programs and displays the pop-up window shown in Figure 3-4 after Windows has restarted. Click **OK** to close this window. When you are finished using the Configuration Utility, check the **Don't Show This Message . . .** option in the pop-up window.

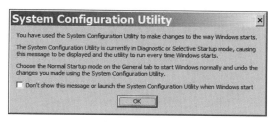

Figure 3-4: The System Configuration Utility opens
this window after the computer restarts.

Once you have identified the program that is giving you grief, there are several things you can do. If it's not an essential program, the best thing to do is to uninstall it. If it's a program you use all the time, try uninstalling it and reinstalling from the original CD or other media. If the problem reappears, use the Configuration Utility to temporarily disable the program and look for help from the software developer, from the Microsoft Knowledge Base, or from one of the other sources of troubleshooting advice described in Chapter 1 of this book.

Using the Configuration Utility to Streamline Startup

When you open the System Configuration Utility, you probably won't recognize all of the programs and services listed in the Services and Startup tabs. Some of these might be useful programs or obscure parts of Windows, but it's quite possible that some other programs have added themselves to the startup list without your knowledge or permission. Each of these programs increases the amount of time needed for Windows to start and ties up some small amount of the computer's memory that could otherwise be used for more valuable work, so it's a good idea to permanently disable them.

But how can you tell which programs and services are essential and which are junk? In some cases, the name of the startup item or service or the text of the command is a giveaway, but other names are more cryptic. For an explanation of any unfamiliar program or service, use a web search tool (such as Google) to find a description of the name you see in the Startup Item or Service column. Several websites are dedicated to explaining most of the items that appear in the Configuration Utility, with a recommendation for each item to either keep or disable it.

Here are some websites that offer useful explanations of startup items:

www.auditmypc.com

www.tasklist.org

www.answersthatwork.com/Tasklist_pages/tasklist.htm

www.bleepingcomputer.com/startups

These sites tend to come and go without warning, so you might not find the information you need on all of them. If you can't find a startup item in the first place you look, try another site, or run a Google search on the name of the item. However, be warned: Several other sites that claim to offer similar lists are really just come-ons to paid subscription services; you should be able to find the same information without paying for it.

Don't worry about turning off an essential program by accident. If Windows won't restart properly, you can restore a startup item by replacing the check mark next to its name. You might have to work through the list and turn startup items on one at a time to find the essential one, but you won't do any permanent damage by turning something off just to see what happens.

The Boot Log: A History of Startup Programs

When Windows fails to start correctly, the failure may occur because one or more of the programs in the boot sequence does not load. A list of startup programs that shows whether each program has started can help you find the specific source of the problem. There is one; it's called the Boot Log.

The Boot Log does not store this information every time Windows starts, but when Windows fails to start properly, you can turn on the logger and then restart the computer to create a new log.

The Boot Log itself is contained in a file called ntbtlog.txt, located in the system root directory (usually C:\Windows). If you can't find ntbtlog.txt in that directory, just search for it (**Start ▸ Search**).

To turn on the Boot Log, follow these steps:

1. Find the existing ntbtlog.txt file, and rename it ntbtlog-old.txt.

2. Restart Windows.

3. Once the computer shuts down and begins to start again, press F8 repeatedly to open the Windows Advanced Options menu.

4. Select **Enable Boot Logging** from the Options menu, and press ENTER. Windows will load normally, but it will also create a new Boot Log.

If Windows does not start successfully once you have turned on the Boot Log, restart the computer in Safe Mode. (You may have to use the Reset button on the front panel to turn the computer off and back on again.)

To read the Boot Log, change to the system root directory (probably C:\Windows), and double-click the ntbtlog.txt icon. The Boot Log will appear as a text file, as shown in Figure 3-5.

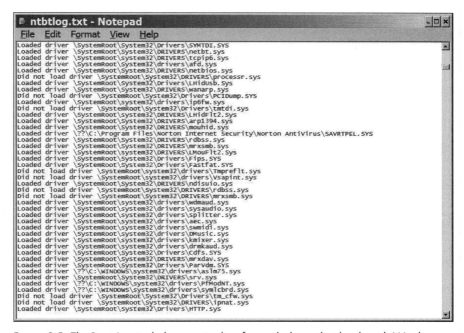

Figure 3-5: The Boot Log includes a status line for each driver that loads with Windows.

The top line of the Boot Log shows the version of Windows and the date and time that the log was created. Each of the following lines lists the status of a driver: either Loaded driver or Did not load driver. A Did not load driver log entry tells you that Windows could not find the driver file or the file is damaged.

The Boot Log lists the drivers in the order in which Windows tried to load them. In most cases, the most important entry in a Boot Log for a failed startup is at the bottom of the list because that entry probably shows the name of a critical file that failed to load.

NOTE *When the name of a driver file appears in the Boot Log without a path, that file is located in the root directory, which is the one that contains the ntbtlg.txt file. If a driver file is in a different folder, the Boot Log shows the file's full path address (such as \WINDOWS\System32\DRIVERS\filename).*

Solving Those "Did Not Load" Errors

You will probably see several Did not load items in the Boot Log, even if Windows seems to have loaded successfully and appears to be working properly. Some of the drivers or services that do not load will be relics from programs or devices that you have removed from your system but still contain references in the Registry. You can remove those references with a Registry cleaner tool, but they're basically harmless.

However, if you find one or more `Did not load driver` items at the end of the Boot Log, they are probably the ones that caused Windows to stop loading. With this information in hand, the best approach to repairing the startup routine is to work backward from the end of Boot Log.

Once you identify the drivers that failed to load, you can determine if a driver is damaged by examining the file properties for the driver file. To view a file's properties, move your mouse cursor over the name of the file in the Windows directory in My Computer, and click the right mouse button.

If the file is completely missing, or if the file properties list show that the file size is 0 bytes, or if the date and time stamp shows a date that is different from the date you installed Windows XP (the "Created:" and "Modified" date stamps should be the same as the ones for C:\Windows\explorer.exe and C:\Windows\notepad.exe), the file is damaged. That's what "did not load" means.

If your file is damaged, you can do one of two things:

- Copy the damaged or missing file or files from another computer running the same Windows version and the same service pack.
- Reinstall Windows from the distribution CD. Use the repair option rather than a full Windows installation.

If another driver fails to load after you restore the first damaged file, you may need to run a new Boot Log to identify and restore that driver file.

4

BLACK SCREENS AND BLUE SCREENS

When a problem in Windows forces the operating system to fail, the computer often displays an error screen, known as a *Stop message*, that describes the cause of the problem. At least that's the official name; most people who are not on the Microsoft payroll call them *Blue Screens of Death (BSODs)*, or just *Blue Screens*, because these messages display text on a solid blue background. When the failure is so complete that it interferes with the computer's ability to display an error message, the screen goes completely dark. Microsoft calls this a *black screen error*. And as you might expect, the rest of the world calls it the *Black Screen of Death*. Rumor has it that the next version of Windows will also include a Red Screen of Death that presumably will appear when a new and even more horrible form of failure occurs.

Both Black Screens and Blue Screens are symptoms of very serious problems. When one of these screens appears, it almost always means that Windows has shut down everything that was running when it detected the problem and any text, image, or other open file has been lost. This is one good reason to save your work frequently (many programs have autosave functions) and keep backups.

Black Screens

More often than not, a Black Screen is a symptom of a hardware failure. Unfortunately, though, a Black Screen doesn't provide any specific information about the cause of the failure; since it can't display any text at all, Windows can't tell you anything about the problem, so you must resort to more general troubleshooting methods.

Open Windows in Safe Mode

To begin trying to fix this problem, first try restarting the computer with either the power switch or the reset button on the front panel of the processor case. In some cases, the failure will have been caused by a temporary problem that disappears when you reboot. This kind of temporary glitch can be hugely irritating, but the repair is relatively painless, except for the data you might have lost when Windows failed.

If that doesn't work, or if the Black Screen occurs again after the computer has been running for a short time, try restarting Windows in Safe Mode. If Windows appears to start properly in Safe Mode, take a look at the Device Manager (**Start ▶ Settings ▶ System ▶ Hardware ▶ Device Manager**) to confirm that all of the controllers, adapters, and other devices are working. If there's a red exclamation point (!) or a yellow question mark (?) next to any of the items listed in the Device Manager, double-click that item and follow the troubleshooting procedure in the Properties window. If there's no apparent hardware failure, and if the Black Screen occurred during startup, go to the System Configuration Utility (**Start ▶ Run ▶ msconfig**) and try turning off the programs or services listed in the Services and Startup tabs, one at a time. Let the Configuration Utility restart Windows in Normal Mode. If the Black Screen doesn't come back, you have identified the source of the problem; if it does reappear, go back to the Configuration Utility, restore the check mark that you had previously removed, and uncheck the next item in the list. Keep trying until Windows starts successfully.

Look for a Hardware Problem

If Windows won't start in Safe Mode, the problem is almost certainly in the computer hardware. Try restarting the computer again, and this time watch the screen as the startup testing information scrolls past. You might see a text message that identifies the problem.

If there's no obvious source for the problem, turn off the computer, disconnect the power cord, and open the case. Look for power and data cables that might have come loose from the motherboard or some other component, and confirm that the memory modules and the main CPU processor are properly seated in their sockets.

Of course, if the computer doesn't respond at all when you try to turn it on—no lights, no noise, no nothin'—it's likely that the problem is a power failure. Either the computer is getting no power from the AC outlet or battery or the internal power supply has failed.

Blue Screens

Blue Screens are more common than Black Screens, but they're often equally irritating. Fortunately, because the computer has enough life left in it to display text on the screen, Blue Screen errors do provide some information that can help identify the reason for the failure, although the messages can be rather cryptic.

How to Read a Stop Message

All Stop messages use the same format, like the one shown in Figure 4-1. The stop error number at the top of the screen identifies the specific type of problem that produced the error. Stop error numbers are in hexadecimal numeric format, and they always begin with an *0x* prefix. The stop error number (also known as the *bugcheck code*) is followed by a series of additional hex codes in parentheses.

```
***STOP: 0x000000D1 (0x00000000, 0xF73120AE, 0xC0000008, 0xC0000000)

A problem has been detected and Windows has been shut down to prevent damage
to your computer

DRIVER_IRQL_NOT_LESS_OR_EQUAL

If this is the first time you've seen this Stop error screen, restart your
computer.  If this screen appears again, follow these steps:

Check to make sure any new hardware or software is properly installed.  If this is a
new installation, ask your hardware or software manufacturer for any Windows updates
you might need.

If problems continue, disable or remove any newly installed hardware or software.
Disable BIOS memory options such as caching or shadowing.  If you need to use Safe
Mode to remove or disable components, restart your computer, press f8 to select
Advanced Startup Options, and then select Safe Mode.

*** WXYZ.SYS - Address F73120AE base at C00000000, DateStamp 36b072a3

Kernel Debugger Using: COM2 (Port 0x2f8, Baud Rate 19200)
Beginning dump of physical memory
Physical memory dump complete.  Contact your system administrator or
technical support group.
```

Figure 4-1: Blue Screen error messages always follow the same format.

Each stop error number corresponds to a "symbolic name" that appears beneath the generic "A problem has been detected . . ." text, a few lines down the screen. For example, a stop error with a 0x000000000A code always uses the symbolic name "IRQL_NOT_LESS_OR_EQUAL." Unfortunately, most of the symbolic names in Blue Screens are just about that cryptic. They meant something to the programmer who wrote the code, but they don't mean much to the rest of us without a detailed explanation.

The next part of the screen contains a block of plain text that offers one or more suggestions for recovering from the problem that produced the error. Some of these recommendations are more useful than others, but they're always worth trying.

NOTE   *Before you reach for the reset button or the power switch, remember to copy the text of the Stop message, including the stop error number, the symbolic name, and the driver information; you will need this information to troubleshoot the problem.*

Look for More Details

In too many cases, the recommended user action is not enough to solve the problem because it often doesn't say much more than "restart the computer and undo whatever you just did." But the Microsoft Knowledge Base and other online sources can usually provide more details when you run a web search on the stop error number or the symbolic name.

Replace the Driver File

If a corrupted driver file has caused the problem, the third section of the stop error screen shows the name of a driver file. To restore a bad driver file, follow these steps:

1. Note the name of the file identified in the Blue Screen error message.
2. Restart the computer in Safe Mode.
3. Use the **Start ▶ Search** tool to find the bad driver file.
4. Right-click the name of the driver file, and compare the date with the dates of other driver files; if the "Created" date is more recent, it's likely that the driver file is corrupt. Confirm that the size of the file is greater than zero.
5. If the driver file has been damaged, use the device driver rollback tool to restore the file to its original condition. In **Start ▶ Run**, type **devmgmt.msc** and click the **OK** button. The Device Manager window appears on the screen.
6. Find the device whose driver appears to be damaged. You will probably see a red or yellow mark over the name of the device. Double-click the device name. A Properties window appears.
7. Select the **Driver** tab and click the **Roll Back Driver** button.

If Windows can find another, earlier version of the driver file on your hard drive, it will install that one in place of the current, apparently defective file. If it can't find another driver file, it will display a message that offers to run the Troubleshooter.

If That Doesn't Work . . .

The Troubleshooter will probably tell you to uninstall and reinstall the driver, but if you already know that the driver file is corrupted, that's not much help. If the advice in the Troubleshooter doesn't restore the driver, try the following.

1. Find the original driver disk that was supplied with the device, or use another computer to download a new driver file from the Internet. Try www.driversplanet.com, www.driverzone.com, or www.pcdrivers.com for links to most manufacturers' download sites.

2. From the Device Manager, right-click the name of the device and select **Update Driver** from the pop-up menu. The Hardware Update Wizard (shown in Figure 4-2) appears.

Figure 4-2: Use the Hardware Update Wizard to install a new driver file.

3. Choose the **Install From A List Or Specific Location** option and click the **Next** button.

4. In the Choose Your Search And Installation Options window, choose the **Don't Search** option and click the **Next** button.

5. In the Select The Device Driver window, click the **Have Disk** button.

6. In the Install From Disk window, click the **Browse** button and find the location of the driver file either on the driver disk or in the directory folder where you stored the downloaded driver.

7. Follow the instructions in the wizard windows to complete the driver installation.

8. Restart the computer in Normal Mode.

NOTE *At the bottom of the Blue Screen message, you might see a block of text that shows Debug port and status information. If the kernel debugging option was turned on when the failure occurred, this text will show where the debugging information was stored. It's unlikely that this option was active unless you've been working with a help desk or tech support person.*

Wait, Wait! Don't Let the Message Disappear!

Many Blue Screens display the failure message (blue screen) for a few seconds and then automatically restart the computer before you get a chance to read the message text. If the restart clears the problem, that's great. But that automatic restart can drive you 'round the bend if it happens over and over and over. If you can't read the @#$%! message, you probably can't do much troubleshooting.

To shut down the automatic restart, follow these steps:

1. When the computer restarts, press the F8 key several times until the Windows Advanced Options menu appears.

2. Use the up and down arrow keys to highlight Safe Mode, and press the ENTER key.

3. After the computer opens in Safe Mode, select **Start ▶ Settings ▶ Control Panel ▶ System**. The System Properties window opens on your screen.

4. Choose the **Advanced** tab to open the dialog box shown in Figure 4-3 and click **Settings** in the Startup And Recovery box.

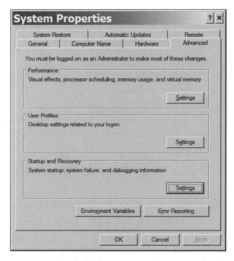

Figure 4-3: Click the Settings button in the Startup And Recovery box to turn off automatic recovery.

5. In the Startup And Recovery window (shown in Figure 4-4), click the **Automatically Restart** option to remove the check mark.

6. Click the **OK** buttons to close the Startup And Recovery and System Properties windows.

7. Restart the computer. This time, the Blue Screen should remain on the screen until you turn off the computer.

Finding a Fix

It may not be obvious, but the text of a Blue Screen error message is Windows's best effort to tell you exactly what has gone wrong with your computer and how to deal with it. Using the text of the message, you can look for helpful advice from Microsoft's own technical support infrastructure and plug yourself into the collective wisdom of other users who have faced the same problem themselves.

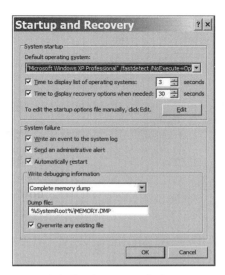

Figure 4-4: The Automatically Restart option is located in the System Failure section of the Startup And Recovery window.

The Microsoft Knowledge Base

The first place to look for an explanation of a Blue Screen error message is the Microsoft Knowledge Base at http://support.microsoft.com. The Knowledge Base contains articles written by Microsoft's developers and technical support experts that identify and explain real and potential problems. When a new and previously unseen problem arises, Microsoft uses the Knowledge Base to distribute information to their own support staff and to outside users. When you request help from Microsoft via e-mail or telephone, the first-level support advisors who take your call or message are almost always using the Knowledge Base to find the information they provide to you.

NOTE   *Because the computer that suffered the Blue Screen error is for all practical purposes out of service, you will probably need a second computer to connect to the Internet and search for articles in the Knowledge Base. Your best bet is to set up a laptop or some other more-or-less portable computer next to the one you're trying to fix so you can read instructions off the screen and enter commands directly into the machine you're trying to fix.*

Search for an Explanation

It seems as if Microsoft changes the layout of their Help and Support Center home page every few weeks, but there's always a "Search the Knowledge Base" section someplace on the page. To find a description of a specific Stop message, type the stop error number (the hex number that begins with *0x* in the top line of the Blue Screen) into the Search field. Try the error number immediately after ***STOP: first; if that doesn't produce anything useful, return to the Search page and try the entire series of numbers within the parentheses.

For example, if the stop error number is 0x0000007F, the Knowledge Base will return a long list of links to Knowledge Base articles that describe different situations in which this error can occur, as shown in Figure 4-5. Double-click the link that seems to come closest to your own problem to open that article.

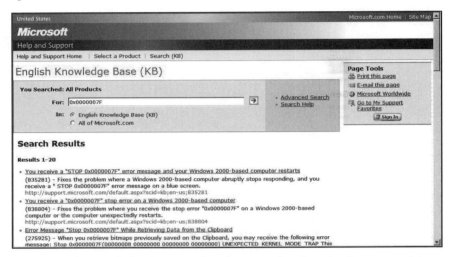

Figure 4-5: The Knowledge Base search tool returns a list of articles that may explain an error message.

NOTE *If the Search page offers a choice of either "Search the Knowledge Base" or "Search the whole Microsoft.com site," choose the second option. Sometimes the essential nut of information you need is buried in an obscure article targeted at programmers. If there's something useful hidden in another portion of the site, you should do what you can to find it.*

Figure 4-6 shows a typical Knowledge Base article. If the problem you are facing is similar to the one described in the Symptoms section, read the Cause section for an explanation, and follow the steps in the Resolution section *exactly* as they appear in the Knowledge Base article. If the trouble-shooting advice in the Resolution section doesn't solve the problem, read the More Information section and the other articles linked from there for more ideas.

Each Knowledge Base article includes these sections:

Symptoms
   A description of the problem, including the text of the error message

Cause
   An explanation of the conditions that produced the error message

Resolution
   One or more detailed step-by-step procedures for solving the problem and restoring Windows to normal operation

More Information

Additional advice about the cause of the problem and links to other Knowledge Base articles with related information

Applies To

A list of the Windows versions or other Microsoft products in which the problem described in this article might occur

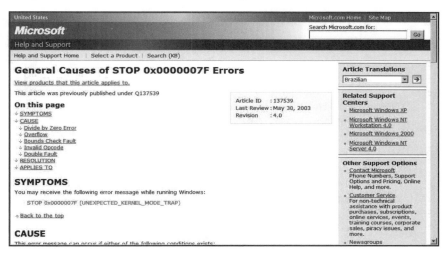

Figure 4-6: Every Knowledge Base article follows the same format.

Look in the Newsgroups

If there's nothing useful in the Knowledge Base, the next place to look for help is in the community newsgroups that Microsoft maintains to allow their users to exchange advice and help (http://support.microsoft.com/newsgroups). There's an excellent chance that your question has already been asked and answered by somebody else facing the same symptoms, but if not, you can post your own question to a newsgroup and wait for somebody to send an answer. Hundreds of experienced Windows users and Microsoft employees monitor the newsgroups, so your question will probably receive one or more replies within an hour or less.

To read old messages or send a new one, drill down from the top-level menu through the language list to the specific product that you are trying to work with. Within each product, there's a submenu of versions and individual topics. For example, questions about Windows XP are located in the English/Windows/General Discussion/Windows XP Help and Support newsgroup.

Before you jump in and submit a new question, use the Search tool at the top of the list of messages to look for an earlier posting on the same subject. Type the stop error number that appears at the top of the Blue Screen in the Search For field to look for previous questions and answers about that error message. If that doesn't produce any hits, try again using the exact text of the symbolic name, including the underscore characters between words.

If you can't find an old question about your problem, go ahead and send one of your own to the newsgroup. Be sure to include both the stop error number and the symbolic name in the text of your message, and describe everything you've already tried. Remember that most of the people in the newsgroup who are trying to help you are volunteers, so it's best to give them as much information to work with as possible.

Try Other Internet Resources

The Microsoft websites aren't the only places on the Internet where you can find help interpreting a Blue Screen error message. One particularly useful web page for finding help with Blue Screens is James Eshelman's Trouble-shooting Windows Stop Messages (http://aumha.org/win5/kbestop.htm). This site offers an extensive list of stop error numbers and symbolic names, with links to specific explanations for each one. It's often faster to find a link from this page than to use the search tool on Microsoft's own website.

Many other sites also offer advice, user forums, and technical information about troubleshooting Windows problems. Some are more helpful than others, but sometimes there's a nubbin of essential information buried in an otherwise useless site. To look for information about a Blue Screen, use a web search engine such as Google to search for the stop error number or the symbolic name that appeared in the Blue Screen message.

Some of these sites supplement information in books and magazines, and others are there to create online communities of users or generate sales for shareware products. Whatever the reason, if somebody offers a possible fix for your broken computer, grab it and hope that it will solve the problem.

Of course, some of these self-appointed experts are more reliable than others, and there's no way to know which ones are which without trying their suggested fixes. So it's always important to keep careful track of exactly what you have done; if the fix creates new problems, you should try to restore the system to its original (if broken) condition before moving on to the next good idea.

And remember that the whole system of strangers helping strangers through the Internet works both ways. If you discover somebody asking a question about a problem that you know how to solve, please share your knowledge. This isn't a chapter about Eastern religion, but you can think of this as a form of karma: Assume that good deeds (in the form of contributions to the Collective Wisdom of the Internet) will lead to positive consequences.

5

SOLVING DEVICE DRIVER PROBLEMS

Windows was designed as a general-purpose operating system that would work with just about any kind of peripheral device. If there's a way to convert information to or from digital form, Windows should be able to handle it.

But two complications make these design goals difficult to achieve: First, every device may handle information slightly differently, so Windows needs a different set of commands and controls for each device. Second, new and different devices come to market all the time. In order to support this tremendous variety of inputs and outputs, Windows uses device drivers to convert between the specific commands and data used by a particular device and the generic commands and data that the computer processor knows how to handle.

One of the keys to Windows's design is its modular structure. The core operating system calls out to separate modules that provide support for many types of hardware and software, so the developers of that hardware and software can create their own feature sets rather than limiting themselves to the ones built into Windows. The modules that act as the interfaces between the central computer and external devices are called *device drivers*. The modules that add functions that are not part of the executable code in a process are called *dynamic link libraries (DLLs)*.

As a user, it's not essential to understand exactly how individual device drivers and DLLs work, but it is important to know that they're out there and that you must find and install them in order to make many kinds of hardware and software work with Windows.

If an essential driver fails, or if the file that contains the driver becomes damaged, either Windows will disable the device controlled by that driver or, if the driver is essential to Windows's operation, it will shut down and produce a Blue Screen error message.

Every peripheral device connected to your computer—whether it's your keyboard, the video display, the hard drive, or another device—uses a device driver to exchange data with the computer's central processor. Windows uses device drivers to convert generic input and output signals to and from the specific commands and responses that each device uses to perform its particular activity. Many device drivers also include a configuration program that allows a user to change individual settings.

For example, a mouse driver will specify the number of buttons on the mouse, the way the computer responds when a user clicks each button, the rate at which the cursor moves across the screen as you move the mouse, and so forth. Still other device drivers control internal functions such as the IDE channels and the system clock.

Each device driver is a separate file. If one or more of these files is damaged or missing, or if the device driver is not consistent with the device it's supposed to control, the device will not work properly, if it works at all. When a mouse or keyboard does not respond the way you expect, or when a scanner or a CD drive does not show up in Windows Explorer, a device driver problem is probably the cause.

Device Drivers

A computer without device drivers is just a box. Without the right device driver, the computer won't know how to operate the devices that it uses to perform useful work and convey the products of that work to the world outside the computer. The device driver recognizes incoming instructions and data from an external device and translates them to a form that the operating system can understand, and it translates outbound commands and data from the processor into the specific controls that a peripheral device can use. For example, the device driver for a printer might receive an instruction from the processor to print the letter X on a page. It's up to the device driver to know if the printer should strike a particular type bar or a particular set of dots against a ribbon or deposit ink or laser toner in a specific pattern directly onto the paper.

Another device driver might tell the computer which input/output (I/O) port carries data to and from the keyboard, tell it how to convert keystrokes into input data, and turn the Caps Lock, Num Lock, and Scroll Lock lights on or off.

In general, device drivers will specify whether the device uses a serial or parallel port, a USB port, a PCMCIA socket, one of the internal expansion slots on the computer's motherboard, or some other form of data exchange. The device driver also deals with memory management and timing, and it specifies the input and output ports and the methods that the device will use to exchange data with the processor. Figure 5-1 shows how a computer exchanges information with a peripheral device through a device driver.

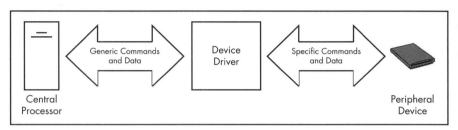

Figure 5-1: A device driver is the interface between the central computer processor and an external device.

Windows isn't the only operating system that uses device drivers. Just as a device driver can convert generic Windows commands to the specific instructions that a particular device needs, a different driver can exchange commands and data with Unix, Linux, or a Macintosh operating system. Because each driver presents the same appearance to the external device, it's possible to use the same printer or monitor or other device with many operating systems.

Device drivers make Windows more flexible by separating the specific requirements of an external device from the general requirements of the operating system. Therefore, when the designers of a peripheral device introduce a new or updated product, they can include new device drivers that will make that product compatible with Windows. And when a new version of Windows appears, they can create updated device drivers that take advantage of the operating system's new features and functions.

As a general rule, you need one or more device drivers for every device that you want to run with Windows. When you upgrade to a newer Windows version, you may have to find and install new drivers at the same time. Some of these drivers are included in the Windows upgrade package, but others will require some detective work. You can find pointers to several sources for information about obscure device drivers later in this chapter.

DLL Files

A dynamic link library (DLL) provides a way for a process to perform a function that is not written into the process's executable code. The code inside the DLL is linked to the process that uses it, but it's stored in a separate file, which can be shared by two or more processes. Therefore, updating or replacing a DLL can add or change a function without the need to replace the original process, and a single DLL can respond to calls from more than one application, so it can add or change more than one program at the same time.

From the user's perspective, the important difference between a DLL and an application program is that it's not possible to run a DLL directly; you must execute it through an application that calls the DLL.

Many Windows programs and processes use DLLs to add or update the functions that they can perform. So it's not uncommon for software developers to distribute new DLLs as a convenient way to update their products. You probably won't find DLL files as separate downloads, but many application programs and utilities include DLL files in the updates to their software.

Diagnosing a Driver Problem

If a device connected to the computer—such as a sound card, a CD drive, or a scanner—does not work the way you expect it to be working, there's an excellent chance that the driver that controls that device is causing the problem.

To check the status of all the device drivers in a Windows system, open the Device Manager (**Start ▶ Settings ▶ Control Panel ▶ System ▶ Hardware ▶ Device Manager**, or type **devmgmt.exe** in the Start ▶ Run window) and look for either a yellow exclamation point (!) or a red X over the icon next to the name of a device. Figure 5-2 shows the Device Manager with a damaged device driver.

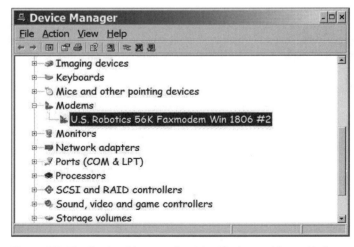

Figure 5-2: The Device Manager has identified a problem with the modem driver.

NOTE *When the Device Manager detects a problem, it automatically expands the category list that includes the damaged driver, so there's no need to open the compacted category item listings.*

Both red and yellow flags indicate that a problem exists with the device named next to the icon; the red X is more serious than the yellow exclamation mark, but both tell you that the device is not working properly. The red X generally indicates that the device has been completely disabled.

For detailed information about a particular device problem, double-click the device's name to open its Properties window. The Device Status box in the General tab (see Figure 5-3) will explain the problem and offer advice for repairing it. If the fix is more complicated than "reboot the computer," the Properties window will include a Troubleshoot button that opens another window with more detailed instructions. The Device Status box might also include a code number.

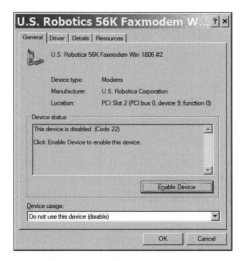

Figure 5-3: The Device Manager links to Properties windows that identify driver problems.

NOTE *If the Troubleshoot instructions don't solve the problem, see Appendix A of this book for explanations of the most common Device Manager error codes. For more recent information, go to the Microsoft Knowledge Base and search for Article No. 310123. This article contains Microsoft's latest updates to its list of error codes.*

Regardless of the cause, the most common fix for driver problems is to reinstall the driver. If the version already installed on your computer doesn't load, or if it does but the problem comes back again, it's always a good idea to search online for an updated version of the device driver file. And even if the existing copy is the latest release, go ahead and download a new copy from Microsoft or the manufacturer's website—it's possible that the copy on your computer is damaged or corrupted.

Where to Find New Drivers

Microsoft and the manufacturers of equipment that works with Windows make a strong effort to distribute the drivers necessary to support most popular peripheral devices. The Windows CD and the Windows Update website contain drivers for hundreds of external devices, and there's almost always a software disk included with your new printer, hard drive, mouse, or other external device that contains drivers for Windows and other operating systems.

When you install Windows or upgrade to a newer Windows version, the Setup routine includes an automatic update that connects your computer to Microsoft's online Windows Update center and finds the latest drivers for the hardware your system is using. When you connect a new piece of hardware, Windows will probably detect it automatically, and it will try to find and load a driver from your computer's hard drive, from the Windows distribution CD, or from a file supplied by the hardware vendor. If it fails to find the right driver file, Windows won't complete the installation.

But what if the driver file's not on the Windows CD? The first place to look is the Microsoft Windows Update center. If the latest device driver has passed the "Designed for Windows" requirements, Windows Update can automatically detect and install the latest version.

To find device drivers through Windows Update, follow these steps:

1. From the Windows Start menu or the Internet Explorer Tools menu, choose **Windows Update**.
2. When the top-level Windows Update web page appears, choose the **Custom** option, and scroll down to Optional Hardware Updates.
3. Click the **Review And Install Updates** link to view a list of available new device drivers.

If Windows Update can't supply a new driver, try the hardware manufacturer's website. If you can't find a web address on the package, try www.*companyname*.com or use a web search tool to find them. That will probably work most of the time. If not, go to one of the websites that offer links to every known source of drivers:

www.windrivers.com/company.htm

www.pcdrivers.com

www.driverzone.com

www.driverguide.com

www.helpdrivers.com

www.winguides.com/drivers

www.driversplanet.com

www.totallydrivers.com

If you can't find a device driver that was specifically designed for Windows XP, try installing the driver for Windows 2000. At the device driver level, the two versions of Windows are very similar, so Windows 2000 drivers will often work just fine with Windows XP.

As a last resort, try the Driver Forum at www.totallydrivers.com/forum, the forum at www.driverforum.com, or the user forums at the device manufacturer's website. Search the forums for the specific make and model of the device you're trying to install; if somebody else has asked about the same device, there's probably a reply with a pointer to an obscure source for the driver file. If you can't find anything about your device, try posting your own request.

Installing New Drivers

Installing a new device driver is easy. If the driver disk or download includes a Setup or Install program, go ahead and run it. If not, run the Add Hardware routine from the Control Panel and follow the instructions in the Add Hardware Wizard. When the wizard displays a list of devices or manufacturers, click the **Have Disk** button, as shown in Figure 5-4. If the driver is on a floppy disk or a CD, insert the disk with the driver file in the computer's drive; if it's on your hard drive, use the **Browse** button in the Install From Disk dialog box to find the driver file.

Figure 5-4: Use the Have Disk button to install a device driver from a file.

If a driver is supplied as an information file (with a .inf file extension), you can bypass the Add Hardware Wizard and install the driver by opening the folder that contains the file, right-clicking the file, and selecting **Install** from the pop-up menu.

Returning to an Earlier Version

Sometimes a new device driver creates more problems than it solves. This may occur when you're using an older device that doesn't have the latest internal firmware or simply because the new version is defective. If this happens, Windows offers an easy way to remove the newer driver and restore the one that was in use before.

Follow these steps to roll back a device driver:

1. From the Control Panel, open the **System Properties** dialog box (**Start ▸ Settings ▸ Control Panel ▸ System**).

2. Choose the **Hardware** tab and click the **Device Manager** button.

3. If it's not already expanded, click the category that includes the device whose driver you want to roll back.

4. Double-click the name of the device whose driver you want to restore.

5. In the Properties window for that device, click the **Driver** tab and click the **Roll Back Driver** button.

6. Click **Yes** to confirm that you want to roll back this driver.

If the Roll Back Driver program can't find an earlier version of the device driver, it will display a message like the one in Figure 5-5, offering to run a Troubleshooter. In this case, the Troubleshooter probably won't offer any useful advice, so your best bet is to choose No.

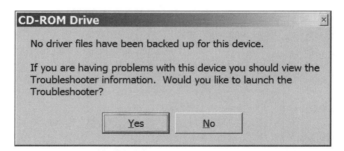

Figure 5-5: If the Roll Back Driver program can't find an earlier device driver, it will display this dialog box.

When it works, rolling back the device driver can save a lot of time and trouble, but it does have a few limitations. First, it can return to only the driver version immediately preceding the current one; therefore, you can't go back to a driver older than the last one. If you try one new driver that doesn't work and then install a second driver from a different source, you can't return to the original driver because that one is now two generations behind you. And second, the Roll Back Driver tool does not work on printer drivers. Finally, if you're using a device that uses more than one device driver (such as a combination card or a complex audio device), you must roll back each device driver separately.

Storing and Organizing Your Drivers

Once you download and install new device drivers and software updates, you should store copies of the update files along with the distribution copies of Windows and your application programs on CDs or floppy disks. You won't need to use those files again unless you have to replace a hard drive or move a device to a different computer, but remember that you won't be able to read these files from a hard drive when you're trying to recover from a disk crash.

NOTE   *When you do have to reinstall a driver or restore a drive, you might want to go back to Microsoft or the original manufacturers' websites to download new copies of all your drivers rather than loading your older copies. This will assure that you can take advantage of the latest version of each driver, including any improvements, patches, and bug fixes that may have been added since your last install.*

If you travel with a laptop and other portable computer users, create an emergency repair CD that will live in one of the pockets of the computer case or bag. In addition to any utilities supplied by the computer manufacturer, the CD should have a top-level directory folder called Device Drivers with a separate subfolder for each peripheral device—mouse, network interfaces, modem, and so forth. It wouldn't hurt to include some additional top-level folders with other important programs and data, including your e-mail address book, a text file that lists the configuration settings for your Internet accounts (e-mail server addresses, DNS servers, and other information supplied by your service provider), your web browser's Favorites or Bookmarks list, and an antispyware utility. With luck, you won't ever need the files on this CD, but if you do, they will save a lot of time when you have to restore your portable computer while you're away from home base.

Use Device Driver Rollback to Solve a Conflict

If an existing device stopped working after you installed a new device driver, try using the Device Driver Rollback tool to return to an earlier driver. Follow these steps to use this tool:

1. Open **Start ▸ Settings ▸ Control Panel ▸ System** (from the Classic menu) or **Start ▸ Control Panel ▸ System** (from the XP Start menu).

2. Select the **Hardware** tab and click **Device Manager**. When the Device Manager window appears, see if any devices have a yellow exclamation point (!) next to the device name. If so, double-click the name of the device to open a Properties dialog box (see Figure 5-6).

Figure 5-6: Use Roll Back Driver to return to an earlier version of a device driver.

3. Choose the **Driver** tab and click the **Roll Back Driver** button. If any older drivers are available, Windows will display a list.

4. Choose the old driver you want to install and click the **OK** button.

6

USING THE MICROSOFT KNOWLEDGE BASE AND OTHER ONLINE RESOURCES

If you can't solve a problem using the obvious troubleshooting methods—following the instructions in an error message, shutting down and restarting the computer or an individual program, looking for a disconnected cable, reading the instruction manual——the next step is to search for advice from Microsoft, from the hardware and software manufacturers, and from other users. Someone, somewhere has probably seen and solved the particular problem that you're having; you should take advantage of their experience rather than starting from a blank slate.

The Internet is the key to finding all of this information because answers to Windows questions are spread among hundreds of web pages, users' forums, lists of frequently asked questions (FAQs), and independent user groups.

Try the Help Screens First

Before you start looking for information on the Internet, check the help screens that come with most software programs. In Windows XP, the help system is called Help and Support, but in most other programs, it's just plain Help. The Help menu in most Windows programs, but not always in Windows itself, is the rightmost menu in the program's menu bar. In Windows, Help and Support is accessed via the Start menu (**Start ▸ Help And Support**) or the Help menu in any Windows Explorer (My Computer) window.

Unfortunately, the quality of the information supplied in online Help varies from one program to another. Some software, like Windows XP, includes a tremendous amount of useful advice and instructions with a detailed index and direct links to additional information on the Internet. Others offer little more than the text of the hard-copy documents supplied with the program or, worse, just a page or two that might explain how to install the program (which you have already figured out or you wouldn't be using the Help command), or a web address.

The amount and quality of the Help information supplied is often a case of "you get what you pay for." A program that costs a couple of hundred dollars (or the equivalent in euros, pounds, or yen) is more likely to include extensive Help than a piece of shareware that sells for peanuts. Of course, you may find some exceptions on both sides; there are expensive programs with lousy Help and freebies with excellent Help.

In Windows XP, the Help and Support Center offers several ways to find information about a specific problem. The home page, shown in Figure 6-1, includes both a search tool and a list of common Help topics. There's also a link in the toolbar to the Help index, which offers both another search tool and a more detailed list of Help topics than the one on the home page.

Most of the items in the list of Help topics at the right side of the home page are top-level headings that link you to a list of more specific topics and eventually to an article about a single subject. In most cases, you come to Help because you're looking for very specific information, so you can eliminate some of the intermediate steps by using the Index function from the toolbar or the Search function from the section directly under the toolbar. If you don't see either of these tools, click the Change View icon at the top of your Help window.

The two search tools produce two different sets of results: The Index tool limits the search to the Help articles that are supplied with Windows and stored in your own computer; the Search function finds articles from the Microsoft Knowledge Base on the Internet and provides links to both local and online articles.

The major advantage of the Index tool is that it displays a complete list of all the local Help articles related to Windows XP. As Figure 6-2 shows, the left side of the Index window contains a long list of keywords. In many cases, it's easier to browse through the list than it is to guess the right keyword for a search. When you choose a keyword, the computer will either display a list of related topics or take you directly to a specific Help article.

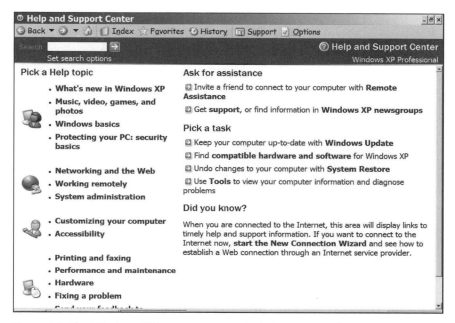

Figure 6-1: The Windows XP home page contains links to many information resources.

Many Help articles include a Related Topics link at the bottom of the page. If the current article doesn't include the specific information you need, or if you want to find more details, try one of the linked articles.

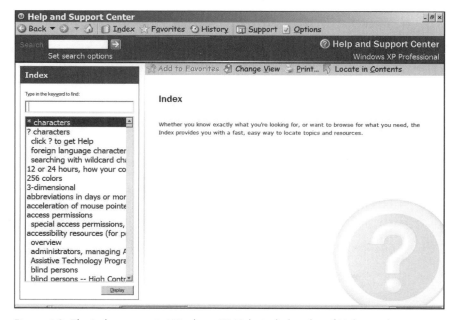

Figure 6-2: The Index pages in Windows XP Help include a list of Help articles.

Many of the programs and utilities that are part of Windows XP include their own Help files that contain information that may not be included in the general Windows XP Help and Support Center. So the first place to look for Help about the program you're currently using is the Help menu in that program's toolbar. Within the Help menu, the link to the Help system might be called Help Topics, Contents, or something similar. If you can't find the information you need in a program's Help files, try the Windows Help and Support Center.

README Files

Many software vendors add a file called README to their distribution packages at the very last minute before they release the product to manu-facture. This file, which might be called ReadMe.txt, readme.htm, or some other obvious variation, contains information that they discovered too late to include in the user manual or other formal documentation. It often includes instructions for fixing bugs, compatibility problems with other software or hardware, and other possible problems. It's always a good idea to look for a README file before you install a new piece of software and when you encounter a problem after installation that isn't described in the online Help or the user manual.

In Windows XP, the README.HTM file contains a web page with links to three additional pages with last-minute information about installation and setup and general release notes. On the Windows XP Service Pack 2 CD, the file is READMESP.HTM

The Microsoft Knowledge Base

Knowledge base is a fancy name for a collection of articles and other technical information that has been organized for easy searching. Microsoft uses their Knowledge Base to distribute technical information about their products to their own technical support staff and to outside organizations that support Windows users. More than 150,000 Knowledge Base articles explain how to interpret and respond to error messages, work around bugs in Microsoft products, and find solutions to problems. Most of the same Knowledge Base articles are available to the rest of us through the Internet.

Whenever somebody within Microsoft discovers a new Windows problem (or a problem with some other Microsoft product), or a new fix for an old problem, or a new way to improve performance, that information will be added to the Knowledge Base. It's a living document (or set of documents) that keeps dozens of people at Microsoft busy writing and posting updates.

When you telephone or e-mail Microsoft tech support, the person who takes your call could be located at Microsoft headquarters in Redmond, Washington, or at a support center in Texas, Nova Scotia, or India; wherever they might be, they all use the Knowledge Base to find answers to your questions. Microsoft charges for many of those support calls, and others require a long-distance telephone call that might last an hour or more, so it's often better (and less costly) to go to the online version of the Knowledge Base first to try to find the same information on your own.

If your copy of Windows XP came with a new computer, you might have to depend on the computer manufacturer's tech support center for help with Windows. Microsoft expects the support representatives in those centers to use the Knowledge Base to help you find solutions to your computer problems, but there are plenty of horror stories about poor training, pressure to get rid of every call within six minutes or less, and one-solution-fits-all-problems policies. ("Have you tried rebooting the computer? It still doesn't work? Try reformatting your hard drive and reloading everything. You tried that? Well, it must be a bad motherboard. Let me transfer you to shipping, where they'll take your address and credit card number.") Microsoft may not always allow their own tech support people to talk with you, but they're happy to let you consult the Knowledge Base on your own.

The Knowledge Base is not limited to problems caused by Microsoft products; because many users call Microsoft for help with problems that were actually caused by some other company's products, the Knowledge Base often includes information about fixing those problems and pointers to the other company's website or tech support center.

Opening the Knowledge Base

To find an article in the Knowledge Base, start at the Microsoft Support home page, http://support.microsoft.com, shown in Figure 6-3. Microsoft changes the layout and content of this page all the time, but it always includes a "Search the Knowledge Base" field someplace near the top.

Figure 6-3: Microsoft's Help and Support web page is the gateway to the Knowledge Base.

Back in Chapter 1, I told you that the first step in solving a problem is describing it. This is where describing the problem becomes important. To find one or more Knowledge Base articles related to a specific problem, type a keyword that describes the problem into the Search box. If Windows or another program has generated an error message, type the first three or four words of the message in the Search box. If there's an error code number or other unique identifier, try using that as a keyword.

For example, if you see an error message that says, Smrtbltz.dll is damaged, use Smrtbltz.dll in your keyword search. The search tool will give you a list of all the Knowledge Base articles that mention Smrtbltz.dll.

If you chose a keyword that appears in one or more Knowledge Base articles, the search tool will display a list of articles related to that keyword or phrase. If you're lucky, one of the articles will contain exactly the information you're trying to find. So click each link in the list and read the first couple of paragraphs to find out if the article is related to your specific problem. If the first article is not what you need, use the browser's Back button to return to your search results and move on to the next article in the list.

If the list of articles that match your keyword search appears to include a lot of items that apply to programs other than Windows, try refining your search. Either choose the version of Windows you're using from the list at the left side of the search page or add *XP* or some other identifier to the keywords in the Search field.

Sometimes a short phrase is more effective than a single keyword, so a brief description of the problem, such as "won't start" or "green smoke," will produce something more useful than a search for a single word.

If your first search doesn't lead you to an answer to your problem, try a different keyword unless it's absolutely obvious that your original search was unique (such as the text of a message or a code number). The people who maintain the Knowledge Base are very good about including as many useful keywords as possible in each article, but sometimes you might come up with one that is slightly different from the ones in the article. So it's always good practice to try additional keywords if the first search does not produce a useful result.

Sometimes a Microsoft document or some other company's tech support website will mention a Knowledge Base article by number. To open an article when you know its number, type **KB*xxxxxx*** (with the article number in place of *xxxxxx*) in either the "Search the Knowledge Base" or the "Search Microsoft.com for" field in any Microsoft support web page.

Reading a Knowledge Base Article

Every article in the Knowledge Base follows a standard format. Most articles do not include every standard heading, but headings almost always appear in the same order. Figure 6-4 shows the top of a typical Knowledge Base article.

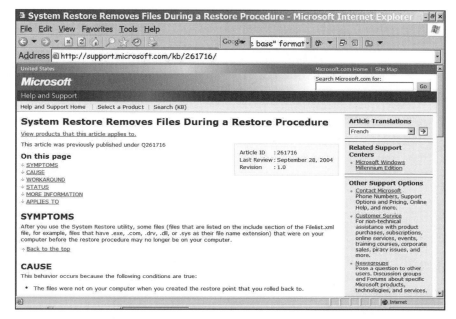

Figure 6-4: Knowledge Base articles always include standard elements.

The sections of Knowledge Base articles appear in this order:

Title

The title of a Knowledge Base article is a description of the article's subject. In most cases, the title is a single sentence or phrase that identifies a problem, condition, or procedure.

Knowledge Base Information

Each article includes a box at the upper right, under the title, with the Article ID number, the date of the most recent review, and the revision number.

Summary

The summary contains a short explanation of the information that is presented in more detail later in the article. In most cases, the first few paragraphs of the summary are enough to tell you whether or not the article applies to the problem you are trying to solve or the condition you want to understand. However, when you're trying to interpret an error message, you should also look for the text under the More Information or Symptoms headings.

Symptoms

The Symptoms section contains descriptions of the visible or audible effects of the condition described by this article.

Cause

The Cause section explains why the problem or condition occurs.

Workaround

A workaround is a technique for bypassing a problem. It does not solve or repair the underlying condition, but it does give you a way to avoid the symptoms. A workaround might be the best approach if Microsoft has not yet figured out the cause of a problem or if the new software necessary to permanently fix it is not yet available.

Resolution

The Resolution section contains specific instructions for correcting a problem. It might include a step-by-step procedure, links to a downloadable software patch, or a telephone number for a particular technical support center.

Status

The Status section shows the current state of the problem. If Microsoft has not yet identified a fix for a problem, or if it has decided that it's a normal condition or some other company is responsible, the Status section will reflect that determination. If Microsoft or some other supplier has solved the problem in a later release or a service pack, that information will also appear under Status.

More Information

The More Information section contains additional facts about the condition or problem described in the current article. For example, this appears in one article under More Information: "This problem stops occurring one week after the transition to daylight savings time."

Other Knowledge Base articles might include a step-by-step procedure for reproducing the behavior described in the current article in the More Information section.

References

References are links and pointers to additional Knowledge Base articles and other Microsoft web pages that contain more information about the subject of this article.

Applies To

The Applies To section always contains a list of one or more Microsoft products in which the condition described in this article is known to exist.

Keywords

At the bottom of each Knowledge Base article, there's a list of keywords that Microsoft uses for automated searches. In most cases, these keywords are not useful for plain-language searches. They don't contribute anything useful to the content of the article itself.

Buried Treasure in the Knowledge Base

In general, articles in the Microsoft Knowledge Base don't offer much opportunity for entertainment. Most Knowledge Base articles are sober, no-nonsense descriptions of problems and solutions in Microsoft products, but a few go beyond the usual boring content to offer some Really Strange content. For example, take a look at Article No. 152697, "Koi and the Kola Nuts: The Story of Koi and the Kola Nuts."

Still others are explanations of odd error messages, like this one (Article No. 330358):

```
Keyboard Error or No Keyboard Present
Press F1 to continue, DEL to enter setup
```

Or this one (Article No. 276304):

```
Your password must be at least 18770 characters and cannot repeat any of your
previous 30689 passwords. Please type a different password.
```

There are other more productive places to look for amusing material online, but it was probably inevitable that somebody has created a list of pointers to goofy stuff in the Knowledge Base. You can find lots more of this stuff in Jill Dybka's Funny Microsoft Q Articles web page at www.jazzkeyboard .com/jill/qarticles.html.

Hardware and Software Manufacturers' Websites

Many other hardware and software manufacturers offer their own online technical support services, including their own knowledge bases, downloadable updates to software and firmware, lists of frequently asked questions (FAQs), and bulletin boards or forums where users can share their experience with the sponsor's products. If you can't find a satisfactory solution to a problem on the Microsoft site, it can often be productive to look at another company's support center.

However, it's not always easy to know exactly where to look. If, for example, you have a Gateway computer with an Intel Pentium processor and a motherboard made by Tyan, you might have to look at all three companies' support sites to find the solution to a problem (that's a hypothetical combination; I don't know whether Gateway uses Tyan boards or not).

If you're having trouble with a video display adapter card, you might find support at both the card manufacturer's site and the site maintained by the people who made the video controller on the card. For network or Internet access problems, try your Internet service provider first and then the makers of your network gateway or router. In general, if you can't find an answer in the first place you look, try to find another possible source. As a rule, most corporate sites use a web address in this format: www.*brandname*.com, with the name of the company in place of *brandname*. If that doesn't work, try using a web search tool such as Google to find the company's main site.

If your computer is still under warranty, or if the problem appeared after you installed a new or replacement hardware component or software product, call or e-mail the company behind that product first, before you try any major repairs. You don't want to give anybody an excuse to say, "You voided the warranty when you followed some other company's advice." And if your employer has a help desk or your computer is covered by a service contract, call the service provider before you get in too deeply; you (or your employer) have already paid somebody to help you fix the computer, so you should let them do their job.

Every manufacturer's website has a different layout and design, so it might take some detective work to find the section of each site devoted to technical support. In most cases, there's a Support link at or near the top of the page or along the right or left side. On other sites, you'll have to jump to a page devoted to the specific product or service you're trying to troubleshoot and then look for a support page.

Newsgroups and Independent Support Services

Today, the online technical newsgroups are still among the best places to find help with computer problems.

The worldwide Usenet system of newsgroups has been around since 1979, when a group of graduate students in North Carolina set up a small network that used dial-up telephone connections to share information among computer users at several universities. The system rapidly expanded and adopted other network connection types to connect millions of participants around the world who use it to discuss thousands of separate topics. Each topic occupies a separate newsgroup.

Many newsgroups are dedicated to technical topics, including most computer operating systems and applications, individual computer makers, and other related subjects. In many cases, the newsgroups devoted to obscure or obsolete computers and software may be the only places left to find information about keeping those virtual dinosaurs alive. If you're trying to restore an old mainframe computer (or some other old technology), there's probably a newsgroup where you can find others who share your interest.

More to the point, there are plenty of active newsgroups for discussing current computer hardware and software. The regular participants are often some of the most knowledgeable users of the products, sometimes including their designers and product managers. Many of the regulars are happy to answer questions from newcomers. Of course, it's best to look for those answers in the manual, the on-screen help, and other sources first, but asking for help in a newsgroup can sometimes produce results that are not available anyplace else.

It's also good practice to read some recent messages in a newsgroup before you post your own question. There's an excellent chance that somebody else has had a similar problem and your question has already been asked and answered. If your newsreader program has a search tool, you can use the tool to scan the entire newsgroup for messages related to your own problem.

In many technical newsgroups, one or more of the regular participants have created a list of frequently asked questions, or FAQs, that new readers ask all the time. An FAQ document is a list of common questions with an answer to each one. These might include the basic "How do I change fonts on my desktop?" type of questions, along with questions about widespread bugs in software. If there is an FAQ document for a newsgroup, the creators probably post a new copy once a month, or once every few months. It's a courtesy to the regulars in a newsgroup to read the FAQ before jumping in with yet another version of the same old question.

There are several ways to participate in public Usenet newsgroups. If your Internet service provider (ISP) offers access to a news server, you can use a dedicated newsreader program such as Agent or Free Agent from Forté (www.forteinc.com) or a combined news and e-mail program such as the Outlook Express program included with Windows XP, or Mozilla Thunderbird. Your ISP's tech support center can tell you how to set up your news program to connect to their server.

Unfortunately, some of the largest ISPs no longer offer access to Usenet newsgroups. If you use America Online, MSN, or some other ISP that does not have a news server, you can either connect to a public news server or use a website that publishes Usenet messages on web pages.

Public news servers are subscription services that will allow anybody to connect to Usenet through their systems. Most of them offer free read-only access, but they charge for the privilege of sending a message to a newsgroup. For a huge list of public news servers, take a look at www.newzbot.com or http://dmoz.org/Computers/Usenet/Public_News_Servers.

If you prefer to use your web browser, you can reach Usenet groups through Google's Groups service. Start at http://groups.google.com and choose the Browse All of Usenet link near the bottom of your screen to open the first of many pages of links to individual newsgroups. The Google site is free, so it might be a better method than one of the paid subscription services. However, it's not always easy to find a specific Usenet group in the Google list unless you already know its name. So the best approach might be to use Outlook Express or another news reader program to find the group you want, and read existing messages and then go to Google to post your own questions.

Because there are more than 50,000 separate newsgroups within the Usenet system, it can be difficult to find the one that contains the information you want. To find a newsgroup dedicated to a particular product, use the search tool within your newsreader program or on the website.

In addition to the public Usenet newsgroups, some companies, including Microsoft and Symantec, maintain their own news servers that are devoted exclusively to discussions of their own products. Sometimes, the same newsgroups are accessible both through Usenet and through the company's own website. You can find Microsoft's newsgroups on Usenet under the Microsoft.public.*product name.topic* hierarchy or on the Web at www.support.microsoft.com/newsgroups or through www.windowsforums .com. Hundreds of paid and volunteer experts watch the Microsoft newsgroups and are ready to jump in and answer questions from perplexed users, so the quality of the information in the newsgroups is at least as good as the advice provided by the tech support staff.

The newsgroups on Usenet and on the Microsoft support site are exactly the same; if you post a message on either system, it will immediately appear in both places. Figures 6-5 and 6-6 show the same message on Usenet and the Microsoft site.

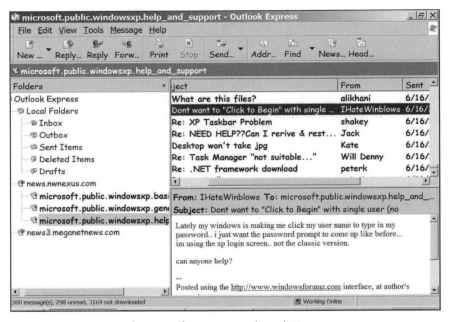

Figure 6-5: You can reach Microsoft newsgroups through Usenet . . .

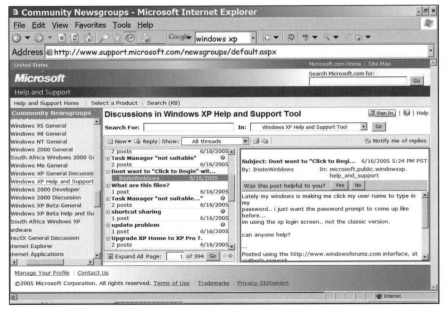

Figure 6-6: . . . or through Microsoft's Support web pages.

Search Online for the Symptoms

In addition to the support sites maintained by Microsoft and other hardware and software developers and the Usenet newsgroups, the Internet is full of independent websites that offer Windows hints and tips and bulletin boards where users can share their experiences and answer other users' questions. Some are operated by hobby groups and magazines, and others are stand-alone projects created by self-appointed experts who want to inflate their own reputations and generate some income from on-screen advertisements.

Whatever the source, if some crucial snippet of obscure information can solve a problem for you, go ahead and take advantage of it. The trick is knowing how to find the particular snippet you need when you need it.

That's why search tools like Google, Alltheweb, and Ask Jeeves ought to be essential parts of your troubleshooting tool kit. A web search for the text of an error message or a description of a problem often produces links to independent sites along with the Microsoft Knowledge Base and other "official" information sources. The search tools don't examine every message in places like the Microsoft newsgroups and the user forums on other manufacturers' websites, so you can't ignore the other methods in this chapter, but sometimes a general web search will come up with items that you would not find any other way.

So once again, the key to finding the web page with the information you need is to choose the right keyword or phrase for your search. Try the exact text of an on-screen message, a message number combined with the name of the program, or the model number of the product. If that doesn't apply to your specific situation, try a two- or three-word description of the problem.

Sometimes a keyword search will produce a huge number of hits, most of them irrelevant to the problem you want to solve. When that happens, try to refine the search with one or more additional words or phrases in the search field, or try to frame the problem as a question.

Don't Panic (Yet)

There's nothing like the unique combination of horror, panic, and help-lessness you experience when you watch your computer crash—that horrible feeling in your gut when the only copy of an important document disappears from your screen or an unintelligible error message pops up when you turn on the machine.

When this happens to you, it's important to remember two essential facts: First, computers do not suffer from random failures—there's a reason for everything; and second, it's almost certain that you're not the first person whose computer has suffered from this particular type of failure. And thanks to the Internet, somebody has probably posted an explanation of the problem and instructions for repairing it on a website or newsgroup.

So the forums, bulletin boards, knowledge bases, and other online resources are among the most valuable troubleshooting tools you can use. Take advantage of them. The feeling of relief after you have recovered from a computer problem is almost worth the original pain.

7

USING SYSTEM RESTORE AND OTHER ROLLBACK TECHNIQUES

A huge proportion of all Windows problems occur immediately after you install a new program, update a device driver, or change configuration settings that create a conflict with the setup that had been working properly up to that time. For example, when you install a new video card or sound card, the software associated with that card could cause other devices to stop working.

As such, the best way to recover from a Windows problem is often to undo recent changes and return the machine to the state it was in before the problem existed. Windows XP's System Restore tool makes it easy to automate this process.

System Restore is like an "undo" command for Windows configuration settings. It saves snapshots of the Windows Registry and other important configuration settings (called *restore points*) on a regular schedule and whenever there's a significant change. If a configuration change causes Windows to fail, the System Restore tool can return the system to a state that was (presumably) problem free.

NOTE *The System Restore tool does not remove or change data files, so restoring Windows to an older configuration will not result in the loss of recent documents, e-mail, bookmarks, or other data not directly related to the Windows configuration.*

You can also return the system to an earlier restore point to remove the effects of spyware or a virus from the Windows Registry. It's not a substitute for a complete system scan by an antivirus or antispyware program, but combined with one of those scanning utilities, the System Restore tool might get rid of some residual crud left over from the virus or spyware infection.

NOTE *Windows normally saves older restore points for a couple of months (depending on the size of your hard drive), so you can try an earlier or later configuration if the first one doesn't solve the problem.*

Before You Try System Restore

Although it won't delete data files or e-mail messages, System Restore does change a lot of files and Registry settings at once, which is both its strongest and its weakest feature. While it's much easier to make all those changes with System Restore than to make each one individually, System Restore sometimes changes things that you didn't want to change. For example, if you choose a date two or three weeks ago (or more) as your restore point, System Restore will undo all the changes you have made since that time, including automatic updates to Windows and to your antivirus and antispyware programs.

Therefore, it's often best to try some other, less extreme repair methods first. Before you use System Restore, try the approaches described in this section.

Reboot the computer

Before you do anything else, try restarting the computer. More often than you might expect, many problems will disappear on a reboot.

Return to Last Known Good Configuration

If rebooting doesn't do the trick, try returning to the last known good configuration. To do so, restart the computer and immediately press F8 to open the Windows Advanced Options Menu; then use the up and down arrow keys to choose the **Last Known Good Configuration** option. Press ENTER to restart the computer.

Returning to the Last Known Good Configuration reverts the system to the condition it was in before any changes that you made during the current session. If the problem occurred when you installed a new program or device driver or when Windows or some other program tried to install an updated software version, returning to the Last Known Good Configuration will cancel that installation.

Try the Program Compatibility Wizard

If a problem appears after you install a program that was designed for an earlier version of Windows but isn't compatible with Windows XP, you may need to change the program's compatibility mode before it will work properly. The easiest way to make these changes is with the Program Compatibility Wizard:

1. From the Start menu, choose **Programs** or **All Programs ▸ Accessories ▸ Program Compatibility Wizard**.

2. Step through the wizard until you reach a screen where you can select the program that you recently installed. Select the suspect program, and then click **Next** to move to the screen that offers a choice of compatibility modes.

3. How do you determine which mode to use? If the program was designed for a specific version of Windows, such as Windows 98 or Windows 2000, choose to run it in that mode. If you're not sure, check the software publisher's website.

4. Move on to the Display Settings screen. Again, consult the program manual for the correct setting.

5. At the Test Your Compatibility Settings screen, confirm that the settings you chose will work with this program. If the program does not pass the test, use the **Back** button to return to earlier screens and try a different display setting or compatibility mode.

6. Click **Next** to step through the rest of the Compatibility Wizard.

Try uninstalling a program

A problem that occurs immediately after you install a new program is probably related to that program, so removing the program may be all you need to do to eliminate the conflict with other programs and settings.

Use Device Driver Rollback

If your problem appeared immediately after you installed a new device driver, try using the Device Driver Rollback tool to return to an earlier driver. Here's how to use this tool:

1. From the Start menu, choose **Run** and enter **devmgmt.msc** in the Open field.

2. When the Device Manager window appears, look for a yellow exclamation point (!) next to the name of the device you just installed.
If you find one, double-click the device name to open a Properties
dialog box.

3. Choose the **Driver** tab as shown in Figure 7-1, and click the **Roll Back
Driver** button.

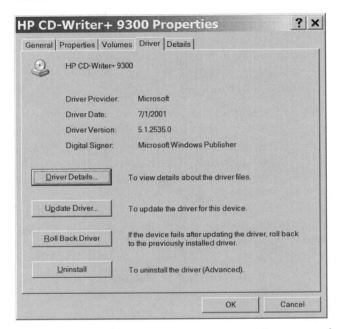

Figure 7-1: Use Roll Back Driver to return to an earlier version of a
device driver.

Creating Restore Points

Windows automatically creates a new restore point every 24 hours or when
it has been more than 24 hours since the most recent restore point was
created (usually because the computer was turned off). It also creates a
new restore point after most device drivers, programs, or automatic
updates are installed.

The daily restore points and the automatic restore points that are set
when a driver, program, or update is installed are almost always enough
to meet your needs, but you can also create an additional restore point at
any time.

To establish a manual restore point, follow these steps:

1. Choose **Start ▶ Programs ▶ Accessories ▶ System Tools ▶ System Restore**.
The System Restore Wizard, shown in Figure 7-2, appears.

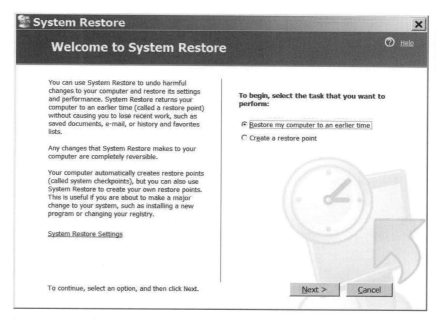

Figure 7-2: Use the System Restore tool to create a new restore point or to return to an earlier configuration.

2. Select the **Create A Restore Point** option, and click **Next**. The Create A Restore Point window appears, as shown in Figure 7-3.

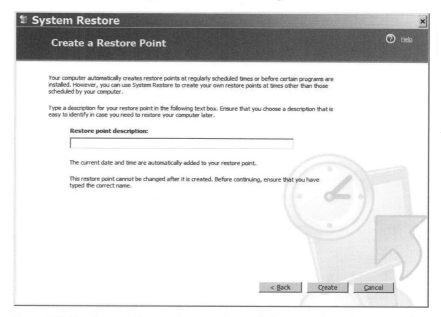

Figure 7-3: The Create A Restore Point window includes space for a description of the new restore point.

3. Type a name for this restore point, and click **Create**. The wizard will create the new restore point and display a confirmation.

Returning to a Restore Point

If none of the suggestions in the previous section solve the problem, it's time to try a full system restore.

Follow these steps to return Windows to a restore point:

1. Shut down any programs that are currently running.
2. Choose **Start ▸ Programs ▸ Accessories ▸ System Tools ▸ System Restore**.
3. Choose **Restore My Computer To An Earlier Time** and click **Next**. The Select A Restore Point window, shown in Figure 7-4, appears.

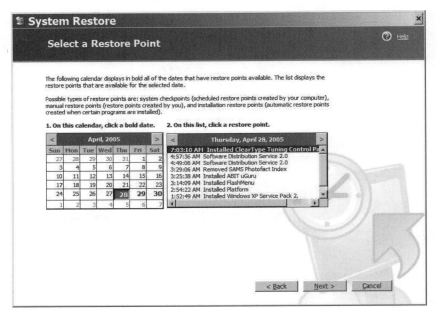

Figure 7-4: Use the Select A Restore Point window to choose the age of the restore point.

4. From the calendar, choose a date just before the problem occurred. For example, if a system failure has just appeared, try using yesterday's date as your restore point. If the problem has been occurring for several days, try a restore point from last week. If you think you know which program or other installation caused the problem, look at the list of restore points for several dates until you find the list that includes that installation.
5. If Windows created more than one restore point on the date you chose, it will list all of them in the right box. Choose one that was set before you made the change you're trying to undo. Click the **Next** button to continue.

6. The wizard will display a window full of warnings and instructions. Read the text to confirm that restoring the system won't do any irreparable damage, and click **Next**. Windows will display a progress indicator while it collects data about the restore point you selected, and then it will restart the computer with the selected restore point settings.

Starting System Restore in Safe Mode

Sometimes the conflict created by a new program or device driver is so serious that it won't allow you to start Windows normally. In that event, you should start Windows in Safe Mode and run System Restore from there. However, if the new program or driver conflicts with certain core Windows programs or services, Safe Mode won't be able to start the Windows Explorer program that controls the Windows desktop, and the desktop simply will not appear.

There is an alternative. Rather than starting Windows in the usual Safe Mode, start in Safe Mode with Command Prompt, which opens cmd.exe (the old DOS command-line interface) instead of Windows Explorer.

When Safe Mode with Command Prompt loads, you will see a cmd.exe window with a C:\ prompt like the one shown in Figure 7-5 (the address in the prompt shows the location of the cmd.exe program file). That prompt indicates that Windows is ready to accept a new text command.

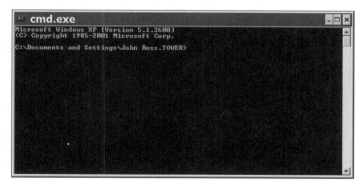

Figure 7-5: Safe Mode with Command Prompt opens a command window instead of the Windows desktop.

To start System Restore from a command prompt, type this command:

```
\windows\system32\restore\rstrui.exe
```

The System Restore window that opens in response to this command is exactly the same as the one described earlier in this chapter.

8

UNDERNEATH IT ALL: THE BIOS

Before Windows starts, the essential functions (such as testing memory and reading software from a hard drive) are under the control of a block of software code called the *basic input/output system (BIOS)*, which is stored on the computer's motherboard. If the computer fails the initial tests, or if it doesn't send or receive signals from essential components (like the keyboard or the video display) before Windows starts, the BIOS is probably at fault—either the code itself is corrupt or an optional setting is wrong. We'll take a look at the configuration and option settings built into the BIOS in this chapter.

One of the first problems that computer designers have to solve is that of loading an operating system (such as Windows) into the computer's memory. Starting with nothing at all running, the computer must use relatively simple internal software to install the more complicated OS. This process is known as pulling the computer up by its own bootstraps, or *booting* the computer. This is similar to the job performed by a car's starter motor, which uses a battery to give the main motor an initial "push" to get it moving.

In a computer that will run Windows (and other operating systems, including some forms of Unix and Linux), the internal boot software is called the *ROM BIOS,* usually referred to simply as BIOS. ROM is an abbreviation for the **r**ead-**o**nly **m**emory chip on the computer's main circuit board that holds the startup software, and BIOS stands for the **b**asic **i**nput/**o**utput **s**ystem that instructs the computer to recognize certain input signals, and to send signals to certain outputs.

Every time you turn on the computer, the BIOS runs the *power-on self test (POST)* to confirm that various components of the computer are operating correctly. Next, it loads a series of instructions into memory that the computer needs to exchange commands and data with the rest of the world. The rest of the computer's world might include the keyboard, system clock, hard drive (and other storage devices), video display, and speakers.

Finally, the BIOS searches for the operating system software which may be stored on a floppy disk, hard drive, or other storage device (perhaps a USB key). Once it finds the operating system, it loads into the computer's *random access memory (RAM).*

Think of the BIOS as the foundation of a building with everything else built on top of it. The BIOS sets the rules and provides the tools that the operating system and the application programs must use to do useful work.

The designers of the BIOS and the designers of Windows consult closely to make sure that everything works together properly. For the rest of us, it's enough to know that some low-level configuration options are set in the BIOS and that a new operating system or a new hardware device might require an updated BIOS in order to take advantage of new features and functions.

NOTE *The BIOS code is the bridge between the generic machine code used by the central processor and the specific commands used by everything else in the computer. Therefore, it's often necessary to add new code to the BIOS when a new operating system or a new type or version of hardware becomes available after the original BIOS was installed.*

The Power-on Self Test

As you read in Chapter 3, the power-on sequence begins as soon as you turn on the computer, and much of the information acquired is displayed on the computer screen. You might not see the first few lines of text if you're starting the monitor after it has been turned off for more than a few minutes, especially if you're using a monitor with a picture tube rather than a flat panel display. Much of this information scrolls past too quickly to read it unless you're already focused on the section of the screen where the text will appear. If you miss a line of text, either because the monitor hadn't warmed up enough or because it zoomed past before you could read it, you'll have to turn the computer off and back on again (or push the Reset button) if you wish to see it again.

Typically, you will see the following information after you turn on the computer:

- Information about the video controller
- Information about the BIOS, including the name of the BIOS supplier, the version and release numbers, and a copyright notice
- A memory test that counts the number of memory bits
- A list of PCI expansion cards
- A table showing the computer's configuration and many of the devices connected to it

You might also see some text that contains other information about the computer and maybe a graphic screen that identifies the make and model of the computer or the motherboard, but they aren't included in every system.

Changing the BIOS Settings

Some of the BIOS activities are organized to offer more than one configuration option. Not every BIOS function is fixed in stone . . . or silicon. It's often possible to instruct the BIOS to ignore certain functions and to use specific values or other settings for other actions. For example, the BIOS includes optional configuration settings that identify every hard drive and other storage device connected to the motherboard and others that allow the computer to start when it receives an incoming instruction through its network interface. There are a couple of dozen of these options in most BIOSes, so there's always a way to examine and change the configuration settings.

Most of the time, however, there's not much reason to mess around with the BIOS settings. In fact, it's likely that a huge proportion of the people who use Windows don't even know that these settings exist. Of course, that means that those people will have to call for help in order to change a setting when something does go wrong. This might be just as well because it's entirely possible to screw up the computer's configuration beyond all recognition by incorrectly changing BIOS settings.

NOTE   *In general, it's a good idea to leave the BIOS alone unless you know what you're doing and have a good reason to make a change.*

You won't look at the BIOS configuration very often, but you should know that it's there and how to get to it as part of your troubleshooting routine. Some of the options are pretty trivial, like the one that turns the Num Lock setting on or off on your keyboard when you turn on the computer, but others can create serious problems if they're set incorrectly. It's important to understand what the BIOS settings can do and how to restore them to a standard configuration when the computer just won't start up or it does something really strange after you tweak a setting.

To make things more complicated, there isn't a single standard for BIOS commands and settings. Most computers use BIOSes made by AMI, Award, or Phoenix, but there are also some other, less common types. Each of the companies that provide BIOS software uses a different set of commands (command set), and the BIOS for each make and model of computer motherboard (the big circuit board inside the computer) includes specific features and options that control that particular motherboard. Therefore, your BIOS settings might use different commands and options from the ones described in this chapter, and the screens you see on your video display might be quite different from the examples here. Each manufacturer uses a different self-test sequence and a different layout for the configuration screens, but the information is similar for all of them. The best place to find a full explanation of your own computer's BIOS-specific settings is the user guide or other manuals supplied with your computer or motherboard. If you can't find the manual, look in the motherboard manufacturer's website for a downloadable copy. And for even more detail, check out "The Definitive BIOS Optimization Guide" at http://www.adriansrojakpot.com/Speed_Demonz/BIOS_Guide/BIOS_Guide_Index.htm.

Opening the BIOS Setup Tool

To change the BIOS configuration settings, you need to open the BIOS setup tool. To do so, press the key identified on screen immediately after the computer finishes its POST. (If you can't figure out which key that is, check the user manual or try F1, F2, or the DELETE key.)

The timing on this can be a bit fiddly because there is usually no visual or audible indication the test has finished unless it identifies a problem. If you press the key too soon, nothing happens, but if you're too late, the BIOS has already begun to load Windows.

If you miss the chance to enter the BIOS setup utility, just let Windows complete its startup routine, and then restart the computer and try again.

NOTE   *It does no harm to hit the key too soon. You can start clicking the key up and down as soon as the computer restarts. It will be obvious when you succeed.*

Changing BIOS Settings

Whenever you consider changing the BIOS configuration, take the time to read the description of the option you want to change in the user manual supplied with your computer or motherboard. Each BIOS configuration utility has a different layout, but they all have similar elements. The instructions on screen and in the manual should give you the information you need for your own system. (Figures 8-1 and 8-2 show two typical top-level BIOS utility menu screens.)

Before you change a BIOS settings, write down the current configuration so that you can return to your original settings if a change creates new and possibly even more dramatic problems. To protect against a future disaster, keep the list of BIOS settings with your computer manuals, lists of Internet settings, and other documents.

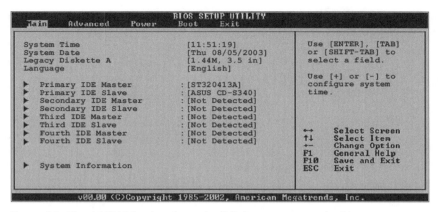

Figure 8-1: This AMIBIOS utility shows the IDE drive settings on the Main menu . . .

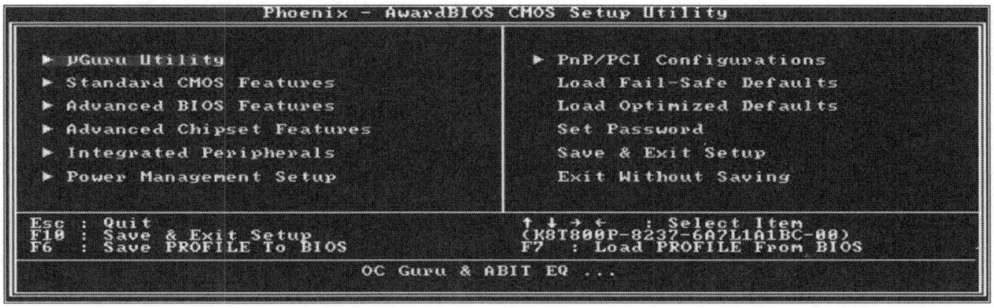

Figure 8-2: . . . while the AwardBIOS main menu contains only links to submenus.

NOTE *If you're troubleshooting the BIOS on a computer without a copy of the original settings, either try the Default settings option if it's available on the top-level menu or check the motherboard manual for the preferred settings.*

Some BIOS options can change things that you probably won't need to worry about, like Resource Exclusion and IRQ assignments. But several, like the ones discussed in the following sections, are more likely to need your attention.

Date and Time

The BIOS setup tool includes menu items that change the time and date settings on the computer's internal clock. You can change the settings here, but it's probably easier to use the Date and Time program built into Windows. Both the BIOS and Windows use the same clock and calendar, so changes from either program also appear on the other.

To change the date and time, double-click the time at the lower-right corner of your Windows desktop to open the Date/Time Properties window.

Configuring Hard Drives and Other IDE Devices

Integrated Device Electronics (IDE) devices are data storage devices that carry their electronic controllers in the same physical package as the device itself.

Hard drives, CD drives, DVD drives, and Zip drives are the most common types of IDE devices.

Each IDE connector on the motherboard can support two devices, which it recognizes as a master and a slave. Every IDE device has a set of jumpers next to the data connector that can set the device as either a master or a slave.

NOTE   *The instructions supplied with a new drive will include the correct jumper settings for that drive; in most cases, the jumper settings are also printed on the device itself. If you're installing an older drive into a new machine, look at the manufacturer's website for configuration information.*

Some IDE hard drives and other devices (such as CD drives) require you to use different jumper settings for the master drive when a slave drive is present, or when there is only a master drive without a slave. Others use the same jumper settings for a master regardless of whether there's a slave or not. If you add a new slave drive to an existing master drive, check the manual or manufacturer's website for the master drive to make sure that the jumper is still in the right place. (For more about setting jumpers and the relationship between masters and slaves, see Chapter 16.)

Almost all motherboards have at least two IDE connectors, which the BIOS identifies as primary and secondary. If there's a third IDE connector, the BIOS will see it as tertiary or third, or identify it with some other word that means the same thing. When two IDE connectors are present, the BIOS will have IDE configuration settings for a primary master, a primary slave, a secondary master, and a secondary slave. Some motherboards also have connectors for SATA (Serial ATA) drives.

When the jumpers are set properly on each drive, your computer's BIOS should detect and identify each IDE or SATA drive automatically, but you might have to use the configuration utility to tweak a new drive. If the BIOS doesn't detect a new drive, Windows won't find the drive either, and if the undetected drive contains your Windows XP software, Windows won't start.

To add a new drive or restore a drive that's missing from the BIOS configuration, follow these steps:

1. Restart the computer, and immediately press the key that opens the BIOS setup utility. The Main BIOS Setup Menu screen will appear.

2. In some systems, the main menu contains links to several submenus. In others, the main menu displays some of the most frequently used configuration settings, including the time and date and links to submenus for each IDE device. If the main menu on your screen does not include links to the primary and secondary master and slave, look for a submenu called Standard CMOS Settings.

3. Use the up and down arrow keys to move around the screen, and then open the submenu for each IDE device, one device at a time. Figure 8-3 shows a typical IDE device configuration screen.

4. Some BIOS tools automatically detect the settings for each drive when you open the submenu; others offer autodetect as a menu option. If the

display does not already show your drive type, select **Autodetect** from the menu, and press ENTER. For most drives manufactured in the last few years, Autodetect should automatically identify the type of drive and configure it properly.

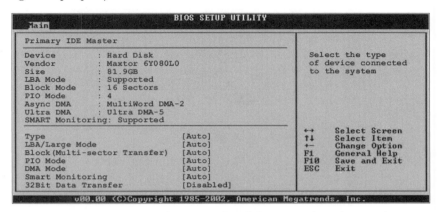

Figure 8-3: The BIOS tool includes settings for all the essential IDE device values.

5. If Autodetect doesn't recognize a device, move down to the other lines in the menu and assign the settings specified in the device's manual, on the manufacturer's website, or printed on the device itself.

6. Follow the instructions on screen to move up one level, and repeat the process for each additional IDE device installed in your computer.

7. Once you have configured all of the IDE devices, follow the on-screen instructions to save your settings, and restart the computer.

Diskette Settings

In the unlikely event that your computer has more than one floppy disk drive, the diskette options specify the size and capacity of each drive. (You probably won't change these settings unless you try to install a second drive to read old 5.25-inch floppies.)

To change these settings, choose the main or CMOS Settings menu item for Drive A or Diskette A to open the submenu for the A: drive. If your machine has a second diskette drive, a B: drive, choose the Drive B or Diskette B menu item to set its configuration.

Boot Sequence

When your computer boots or starts up, it's probably set to look for an operating system on a floppy disk or a CD first. If there's no disk in the drive, it will load the operating system from its primary hard drive (usually the C: drive).

By attempting to boot first from a floppy, CD, or other removable media, the computer can load a a virus scanner or a data recovery program when there's a problem with the hard drive. It can also load the Windows repair tools from the CD to repair a damaged Windows installation or load or reload a new operating system. (The emergency boot diskettes for older Windows versions take advantage of this feature.)

If your hard drive has a problem, if your system won't boot, or if you suspect that you may have a virus, the best way to restore or repair Windows is probably to boot from the Windows CD and run the Repair routine or to boot with an antivirus recovery floppy or CD.

The BIOS setup utility allows you to change the order in which the BIOS reads the drives. To boot from a CD (or other removable media) rather than a hard drive or a floppy, move that drive up to the Number 1 position in the boot sequence list.

Turn Num Lock On or Off

When the Num Lock control is on, the number keys at the right side of most keyboards becomes a 10-key keypad similar to the keyboard on a stand-alone calculator. When Num Lock is off, those keys control motion around a document. The choice of which set of functions should be active when the computer starts is a matter of personal preference, but if the computer always starts with Num Lock in the "wrong" condition, it can be a continuing source of irritation. It's worth setting Num Lock to your liking.

To change the startup Num Lock setting, look for the Boot Up Num Lock Status option in one of the Advanced Options screens. In the Phoenix-Award BIOS setup utility, it's in the Advanced BIOS Features menu; in AwardBIOS, look in the Keyboard Features submenu under the Main menu.

Other BIOS Settings

In general, the other options in the BIOS Settings tool are more obscure than the ones described here, but some of them will be useful to those who like to play with their hardware. Before you change a setting that you don't understand, look in the computer or motherboard manual for an explanation of each option. If the manual doesn't provide enough information, try running a web search on the name of the option.

If All Else Fails, Return to the Default

It's too easy to change some critical BIOS option to a setting that will make things worse than they were before you started. When that happens, the computer might not start at all, or the POST will report one or more errors, or a hard drive or a network connection won't work. This is the point at which you will probably want to throw something through the monitor screen or start shouting obscene curses at your computer.

Stop. Turn off the computer. Take a deep breath. Go get a cup of coffee or a cool drink or something. Eat a chocolate chip cookie. Scratch your cat's ear. Do not give up hope. All is not lost.

When you have (more or less) recovered your composure, follow these steps to return the computer to a BIOS setting that will work in most cases:

1. Turn on the computer.
2. Start the BIOS configuration utility.
3. When the configuration utility appears, find the command that returns the system to a default setting. It might be one of the function keys (F#) or possibly the ESC key. If you don't see a default option on the screen or in the manual, look for it in the list of commands on the screen, and then press that key.
4. If the "set default" command doesn't automatically save the new settings and close the utility program, save your changes and close the BIOS screen.

This should restore the BIOS settings to a configuration that will work. It might not be the most efficient configuration or the one that makes the best use of every component, but it should be adequate to get the computer started and Windows loaded.

If there's still a problem after you have returned to the defaults, it probably won't be as serious. Try again, using the settings that you noted before you started messing around inside the BIOS utility, and read the BIOS Settings section of your manual again. If you still have to make changes, change just one option at a time, save the change, and reboot the computer before changing anything else.

Updating the BIOS

Motherboard manufacturers work closely with the BIOS companies to make sure that a computer built with a new motherboard will work properly with all of the latest keyboards, tape drives, disk drives, sound cards, and other widgets that people are likely to use, and with the newest versions of Windows and other operating systems. But like rust, new product development never sleeps, so the BIOS developers have to provide a way to update the BIOS to support new devices, and new versions of Windows or other operating systems that weren't available when the BIOS shipped.

This is one case where "if it ain't broke, don't fix it" applies. Don't install a new BIOS just because it's a freebie from the motherboard manufacturer; wait until you have a real reason to make the update. If the bells and whistles connected to your computer and Windows appear to be working properly, don't bother with a BIOS update. An update probably won't make the computer work any better unless you install some new device that wasn't supported in the old BIOS, and a failed BIOS update can make your computer unusable. (Of course, when you do need it, a BIOS update can be a lifesaver. Almost as if by magic, that shiny new thing you recently installed will start working.)

Some computers will require a BIOS update in order to take advantage of the features and functions supplied with Windows XP. If you have trouble using some of XP's advanced features, or if the update from an earlier

Windows version doesn't work, check the motherboard manufacturer's website for information for updates required for Windows XP.

There's one more condition that might need a BIOS update: the famous Year 2000 (or Y2K) problem. Remember the Y2K problem? Back in 1998 and 1999, lots of people were convinced that most of the world's computers would break down at the turn of the millennium because they wouldn't understand that the date shown as 1/1/00 was January 1, 2000 and not January 1, 1900, so everything from the electrical grid to traffic lights and soda vending machines would stop working, and we would all have to go back to counting on our fingers and toes. As you might have noticed, it didn't happen, but it did keep a lot of programmers busy fixing old code. Most computers that can handle Windows XP are recent enough that they won't have this problem, but if your computer won't accept the correct year, or if it loses the date every time you reboot, the BIOS may have a Y2K problem. A BIOS update ought to bring the computer into the 21st century.

NOTE *If you lose the time and the date every time you reboot the computer, the problem is likely to be a weak battery. The battery provides constant power for the BIOS and the clock so the time, date, and other settings aren't lost when the computer is turned off. Try replacing the battery on the motherboard before you update the BIOS. Once you replace the battery, you must reset the time and date and change any BIOS settings that should not use the default values.*

If you have a good reason to update your BIOS, follow these steps:

1. Find the make and model number of your computer's motherboard. If you don't have a manual, use a system information utility such as Everest (a free download from www.lavalys.com/products.php) to identify the motherboard. If all else fails, open the computer's case and look for a name on the board itself.

2. Find and download the most recent BIOS update from the computer's manufacturer or directly from the BIOS supplier. (You can find links to most sources of BIOS updates at www.bios-drivers.com or http://simplythebest.net/drivers/bios_updates.html.)

3. The BIOS update file for your motherboard might include a separate update program, or it might be a single executable program that loads the update automatically. Read the instructions for installing the update and follow them carefully. If you're viewing the website or the text file on the machine whose BIOS you're updating, print a copy because you won't be able to see them on your screen while the update is in progress.

NOTE *Remember that the BIOS software includes the very low-level set of instructions that the computer uses to communicate with the rest of the world through the keyboard, the video display, and all of its other inputs and outputs. Without a working BIOS, your computer is simply a box of parts. It's absolutely essential that you follow the instructions supplied with the update tool. Don't assume that you know how to perform an update just because you've done it before. Read the instructions and perform every step exactly as described.*

9

THE WINDOWS REGISTRY: HERE BE DEMONS

Remember those old maps that early explorers used to navigate to unknown parts of the world? In some remote places on the map where there wasn't any reliable information but plenty of frightening rumors, the mapmakers would draw pictures of dragons or sea monsters and include a note that said, "Here be Demons." For most Windows users, the Registry is similar; they look at it as uncharted territory that might produce unthinkable disasters if they go there.

Relax. It's not that bad.

The Windows Registry is the central database that contains almost all the configuration settings and options used by Windows and by most application programs written for Windows. Therefore, if Windows does something that It Has Never Done Before, there's a strong chance that it was caused by a change to one or more lines in the Registry.

Some items in the Registry change automatically every time a program or utility runs. Others change when you install or delete a program or change an option in a Properties window. And still others change after you or someone else edits them directly.

NOTE   *It's also possible to change some Registry items without permission from the computer's owner or users. Many viruses and spyware create problems in Windows by altering the Registry.*

The Registry controls everything from the look of the Windows desktop and the image used as the tiny logo in the upper-right corner of the Explorer window, to the programs that run automatically when you start Windows, and the default folders that store data files created by application programs. Every time you install a new program or change a configuration setting, part of the Registry changes. All the dialog boxes and Properties windows that you use to change Windows settings are really just somebody's idea of an easier way to change one or more Registry listings.

The Registry is located in a hidden subfolder, so items in it don't show up when you use the Windows Search tool. The Registry contains thousands of entries that occupy a lot of space on your hard drive—typically more than 33MB.

NOTE   *If you're curious, you can download a tool to measure the amount of data stored in the Registry from www.microsoft.com/windows2000/techinfo/reskit/tools/existing/dureg-o.asp.*

Because the Registry was designed as an internal database that tells Windows and other programs how to handle various details, it's a very dense set of listings without obvious explanations of the particular function of each line. In fact, it's often impossible to know what a line in the Registry does just by looking at it. And because changing one or two characters in the Registry can render a program or a Windows utility completely useless, trial and error is probably not a productive way to solve Windows problems or to tweak your system.

The conventional wisdom about the Registry is, "Don't mess with it unless you know exactly what you're doing." With a few exceptions, like using a cleanup utility to get rid of orphaned entries that no longer do anything, that's good advice. Still, there are times when editing the Registry is the only way to fix a problem, so it's useful to understand how the Registry is organized and how to modify it safely. Nevertheless, you should always treat changing the Registry as a last resort and approach it with care.

NOTE   *The major exceptions to the "Don't mess with it" rule are certain troubleshooting and repair procedures you may find in the Microsoft Knowledge Base or instructions from some other software support center. These may call for specific changes to the Registry (especially when eliminating certain nasty spyware programs). If you find a Knowledge Base article or a set of instructions for killing a spyware problem or performing some other task that instructs you to edit the Registry, follow them exactly as written.*

If you do try to edit the Registry, be sure to make a backup copy of it first (I'll show you how), and follow the editing instructions as closely as possible. Don't assume that you can apply some kind of logical analysis to the Registry format that will let you figure out what the new entry ought to be; if you don't know exactly what to change and how to change it, don't improvise.

Opening, Reading, and Editing the Registry

While several third-party programs, such as Registry Commander (www.aezay .dk/aezay/regcmd), will edit the Registry, the built-in Windows Registry Editor is fine for most users. The Registry Editor doesn't show up on the Start menu, so choose **Start ▶ Run** and type **regedit** to open it. Click **OK**, and you should be in the Registry Editor, as shown in Figure 9-1.

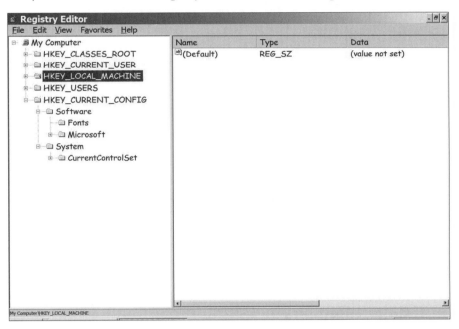

Figure 9-1: Use the Windows Registry Editor to add, change, and remove items from the Registry.

Always make a backup copy of the Registry before you try to edit it:

1. Type **regedit** from Start ▶ Run. You are now in the Registry Editor.
2. Open the **File** menu, and select the **Export** command.
3. Choose a location for the backup copy of the Registry.
4. Type a filename for your backup.
5. At the bottom of the Export Registry File window (shown in Figure 9-2), select **All** in the Export Range box.
6. Click **Save**.

Figure 9-2: Choose All in the Export Range box to save a copy of the entire Registry.

If you discover that the changes you made to the Registry didn't work as expected, you should restore the Registry to the condition it was in before you started to fiddle with it. If you changed just one or two entries, the easiest way to do this is to edit those entries back to their original form. But if you aren't sure what you changed, of if you made a lot of changes, you can restore the Registry from your backup. To do so:

1. Open the Registry Editor.
2. Choose **File ▸ Import**.
3. Select the file that contains the backup you want to restore, and press **Open**.

How the Registry Is Organized

As you may have noticed in Figure 9-1, the Registry Editor displays the Registry as a tree structure, similar to the way Windows Explorer displays files and folders. In Windows XP, the Registry is organized into five top-level folders or branches, known as *hive keys* or *handle keys*. (In earlier Windows versions, the Registry contains six top-level folders.)

The top-level folders are:

HKEY_CLASSES_ROOT

This folder contains instructions that control the Windows user interface. It specifies the properties of every type of object (Microsoft defines an *object* as "any resource that can be manipulated by a program or process"), including files, directories, links on the desktop, shortcuts, drives, and network resources. Properties specified in this folder include the association between file extensions and object types, the icons used by each type of object, the options that appear in the pop-up menu when you right-click an icon, and those that appear in each of the Properties windows. Among other things, this information tells Windows Explorer which program or document file to open when you click an icon.

HKEY_CURRENT_USER
This folder controls the profile that applies to the user currently logged on to Windows. It specifies personalized options such as screen colors and Control Panel settings.

HKEY_LOCAL_MACHINE
This folder controls the options that apply to the hardware and software installed on this computer. Among other things, entries in this folder contain the version numbers of individual programs, options that apply to each program, display settings, and communication options and settings.

HKEY_USERS
This folder contains the hardware and software profiles for all users who have accounts on this computer, along with the default settings that apply to all users.

HKEY_CURRENT_CONFIG
This folder contains the computer's active hardware profile and controls the settings that Windows applies at startup. If the computer holds only one hardware profile, the Current_Config folder contains the same information as the Local_Machine folder.

HKEY_DYN_DATA (Not in Windows XP)
This folder contains temporary data that Windows uses to monitor the status of certain hardware functions.

As a group, these keys control everything about the way Windows operates, so changing an entry in the Registry is the ultimate way to change a feature or function: a desktop image, the text that appears in the bar across the top of a window, the port that a network device uses to communicate, or anything else. For example, the HKEY_LOCAL_MACHINE\SOFTWARE\Microsoft\ Windows\CurrentVersion\Run folder contains a list of the programs that run automatically when you start Windows, and the . . .\CurrentVersion\Fonts folder contains an entry for every typeface that Windows can use.

Using the Registry to Repair or Modify Windows

Entire books have been written about the Windows Registry and how to use it to modify the way Windows performs, but we won't go into that sort of detail here.

Other than modifying some obscure things (like the text in a configuration window), you'll probably find a Properties window or tweaking tool that will let you modify something that is controlled by the Registry, without actually having to edit the Registry yourself. Unless you want to carefully study the Registry's syntax and structure, you're better off leaving things alone rather than trying to edit the Registry directly. But if you don't have any other choice, here are some things you will need to know.

Deleting a Registry Item

You may find it necessary to delete a Registry item to remove a virus, spyware infection, or leftover fragments of an old program. In a few (uncommon) cases, a Registry item might be the source of a conflict that interferes with the operation of another program or configuration setting.

NOTE   *Do not delete anything from the Registry unless you know exactly what you are doing. If a procedure tells you to delete a particular item, don't assume that you can use the same procedure to delete something else.*

To delete an item from the Registry:

1. Choose **Start ▸ Run** and type **regedit** to open the Registry Editor.
2. Highlight the item you want to delete in the tree structure on the left side of the editor screen. To expand a branch or subbranch, click the plus (+) box next to the name of the branch. (Figure 9-3 shows a typical entry.) To search for an item by name, open **Find** in the Edit menu.

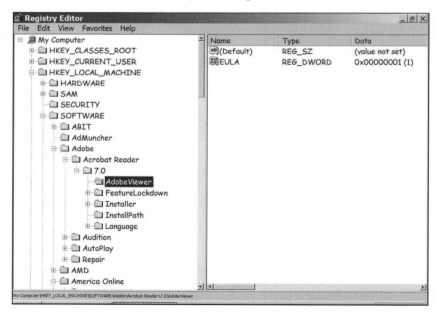

Figure 9-3: Many Registry items are nested several layers into the tree structure.

3. Delete the currently highlighted item with the DELETE key.

NOTE *If you select and delete a branch or subbranch rather than an individual item, you will remove all of the subbranches and items under that branch.*

Disabling a Registry Item

It's sometimes helpful to temporarily disable a branch or an individual Registry item (rather than to remove it completely), because you might want to restore it if the deletion creates more problems than it solves. To disable a branch or an individual item, change its name as follows:

1. Open the Registry Editor.
2. Find and highlight the name of the item you want to disable.
3. Choose **Edit ▶ Rename**. You should see brackets around the item name.
4. Click the highlighted name to insert the cursor in the highlighted text.
5. Move the cursor to the end of the item name, and add **xx** to the name. For example, change EULA to **EULAxx**, as shown in Figure 9-4.

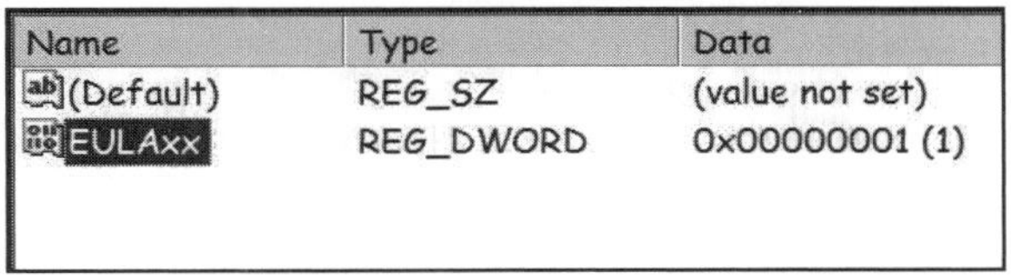

Name	Type	Data
(Default)	REG_SZ	(value not set)
EULAxx	REG_DWORD	0x00000001 (1)

*Figure 9-4: To temporarily disable a Registry item, add **xx** to the name.*

6. Move the cursor away from the item you want to change, click to save the edited name, and then close the Registry Editor.

If the name change produces the result you want, you can either leave the edited version alone or delete the edited item (though it's best to leave it in the Registry, just in case a problem appears later). If the edited name creates a new problem, repeat the name change procedure, but this time, remove the *xx* from the item name.

Adding a New Registry Item

In most cases, new items are added to the Registry as part of a program or a device driver's installation routine. However, you may need to add a new item or key to the Registry in order to create a new option setting from scratch, or to add a new setting to an existing entry.

Any procedure that calls for adding a new registry item should include specific instructions that tell you exactly where to place the new item, what type of item to add, and the exact text of the item. Follow these instructions closely. Don't assume that you can add a similar item in a different location or that you can use a slightly different name or data format.

Editing an Existing Registry Item

When a procedure instructs you edit a Registry key, it will probably include step-by-step instructions for finding and editing the key. If you don't get detailed instructions, follow these steps:

1. Open the Registry Editor.
2. Find the item you want to change. In most cases, the repair procedure will include the item's exact location. If not, use the **Find** tool in the Edit menu.
3. Select the name of the item you want to edit in the list on the right side of the Registry Editor window. (You might have to scroll to the right to read the entire text of the key.)
4. Choose **Edit ▸ Modify** to open the Edit String dialog box, as shown in Figure 9-5.

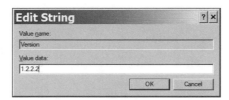

Figure 9-5: Use the Edit String dialog box to change the value of a Registry key.

5. Edit the text in the Value Data field to match the value specified in the procedure. Click **OK** to save the change and close the dialog box.

Getting the Junk Out: Registry Cleanup Tools

Every time you turn on your computer or restart Windows, the computer scans the Registry to set all the configuration options that define the way your computer looks, feels, and performs. When Windows takes too long to start and its response to your commands is sluggish, the Registry probably contains too many entries and Windows is spending too much time reading it. A Registry loaded with junk takes longer to scan than one that contains only useful information.

Registry junk can take many forms. For example, many badly constructed programs won't completely remove every trace of themselves from the Registry when you uninstall them. Other Registry items might be remnants of old, deleted, desktop shortcuts.

Hardware can leave even more junk behind: For example, when you connect a plug-and-play device to your computer, Windows adds configuration information about that device to the Registry. However, if you disconnect the same device, the Registry entries often hang around even though they no longer serve any purpose. Over time, the number of useless entries in the Registry can increase and accumulate to make the Registry (and therefore your computer) less efficient than it ought to be.

The solution is to run a utility program that scans the Registry for unnecessary items and offers to remove them. Some of these programs are stand-alone products, and others are part of general-purpose utility packages. Microsoft's Windows Marketplace (www.windowsmarketplace.com/results .aspx?bcatid=780) offers links to dozens of free or low-cost Registry cleaners, editors, and optimization tools.

Some of these programs are more aggressive than others. For example, compare Norton Utilities WinDoctor (part of Norton SystemWorks) with the stand-alone Registry Clean Expert program. Figures 9-6 and 9-7 show the results of Registry scans on the same computer by Norton WinDoctor and Registry Clean Expert. Notice that WinDoctor found only 8 problems, while Registry Clean Expert found almost 100. That's a significant difference. As a tool for improving slow Windows performance by streamlining the Registry, the more thorough program is probably the better choice.

NOTE *Be careful when removing "found" Registry problems with these Registry tools. Some tools are too aggressive and may result in your damaging the Registry. Remove any Registry entries with care!*

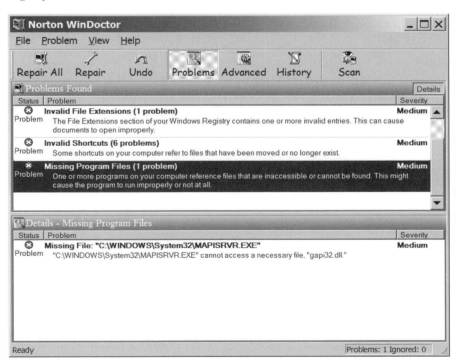

Figure 9-6: Norton WinDoctor scans the Windows Registry and identifies problems.

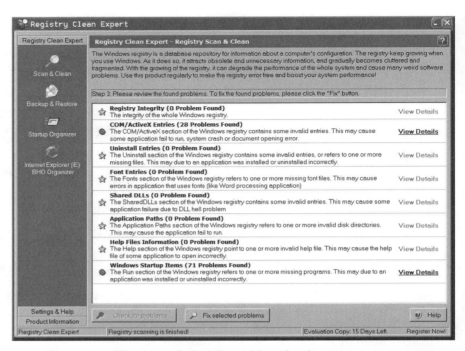

Figure 9-7: Registry Clean Expert finds many problems that the Norton program misses.

Unlike the demons on those old maps, the potential danger inside the Registry is real. If you're serious about troubleshooting problems in Windows, you will probably end up exploring the Registry sooner or later because it contains the rules that control just about everything.

But don't travel without a reliable guide or a set of specific instructions that tell you exactly what to change and how to change it. Otherwise, you can easily do more serious damage without solving your original problem.

10

DEALING WITH INDIVIDUAL PROGRAMS AND FILES

A breakdown in the Windows operating system is not the only possible cause of a computer problem. Sometimes you can isolate the problem to a single program. If everything else appears to be working properly, there's a strong likelihood that the program that is performing oddly (or not working at all) is itself the source of the problem.

In other cases, however, a program appears to work properly, but it refuses to handle a particular file or document. The program has no apparent trouble with anything else, but the document you want to use seems like a lost cause. It won't open at all, or if it does open, it looks as if it has been translated into a combination of Swahili and Martian.

The general rules for fixing problems like these are similar to the ones for troubleshooting Windows—find and isolate the component with the problem, repair or replace the component, test to confirm that the problem has gone away, repeat until fixed—but the specific methods are not exactly the same. When you're dealing with a single balky program, you can probably limit your focus to that program rather than looking at the entire system.

The Program Won't Start

You click the icon on your desktop, or you choose a program from the Start menu, and then . . . nothing happens. If other programs are working properly, the program you're trying to open is in trouble.

In most cases, the solution will be to replace the program software, but you should ask a few questions first.

Have You Used This Program Before?

If you discover that a program won't run immediately after you install it, it's possible that the program is not compatible with the version of Windows installed on your computer. You can think of this as a square-peg-in-a-round-hole problem. This could happen if you are trying to run a very old program that was designed for an earlier version of Windows or a very new program that requires some features of the latest Windows update.

If your newly installed program is not compatible with Windows XP, you can either look for a newer release of that program or try running the program in Compatibility Mode (described later in this chapter). The software manufacturer almost certainly knows about the problem, and they can probably offer instructions for updating. Look for information on the manufacturer's website and in the Microsoft Knowledge Base.

If it's a new program that requires the latest Windows service pack, go ahead and install the service pack. See Chapter 11 for more about Windows updates and service packs. They're free, and they will improve the performance of Windows in general, so what are you waiting for?

Have You Just Upgraded?

If a program stops working after you install a new patch, service pack, or other upgrade to Windows, or when you update the program itself, there's probably some kind of conflict between the program and the operating system. If it's an old program and a new Windows version, the Program Compatibility Wizard (next section) might solve the problem. Otherwise, look in the Support section of the program manufacturer's website for information about using the program with Windows XP. If you don't see any discussion of this problem, telephone or e-mail the manufacturer's support center.

Program Compatibility Mode

Some programs have never been updated; maybe the company that published the program has gone out of business or the developers have decided that there is no demand for a new version. Or maybe you just don't want to spend the money for an upgrade because the old version does everything you want it to do. But now that you have replaced your Old Faithful wood-burning computer with a shiny new machine that runs Windows XP, some of those old programs might not run anymore. And other programs might have trouble with modern video drivers.

Don't give up quite yet: Windows XP includes a Program Compatibility Mode that should help. It won't work with old antivirus or backup utilities and some other system programs, but you will want the latest and greatest editions of those programs anyway because older antivirus programs won't know how to handle the current generation of viruses and old backup utilities can't always deal with today's file formats and structures.

For applications, Compatibility Mode can make XP look (to the balky application) like an older Windows version that the program can work with.

The easiest way to set up a program for Program Compatibility Mode is to use the Program Compatibility Wizard (**Start ▶ Programs ▶ Accessories ▶ Program Compatibility Wizard**). As the wizard steps through the setup routine, you can choose the program and specify the version of Windows that it was intended to use. If you still have the program's original manual, look in the Specifications section to learn which version of Windows to use. If you don't have a manual, you'll have to resort to trial and error: Set the Compatibility Wizard to Windows Me first, and if that doesn't work, try each earlier version of Windows in turn.

If there's a video problem, such as a distorted image or a strange-looking mixture of colors, try changing to one of the alternative display options.

What Else Has Happened Lately?

It's not common, but sometimes two unrelated programs can conflict with one another. If Program B stops working after you install or modify Program A, there's a good chance that the two programs are fighting each other. If both programs depend on the same DLL (dynamic link library) file, the version that was supplied with the newly installed program might not be compatible with the old program.

If you discover that an existing program has stopped working after you installed a new one, contact both manufacturers' technical support centers for advice. In the meantime, you can try reinstalling the older program.

Is There Another Way to Open the Program?

Windows offers several ways to start a program: You can use a shortcut on the desktop or the Start menu, open a data file whose format is linked to the program, enter the name of the program or a data file in the Run window, or use the Windows Explorer shell to run the program. Some programs can also open automatically from within other programs, such as an audio or video player inside a web browser.

If a program fails to run, it's always possible that a problem exists in a short-cut to the program file or the link between the program and a file extension rather than in the program itself. It's often productive to try some other method to run the program before you go to the trouble of reinstalling it.

If you can't open a text or data file from the desktop, try running the program first, and then use the **File ▶ Open** command to load the document or file. For example, if nothing happens when you double-click the name of a text file with a .doc file extension, go to the Start menu and try to open Microsoft Word (or some other word processor) first. If Word won't run from the Start menu, try opening My Computer on the desktop and moving to the Winword.exe program in the C:\Program Files\Microsoft Office\Office folder.

Most program files are normally located in subfolders within the C:\Program Files folder. However, some users prefer their own customized file structure. If you can't find what you want in the Program Files folder, look for some other obvious location, or use the Search tool in the Start menu to find the program file.

The point of this exercise is to separate the application program from the data file. In some cases, a damaged data file won't allow its linked program file to open, so dealing with the two files separately can often solve the problem.

Reinstall the Program

If you have isolated the problem to the program itself rather than a linked data file or a damaged shortcut, and if you know that the program is supposed to be compatible with Windows XP, it's likely that the program file has been damaged. In this case, it's time to reinstall the program. Don't bother to uninstall the old version first, because installing a new copy over the existing version can sometimes allow you to reuse the configuration settings you were using before the previous installation went south.

Find the original CD or other distribution media and run the Install or Setup program. If the program asks if you're performing a new install or a repair, choose the repair option; this will preserve your old settings.

In most cases, this kind of reinstall will load a clean copy of the program into your computer and you can get on with your work. If the program *still* won't run, one of the files left over from the original installation is at fault. Therefore, you will have to remove all vestiges of the program and start again from scratch.

Delete and Reinstall Again

If the program still won't run after you install it on top of an old copy, the next step is to completely delete the program and install it again. Some programs offer their own Uninstall function, but the most reliable method is to use the Add or Remove Programs tool in the Control Panel, shown in Figure 10-1.

To delete a program, follow these steps:

1. Open the Control Panel. From the Windows XP Start menu, select **Control Panel**; from the Classic Windows Start menu, select **Settings ▶ Control Panel**.

Figure 10-1: Use the Add Or Remove Programs tool to delete a damaged program.

2. Open **Add Or Remove Programs** from the Control Panel.

3. Scroll down the list of currently installed programs until you find the name of the program you want to remove.

4. Click the name of the program. The description of the program will expand to display additional information.

5. Click the **Change/Remove** button to delete the program.

Some programs will start their uninstall routine immediately, but others might ask for more information first. Answer any on-screen questions as you step through the removal process.

After the uninstall is complete, restart your computer in order to remove any residual portions of the program from the computer's memory. When the reboot is complete, install the program from the CD or other distribution media just as if you were installing it for the first time. When the installation is complete, check the program manufacturer's website for updates and patches that may have been released since you acquired the program.

A File Opens in the Wrong Program

Many programs establish links to certain file extensions that allow Windows to automatically load a text or data file into a program that can read or process it. For example, files named with .doc extensions might be linked to Microsoft Word or some other word processor, and image files with names ending in .jpg might be linked to Photoshop.

When you open a file, its contents normally appear in a linked program. But sometimes the text, image, or other data will load itself into a different program from the one you were expecting. A sound file plays in Windows Media Player instead of Apple QuickTime, or a text file appears in WordPad instead of Microsoft Word. In some cases, this is just a minor nuisance because you can still view or hear the contents of the file, but at other times the program that opens the file won't recognize all of the file's contents.

This misappropriation of a file extension can happen because another program has taken control of the file extension or when the same file extension applies to two different kinds of data. Certain types of programs, including graphics programs and audio players and editors, are notorious for grabbing control of related data files whether you want them to become the default program or not. Whatever the cause, the solution is to change the file type association:

1. Open Windows Explorer from the desktop or the Start menu.
2. Find the data file whose association you want to change.
3. Right-click the file icon. A pop-up menu will appear.
4. Select **Open With ▶ Choose Program** from the pop-up menu. The Open With dialog box, shown in Figure 10-2, will appear.

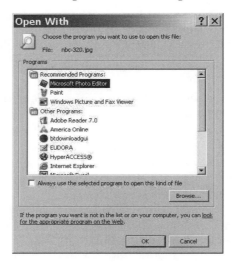

Figure 10-2: The Open With dialog box offers a choice of programs to link to the current file type.

5. Chose the program you want to associate with this type of data file, and turn on the **Always Use The Selected Program** option.
6. Click **OK** to save your choice and close the dialog box.

The Program Freezes

When a program won't do what you tell it to do, it won't accept new commands or data entry, or it refuses to save or open a file, the problem could have one of several causes.

- The document is damaged.
- The document is set to read-only.
- The program file is damaged.

The best way to identify the problem is with a systematic approach:

1. First, try saving the document or file; this probably won't work, but it's worth a try.

2. Try to select the entire document or file, and then use the **Copy** command in the Edit menu to move it to another program. For example, if you're trying to save a text file, open WordPad (**Start ▶ Programs** [or **All Programs**] ▶ **Accessories**) and paste the document into the new program. Save the file in the new program.

3. Next, exit the original program, reboot the computer, and run the program again. This should open the program with no file loaded into it, which will give you a chance to test the program by itself.

4. Load the file into the program.

This might be enough to solve the problem. If not, try loading a different file or document. If that works, the original data file is causing the problem. Sometimes you can salvage the contents of a damaged file by opening it in a different program—try Notepad or WordPad for document files—but often you will have to reconstruct the file from a backup copy or from scratch. You do have a backup, don't you?

If the program can load a file but you still can't change it or save it, find the file in Windows Explorer, right-click the icon, and choose **Properties** from the pop-up menu. At the bottom of the Properties window (shown in Figure 10-3), make sure the Read-only option is not active.

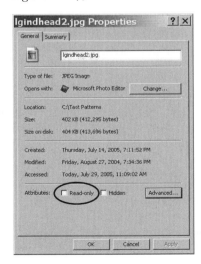

Figure 10-3: The Read-only attribute is at the bottom of the Properties window.

If the program freezes with *any* data file loaded, the problem is in the program itself rather than the data file. To solve the problem, reinstall the program.

I Can't Read a File

If the program is working properly but one particular file won't open, it's possible that the file format and the file extension don't match—either the document is formatted for an older version of the program or somebody has assigned the wrong file extension. For example, Quicken has used many different file formats over the years, so a very old file might not load successfully into the latest version of Quicken without a little help.

Sometimes a program will display a message that flags the file as an unknown format and offer instructions for loading a filter, but just as often, the program will try to open the file. The result might be a block of strange text or odd symbols at the top of the document or an entire document full of gibberish. Or worst case, the file won't open at all.

Windows uses the three-letter file extension at the end of a filename to link a file type to a program. If double-clicking a data file's name opens a program that does not recognize the file format, either the link between the file extension and the program is wrong or the same file extension is used on more than one type of file. Sometimes you can make an educated guess about the nature of the file (maybe the file extension is off by one letter, or you recognize the format when you open it in Notepad), but if it's a complete mystery, use one of these online file extension directories to identify the file type:

http://www.fileinfo.net

http://whatis.techtarget.com/fileFormatA

http://file-ext.com

http://www.webopedia.com/quick_ref/fileextensions.asp

Try a Different Program

If the program linked to a file's file extension won't open the file, try using a different program. Right-click the file's icon in Windows Explorer, and choose **Open With** to choose a new program. If it's a text document, try WordPad or Notepad; if it's an image file, try the Windows Picture and Fax Viewer program.

Check the File Extension

Most programs automatically assign a file extension when you save a data file, but sometimes a file will end up with a different extension or with no extension at all. When that happens, a program might not open the file.

If you know what kind of file you're trying to open (e.g., it's an image file or a text file), right-click the filename and use the **Rename** command to add a file extension.

The File Won't Print

If a file won't print, the first thing to do is to save the file. This will ensure that you don't lose the file's content and allow you to try printing through a different program.

Here are the things to check when a file refuses to print:

- Is the printer turned on? Is the On Line indicator on the printer lit?

- Is the printer displaying an error code or error message? If so, consult the printer manual or the manufacturer's website for an explanation of the code or message and instructions for responding to it.

- Is the correct printer driver loaded into Windows? From the Start menu, open the Printers And Faxes window (**Start ▶ Settings ▶ Printers And Faxes** in the Windows Classic menu) to see links to all of the printer drivers currently loaded on your computer. If you don't see the exact make and model of the printer you're trying to use, double-click the **Add Printer** icon to load the correct driver.

- Is the printer selected as the active printer? Look for a check mark that identifies the active printer next to one of the printer icons in the Printers And Faxes window (like the one in Figure 10-4).

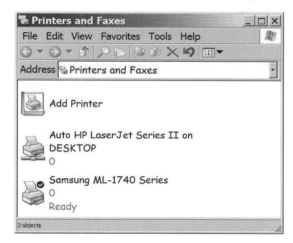

Figure 10-4: The check mark identifies the active printer.

- Is there a printer icon visible in the System Tray next to the clock at the bottom of the screen? This icon indicates that Windows is transferring a document to the active printer. Double-click the icon for details about the current print job and any others that are waiting to print. If the icon is not in the tray, confirm that all the print options are correct (look in the File menu of the program from which you are trying to print) and try again.

- Is the printer out of paper?

- Is the printer out of ink or toner?

• Is the Print To File option in the Print dialog box that opens when you enter the Print command (shown in Figure 10-5) turned on?

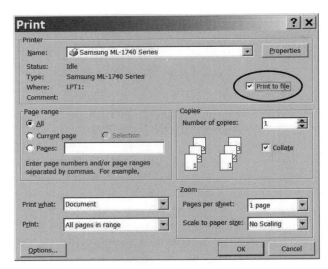

Figure 10-5: Make sure the Print To File option is not active.

The answers to one or more of these questions should identify the reason that your file or document won't print. If your file still won't print, try loading the file into a different program and printing from there. If *that* doesn't work, go to the section on printer problems in Chapter 17 for more information about troubleshooting printers.

The number of possible problems that can be caused by individual programs is limited only by the number of programs installed on your computer. This chapter has offered some "try this first" techniques that will help you solve problems in many programs, but it can't possibly include everything. If nothing in this chapter solves your specific problem, look for specific information about the program in question in the program's help files, the user manual, and the manufacturer's website and support center.

11

SERVICE PACKS, PATCHES, AND OTHER UPDATES

In an ideal world, every computer-related product would work perfectly out of the box, and it would continue to work as long as you own it. Of course, in that world, technical support centers would answer the telephone on the first ring and fine champagne would run out of public drinking fountains.

In *this* world, Windows XP, other software, device drivers, and even your computer's BIOS all require periodic updates that allow them to interact with new products that weren't available when they were first released. These updates also repair recently discovered problems, add new features, and help to protect your software from viruses and other security threats.

Finding and installing updates and patches is an essential skill for every computer troubleshooter. Computer problems that require a software update, new driver, or system patch can be particularly aggravating unless you know that the new software is available. Therefore, looking for an upgrade or a patch should always be part of your troubleshooting routine and your preventive maintenance schedule. The resources are out there, and they're almost always free: It's up to you to use them.

When to Update

When you're trying to find and fix a computer problem, a patch or an update may not jump out at you as the most obvious solution. Unless a manufacturer's support center, or some third-party website or newsgroup points you in that direction, you might never discover that an update is available. Therefore, you should consider checking for updates as a form of preventive maintenance, just like defragmenting your hard drive and backing up your data.

Finding and installing software updates should be part of your regular computer maintenance routine. It's not always necessary to install every update immediately after it becomes available, but it's good practice to install new updates whenever you discover them. Many manufacturers use updates and patches to distribute fixes to known problems (including ones that you may not have discovered yet).

Look for updates (and release notes that might describe other fixes) when you encounter a problem with a newly installed device or piece of software. In fact, even if you don't notice any problems, you should check the manufacturer's website for updates and patches every time you install a new program or peripheral device.

In today's computer world, new security holes are discovered, exploited, and patched all the time; you can't be too careful.

Finding and Installing the Latest Updates

Some software, including Windows XP and many antivirus and Internet security programs, can automatically find and install updates through the Internet as soon as they become available, but many other software publishers simply make their updates available online and wait for you to find them.

Installing Microsoft Windows Updates

Microsoft issues major updates to Windows called *service packs* every couple of years, and additional security patches almost every month. If you haven't already installed the most recent Windows XP service pack, do so now. When this chapter was written, the current service pack was Service Pack 2, also known as SP2. The latest rumors about SP3 say that it's scheduled for late 2007.

SP2 includes improvements to Internet Explorer and Windows Media Player and improved support for wireless networks, but the really important additions are related to security. Microsoft is committed to protecting their users, and many of the new features in SP2 seem to reflect that commitment.

However, there is a potential problem here: Some older programs and device drivers may not be completely compatible with SP2. If you find that one of your programs stops working after you install SP2, or if a device driver fails, check the software or device manufacturer's website for a patch or update. If nothing is available, try using the Windows Compatibility Wizard (**Start ▸ Programs ▸ Accessories ▸ Program Compatibility Wizard**). If that fails, your only remaining option may be to use Add/Remove Programs to uninstall the service pack.

If you have a high-speed Internet connection, it's easy to update Windows XP. Just click the **Windows Update** item in the Start menu or in the Internet Explorer Tools menu. This connects you to a Microsoft web page that will examine your computer to learn which updates you need, and it will download them automatically. (You can do the same thing through a dial-up modem connection, but some of the update files are very large, so it might take several hours to download them.)

Windows Update can also search for new device drivers that have been certified by Microsoft, though more recent versions are often available directly from the manufacturer. The manufacturer's website might also offer some additional diagnostic programs and other software to enhance the performance of its products.

NOTE *If you purchased your computer or upgraded to Windows XP after a service pack was released, that service pack is almost certainly installed already. If it's not, the Windows Upgrade website will let you know about it and offer to download and install the missing service pack along with all of the other recent updates necessary to bring your system up to date.*

Automatic Updating

SP2 also includes an automatic tool that downloads additional updates from Microsoft and installs them on your computer as they become available. After you install SP2, you can turn on the Automatic Updates feature to allow Windows to take care of future updates.

NOTE *The alternative to downloading the service pack through a slow Internet connection is to request the latest Service Pack on a CD from www.microsoft.com/windowsxp/downloads/updates/sp2/cdorder/en_us/default.mspx.*

Patches

In addition to the general-distribution Windows updates and service packs, Microsoft also offers software patches through the Knowledge Base to repair specific problems. Some of these special patches might appear in future service packs, but others are designed to deal with unusual problems that affect only a few users. If you find a link to one of these patches in a Knowledge Base article and it seems like that patch will solve a particular problem that you are having, follow the instructions in the article to install the patch.

Updates for Other Microsoft Products

Unfortunately, other Microsoft products don't offer the same automatic update service as Windows XP, so you must go to the Microsoft website to search for updates. To find the latest improvements to all things Microsoft, go to www.microsoft.com, move to the appropriate product family, and then to either Downloads or Check for Updates.

Updating Security Software

Security updates are a bit of a different story. Because new viruses, spyware, and other threats to your computer appear all the time, the producers of security software release new updates very frequently. Most of these programs include automatic update services that can find and install updates as they become available; be sure to turn on these features.

In general, software products that protect against viruses, spyware, and unauthorized intruders include automatic update features similar to the ones in Windows XP. These programs call home through the Internet on a regular schedule to check for newly available software revisions. When new software is available, the update program either installs it automatically or it displays an on-screen message that encourages you to install the update as soon as possible. Given the choice, it's almost always better to choose the ASAP route unless you're using a processor-intensive program like a video or audio editor or engaged in some kind of real-time activity that might suffer from an unwanted restart when a program update installs itself.

What If an Update Creates Problems?

Unfortunately, some manufacturers don't test their update packages as well as they should, so an update may solve some problems but create new ones at the same time. When that happens, especially with a product as widely used as Windows, the problem usually comes to light very quickly and the manufacturer either announces yet another update, or publishes other instructions for fixing it.

You will probably find third-party websites and newsgroups about most programs, run by users' groups and enthusiastic individuals that offer the latest rumors, gossip, and news. Often, the first information about newly discovered bugs or other problems related to a particular product will appear on one of those unofficial sites rather than the official one. To find the websites devoted to a particular program, try a Google search on the name of the product.

If you can't get help with a problem you're facing on the manufacturer's support center website or through a search, try uninstalling the upgrade if you have the option to do so. (You won't always be able to.) If that doesn't work, you'll have to completely uninstall the original program (including the update), and reinstall it from the original media. (Don't forget to reinstall any earlier updates and patches after you install the main program.)

Updating the BIOS

As you know (or if you don't, go back and read Chapter 8), your computer's BIOS contains instructions that the computer uses to interact with devices such as video cards, as well as the commands necessary to start Windows.

When a new version of Windows appears, or when new devices or new processors become available, the BIOS manufacturer may update the BIOS in order to allow it to recognize and support the newer hardware or software.

For example, if Intel or AMD adds features to new CPU chips, or if a new and better standard for video controllers or network interfaces appears, the computer won't know how to handle those new features unless you update the BIOS software.

The "if it ain't broke, don't fix it" rule applies here. *Don't update your BIOS just because you discover that there's a new release out there on a website.* If your computer is working well, you will add absolutely nothing to its performance by changing the BIOS. But if the computer fails to start after you install a new version of Windows, or if it won't recognize a new piece of hardware, updating the BIOS can often solve the problem.

Use the Right BIOS

Every motherboard uses a specific BIOS, so you must find exactly the right update for the motherboard inside your computer. To identify your motherboard, look in the manual supplied with the computer, call or e-mail the computer manufacturer and ask, or open the case and look for a make and model on the surface of the board.

Information about the make and model of many motherboards is also embedded in the BIOS firmware. Several diagnostic programs can read and display that information, along with many other details about the computer's hardware, memory, and performance. For example, Dr. Hardware (available from www.dr-hardware.com) produces a display like the one in Figure 11-1.

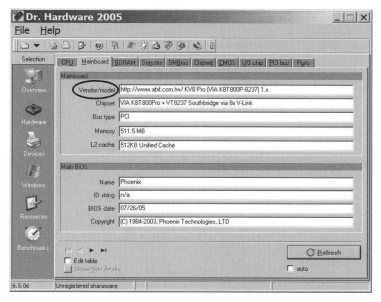

Figure 11-1: Dr. Hardware identifies this computer's motherboard as an Abit KV8 Pro.

Once you know which motherboard you're using, go to either the computer or motherboard manufacturer's website and look in the Support section for the latest BIOS updates. If it offers a separate BIOS installer, download it along with the BIOS itself.

The more enlightened motherboard makers tell you what improvements they have added in each BIOS update. For example, Figure 11-2 shows the BIOS update section of the website for an Abit motherboard that lists the changes in each release. If you can find the specific problem you want to solve in the list of changes, you can be reasonably certain that updating the BIOS will solve your problem.

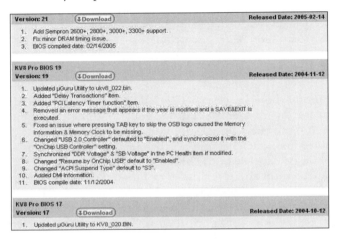

Figure 11-2: In this example, you must update to version 21 to use the motherboard with AMD Sempron processors.

Follow the Instructions

Follow the installation instructions supplied with the BIOS update *exactly* as written. If you don't load the new BIOS correctly, you could disable the original BIOS and your computer. Without a BIOS, your computer won't run which will make it most useful as a doorstop or a boat anchor, but not at all useful as a working computer.

If you have trouble during a BIOS installation, contact your computer or motherboard manufacturer's support center for help. They should be able to either talk you through the repair procedure or send you a new BIOS chip to physically replace the one in your computer.

NOTE *Remember that replacing the BIOS is a form of major surgery; don't try it unless there's no other way to solve a problem. But if you do it correctly, an update can solve a lot of problems.*

12

VIRUSES, SPYWARE, AND OTHER NASTIES

External attacks on your computer come in many forms: viruses, worms, spyware, and Trojan horses are just a few of the most common types. This *malware*, or malicious software, presents threats to your computer's operation, the security of your data, your privacy, and your identity.

If your computer is doing something strange for no apparent reason, a virus or spyware program could be to blame. Sometimes, though, there are no visible signs. For example, a virus could quietly fill up your hard drive with garbage data, or spyware could secretly capture your keystrokes and send them back to an attacker's computer, where the attacker will search your text for account numbers and passwords.

Besides the privacy issues, this stuff is inherently evil because it's theft, plain and simple. Not only does it involve the unauthorized use of computer and network resources, but it also ties up processor cycles, memory, and network bandwidth without permission.

Protecting Your System

Because there are so many kinds of malware out there, and because they can do so much damage, it's absolutely essential to do everything you can to protect your computer. This protection should include prevention in the form of firewalls and filters as well as programs that can remove and repair attacks that might slip through your armor. At a minimum, your computer should have all of the following forms of protection in place:

- A hardware or software firewall (or both) to filter unwanted attempts to connect to and from your computer through the Internet. Windows XP SP2 includes an adequate firewall, but you might want to add at least one more layer of protection with a separate firewall program, or a firewall built into a network switch or router.

- An antivirus program to protect the computer from viruses that duplicate themselves and can interfere with the computer's operation by reformatting a hard drive, deleting or altering program and data files, or loading unwanted programs.

- An antispyware program that filters and removes programs that gather information from your computer and sends that information to a distant host.

As an experienced computer user, you know that security is a problem. And you probably have firewalls, filters, and other security programs in place. But sometimes it's easy to assume that those protective tools are doing their job and that a glitch in the computer's performance must be caused by some other type of problem. In fact, the war between computer miscreants and the good guys who are trying to stop them seems to go on forever, so it's always possible that a new type of attack has been successful.

Therefore, scanning for embedded viruses, spyware, and other malware should be part of every troubleshooting routine. Even when your antivirus, antispyware, and firewall programs are all actively monitoring your system, you can't rule out the possibility that something nasty has found a way into your system.

Viruses, Worms, and Trojan Horses

Computer intrusions can take several forms, including viruses, worms, and Trojan horses:

Viruses

Viruses are snippets of software code that are usually delivered hidden inside another apparently innocuous program or data file. When you open the file that contains a virus, the virus program runs and does whatever damage it was designed to do. Many viruses also attach copies of themselves to other programs or data files so that they can spread to other computers, just like a biological virus spreads from person to person.

An *e-mail virus* is embedded inside an e-mail message. When recipients open infected messages, the virus runs on their computers and also sends copies of itself to e-mail addresses in the recipients' address books.

Worms

A *worm* is software that is designed to take advantage of security problems in widely used programs (often e-mail programs). The worm distributes itself from computer to computer through the Internet and across other computer networks. Many worms also do other damage, such as replacing web pages on infected servers with content created by the worm's originator. Worms can also direct massive attacks on specific computers (computers at the White House and Microsoft are popular targets) in order to overload and crash their Internet access.

Trojan horses

A *Trojan horse* is a program in disguise. For example, it may be identified as a downloadable game or music file, but when it is opened, it's actually something else entirely. That something else usually does some kind of damage, such as erasing the contents of a hard drive or forwarding data to another computer through the Internet.

Antivirus Programs

Obviously, you don't want to let any of these things into your system, but unfortunately, a virus may be secretly active on your computer, even if you don't notice any symptoms. Therefore, you should always run a full-time virus monitor and perform periodic manual antivirus scans as part of your security routine. And just to be doubly sure that your computer is not infected, run an occasional scan of your system using a different antivirus package from the one you normally use.

NOTE   *Some viruses target antivirus software and can shut it down without your knowledge.*

More than two dozen companies offer antivirus programs for Windows XP. For a current list of antivirus programs that Microsoft has tested, go to www.microsoft.com/athome/security/viruses/wsc/en-us/flist.mspx. Several companies offer free versions or free trials of their antivirus products, so you can test a few programs before you settle on one.

Most antivirus programs are effective against all the common viruses, and they all provide frequent updates to add protection against newly discovered threats. The important differences among these programs are cost and ease of use. The antivirus programs that offer free versions for personal use, including Avast (www.avast.com) and AVG (http://free.grisoft.com), are entirely adequate for most home users.

As a supplement to your installed antivirus program, you can also run a free online virus scan from Trend Micro (http://housecall.trendmicro.com), Panda Software (www.pandasoftware.com/activescan/activescan), or BitDefender (http://bitdefender.com/scan8/ie.html). You may need to turn off the installed virus scanner in order to avoid conflicts with an online virus scan.

These websites download and run antivirus programs through the Internet to examine your computer and identify or repair infected files. (The online scans are free because the companies hope that you'll like what they have to offer and buy their more extensive antivirus packages.)

Take Precautions

In addition to your antivirus utility, you must also take other precautions to keep viruses out of your computer:

- Never open an attachment to an e-mail message unless you know what it contains and who sent it. Never open files attached to unsolicited e-mail.

- Keep your antivirus program up to date. New viruses and other threats appear all the time, so it's essential to have the very latest protective software. Most good antivirus programs can automatically update themselves several times per week.

Spyware

As the name suggests, *spyware* is software that spies on you. It gathers information from your computer and relays it to another location. Spyware can capture keystrokes or screen images, identify the hardware and software installed on your computer, and hijack your browser's home page, replacing it with one that displays pornography, advertising, or other messages. More malicious spyware can also collect account login names, passwords, and other personal information. Still other spyware tracks the websites you visit in order to send you targeted advertising. These programs are particularly insidious because they install themselves without your knowledge. They often hide inside another program that offers some kind of useful service, such as a "computer tune-up."

Many advertisers use spyware to distribute advertisements in pop-up windows and web page banners. Some of the worst offenders replace the messages and ads on web pages you visit with their own content, or even force offensive material onto computers where they are not wanted.

Where Did That Come From?

How does spyware make its way into your computer? In most cases, it loads as part of other programs that claim to offer some kind of useful service, such as an added toolbar for your web browser, a file sharing tool (such as those offered in Kazaa, Morpheus, and BearShare), or a file compression tool (such as DivX). Gator, one of the most common spyware programs, claims to help fill out forms and remember passwords, but it also tracks the websites that you visit and sells that information to advertisers; Comet Cursor, a program that can change the appearance of your mouse cursor, also collects marketing information about users; and Xupiter, a search engine toolbar, launches pop-ups and adds advertising links to your Favorites menu. There are dozens and dozens of others.

If your computer is connected to the Internet, and if you have ever downloaded and installed programs from online sources, there's an excellent chance that there are spyware programs lurking beneath the surface of your system. If you share your computer with children or college students, it's even more likely that you're harboring some kind of spyware. Many of the popular file sharing programs used for downloading music files are notorious as channels for distributing spyware.

Protecting Against Spyware

It seems as if some people will grab every possible opportunity to advertise their products or services, whether you want to hear about them or not. Highway billboards, telemarketers, junk faxes, e-mail spam, and spyware are all among the unfortunate forms that advertisers use to force themselves upon potential consumers. There is some debate about whether such marketers are a higher or lower life form than pond scum, but it's a close thing. Either way, it's in your interest to keep these creeps and their programs out of your computer.

It's essential to protect yourself and your computer against spyware. Protection is a three-step process:

1. Identify spyware programs that have already inflicted themselves upon your system.
2. Remove them.
3. Establish a barrier that protects your computer against future spyware infestations.

Like viruses, new spyware appears constantly, and existing programs change their names to escape detection. Because spyware is constantly evolving, you can't just install a spyware filter and forget about it; you must keep it up to date.

Even if you never venture over to the shady parts of the Internet, spyware will find you soon enough.

Finding and Removing Spyware

As soon as you discover that your system has been taken over by a specific spyware program, you're on your way to getting rid of it. For example, if you discover a suspect program in the System Configuration Utility's Startup list (the program that runs when you enter the **msconfig** command from Start ▶ Run), you should immediately disable it in Startup and take steps to remove it completely.

But deleting obvious spyware isn't enough to be sure you have found and disabled all the spyware that has occupied your computer. Several excellent antispyware programs can scan your entire file system to find hidden spyware. Some of the best are free, and others are either try-before-you-buy shareware, or they are included in commercial products. Among others, Ad-Aware (www.lavasoft.com), Spybot Search and Destroy (www.safer-networking.org), Spy

Sweeper (www.webroot.com), Trend Micro Anti-Spyware (www.trendmicro.com), SpyCop (www.spycop.com), and the Microsoft Windows AntiSpyware tool (www.microsoft.com) are all effective programs.

NOTE *The PC Hell Spyware Removal Help page (located at www.pchell/support/spyware.shtml) includes links to pages that explain how to remove many of the most common spyware programs. If you suspect that a program in the Startup list is spyware, but it's not listed at PC Hell, look for it in the list at www.pacs-portal.co.uk/startup_content.htm.*

Because each program takes a slightly different approach, you should install more than one of the freebies, even if you also use a commercial Internet security product. (Unlike antivirus programs, the spyware programs shouldn't conflict with each other.) For example, SpyCop and Spybot Search and Destroy both seem equally effective in finding and removing known spyware, but sometimes a program will slip past one or the other (usually because you're not using the most recent update). SpySubtract also scans cookies placed on your computer by websites that want to track your use of their services. Spy Sweeper seems to find more problems than other programs, including redirected web searches and unwanted additions to your Favorites and startup list. (Webroot's subscription service supplies weekly updates to the Spy Sweeper shields.)

Most antispyware programs will monitor your computer for new spyware infections. When the program detects active spyware, it either blocks it or displays an alert and advises you to remove the offending program. Some programs also run a system scan at Windows startup to make sure that no new spyware processes have loaded. All of the major antispyware packages should perform adequately as long as you keep them up to date. A program that runs an automatic scan during startup might increase the amount of time that Windows takes to load, but if you're committed to keeping spyware out of your computer, that's probably an acceptable trade-off.

NOTE *Several major software companies, including Symantec and McAfee, offer inclusive "Internet Security" products that bundle antivirus, antispyware, and firewall programs into a single package. They also include additional security features and functions, such as an e-mail spam filter and a program that deletes advertisements from web pages. If one or more of those added features is important to you, or if the convenience of a suite of programs that performs several jobs is attractive, then you might want to consider one of these combined packages instead of using separate programs.*

Identifying Malware

If you've run your antivirus and antispyware cleaners, and you still suspect that you have a malware infection, use a systematic approach to identify the specific type of virus or spyware that might be affecting your system:

- Run complete scans with both an antivirus and antispyware program.
- Use the Windows Task Manager to identify all the programs and services that are currently running. To open the Task Manager, press the CTRL, ALT and DELETE keys at the same time. Look in the lists of programs and

services listed in the Applications and Processes tabs to find items that don't seem to belong there. If you don't recognize the name of an item, look in an online list of startup programs such as www.pacs-portal.co.uk/startup_content or www.answerthatwork.com/Tasklist_pages/tasklist.htm, or run an Internet search for the name of that item. If you find a suspect program or service and can't figure out how to kill it, run a web search for its name. There is probably an online discussion of the program that offers instructions for removing it. If you see a pop-up window or a web page you didn't expect, search for the name shown in the title bar at the top of the offending window. For example, if the browser's title bar says "Fubar Spyware Redirector—Microsoft Internet Explorer," search for "Fubar Spyware Redirector."

- Scan your computer with HijackThis (www.spywareinfo.com/~merijn/downloads.html) to find many types of embedded spyware code (see Figure 12-1). Most of the items listed in a HijackThis scan report are not spyware, but the program can often find embedded programs that other tools miss. If you find an item in the results list that you don't recognize, use the **Info On Selected Item** button at the bottom of the window to see an explanation. To delete an item, check its name on the list and note the address in the listing. Click **Fix Checked** to delete the program from active memory, and then use Windows Explorer to delete the file itself. If the same program reappears in another HijackThis scan, run a web search on the filename to find more information.

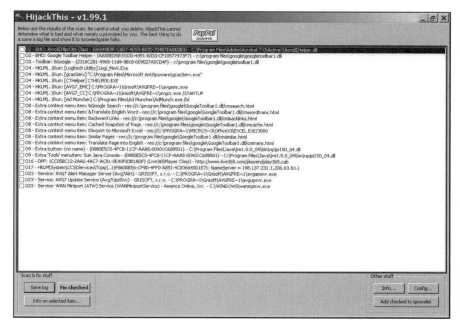

Figure 12-1: HijackThis can find embedded spyware that other programs often miss.

New malware appears all the time, so it's not possible to offer anything like an exhaustive list of symptoms in a stable medium like this book, but the developers of antivirus and antispyware programs devote substantial resources to keeping up with them. Your best defense is to install and use those programs—and keep them current.

Stopping Break-ins: Firewalls

It may seem like an odd form of entertainment, but there's a whole sub-culture out there of people who spend their time trying to break into other people's computers. Some of these people are just in it for the game, but others are cracking into computers as a way to steal personal and corporate information. As anyone who has ever had to deal with identity theft can tell you, taking back control of your life after someone has stolen your credit card numbers, computer passwords, bank account numbers, and other personal data is the bureaucratic equivalent of root canal surgery.

Anytime your computer is connected to the Internet or a local network, there's a possibility that someone will try to break into your files. It's not that the data on your computer is anymore attractive than the data on any of the millions of other computers online, but the most common way for people to find unprotected machines is to systematically scan through every possible numeric Internet address. If your computer is connected to the Internet all the time, attempts to gain access to your system can occur dozens of times every day. Even if you use a dial-up modem, your connection is still at risk.

You can test your computer's potential exposure to intruders by running a security audit through HackerWhacker (http://hackerwhacker.com), AuditMyPC.com (www.auditmypc.com/freescan), ShieldsUP!! (www.grc .com/x/ne.dll), and other websites. These programs scan all possible entry points on your system (known as *ports*) and identify the ones that are not protected. For additional test sites, search the Internet for "security firewall scan."

Use a firewall to protect your computer from unwanted access. A *firewall* is either an external device located between the network port of your computer and the router that connects it to the local network or the Internet, or a software program (like ZoneAlarm) that runs on your computer and monitors network activity. (If your computer is connected to the Internet through a local network, it's common to place the firewall between the network hub and the Internet so that a single firewall can protect the entire network.) Whether it's internal or external, a firewall allows acceptable data to move into and out of the computer or local network, but it restricts attempts to move data to and from unauthorized sources or destinations.

Firewall Software

If your computer is connected directly to the Internet through a broadband connection or a telephone line, a firewall program such as ZoneAlarm (free for personal use), Norton Personal Firewall, or a similar program from McAfee or other suppliers is generally your best choice. The Norton and

McAfee products are often bundled with other programs in those Internet security suites we discussed earlier. The Home PC Firewall Guide (www .firewallguide.com) keeps up with the latest versions of many firewall programs and offers links to sources for free and trial downloads.

Most firewalls compare each connection request to the entries on a list that identifies acceptable or restricted origins and destinations. When an incoming request for a connection to your computer tries to read a file or run a program that should not be available to outsiders, the firewall blocks the connection. But when the request is headed for a safe destination such as your web browser, the firewall lets it pass. The firewall treats outbound communication attempts the same way: If a request to connect to the Internet originates in a program that should not be sending messages, the firewall will block that message.

NOTE *Most firewall programs offer a default configuration that provides the best compromise between protection and convenience. You can generally override the default settings to allow access to a specific program or data port.*

Windows XP SP2 includes Internet Connection Firewall software that can perform many of the same functions as a third-party firewall program. Because you already have it on your system, you might as well turn it on and run a security audit (see the previous section for pointers to online firewall audit services) before spending additional time and money to obtain and install a firewall from another source. If you're connected to the Internet through a local network, turn off the Internet Connection Firewall and use the firewall in your network hub.

To turn on the Windows Internet Connection Firewall, follow these steps:

1. From Control Panel, select **Network Connections** and choose the icon that identifies your connection to the Internet. The dialog box in Figure 12-2 should appear.

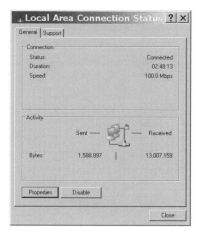

Figure 12-2: The Connection Status window shows the current condition of a network connection.

2. Click the **Properties** button. A Properties window will appear.

3. Select the **Advanced** tab, and click the **Settings** button to display the dialog box shown in Figure 12-3.

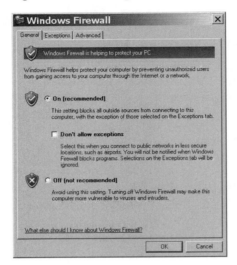

Figure 12-3: The General tab of the Properties window controls the Internet connection firewall.

4. Check the On option to enable the firewall.

Firewall Hardware

A firewall built into a network router or switch is the better choice for users who have more than one computer connected to the Internet through a local area network (LAN). By placing the firewall where the local network connects to the Internet, a single firewall can protect all the computers in the network and still allow file sharing among the computers behind the firewall.

You may already have a firewall in place if you're using a cable or DSL router to share your Internet connection among the computers in your home or small business. If you're on a larger corporate or campus network, the firewall might be a separate device.

The need for firewalls and spyware protection is just another reflection of the evil floating around in today's world. Neither has anything to do with the things you want your computer to do for you, but like locking the door when you leave the house, you have to take some kind of preventive steps to make sure you don't end up spending a lot more time and energy later to recover from the damage that an unprotected computer can sustain. It's unfortunate, but protecting yourself from intruders and snoops is just one of the costs of running a computer.

13

INTERNET CONNECTION PROBLEMS

The Internet has become such an essential part of most people's experience that it's sometimes difficult to know where your own computer stops and the Internet begins. For most of us, it doesn't matter if a particular resource is physically located on a local hard drive (one inside your PC or a network server) or a computer halfway around the world. Either way, it's just a matter of keystrokes and mouse clicks to view it on the screen or listen to it through speakers plugged into your computer.

Of course, this assumes that your connection to the Internet is working properly. If you can't view web pages, send and receive e-mail, or use any other Internet services, there's probably a problem somewhere between your computer and your Internet service provider's (ISP) point of access to the Internet. That problem might be due to a configuration error in your own computer or in the router, modem, or other device that connects you to the ISP. It could even be a breakdown in your ISP's equipment.

On the other hand, there's *nothing* you can do to break the Internet. You can be reasonably certain that the Internet itself—meaning the set of backbone networks and exchange points that connect millions of smaller networks and individual computers to one another—is still out there, no matter how severely your equipment is broken. The Internet was designed to route traffic around damaged links and interconnection points, so it's likely that nothing short of simultaneous explosive charges in about a hundred separate locations around the world could completely shut it down.

Isolate the Problem

As with any computer problem, when you have an Internet connection problem, you must first find the problem before you can fix it. Is it in your computer? Is it in the local network that connects the computer to your ISP? Could it be in the telephone line or broadband connection to the ISP, or at the ISP itself? And once you have located the problem you need to determine the cause.

The first thing to do when your Internet service fails is to locate the problem. It could be in your own computer or your local network, in the distant computer that is providing the data you see on your screen, or someplace between you and the distant machine.

Follow the Signal

The Internet is *huge*. It connects tens of millions of computers together. So it's absolutely essential to have a system that provides a name and location for each of those computers. Therefore, every computer and every intermediate routing device has a unique identity called a *numeric Internet Protocol (IP) address* assigned to it. That identity is a set of four numbers, each within the range from 0 to 255. A typical numeric address might be 206.83.231.2 or 192.168.0.1.

To find a connection problem, you must follow the signal as it passes through the Internet and identify the numeric addresses assigned to each device between your computer and your ISP's access point. If you discover that the signal stops short of its intended destination, that stopping point is probably the source of the problem.

More specifically, you will need the IP addresses for these devices:

- Your own computer
- The local network hub or router
- The ISP's gateway to the Internet

Your Computer

When you set up your Internet account with an ISP, the ISP will provide instructions for setting up your local connection. Your computer's IP address is either assigned *dynamically* by your network (via DHCP), or it is set as a *static* address in the Internet Protocol (TCP/IP) Properties window shown in Figure 13-1.

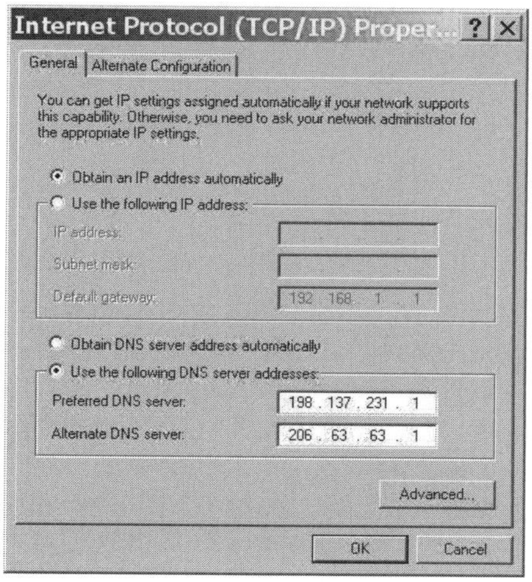

Figure 13-1: In this example, the network automatically assigns an IP address.

To view your computer's IP address, download and install Microsoft's graphic IP Configuration tool from www.microsoft.com/windows2000/techinfo/reskit/tools/existing/wntipcfg-o.asp. You can also view the IP address by choosing **Start ▶ Run**, then entering **CMD** and typing **ipconfig**. (The graphic program was part of the Windows 2000 Resource Kit, but it also works with XP, and it's more convenient than the command-line version.) As you can see in Figure 13-2, the IP Configuration window shows the IP address, along with several other addresses related to your Internet connection.

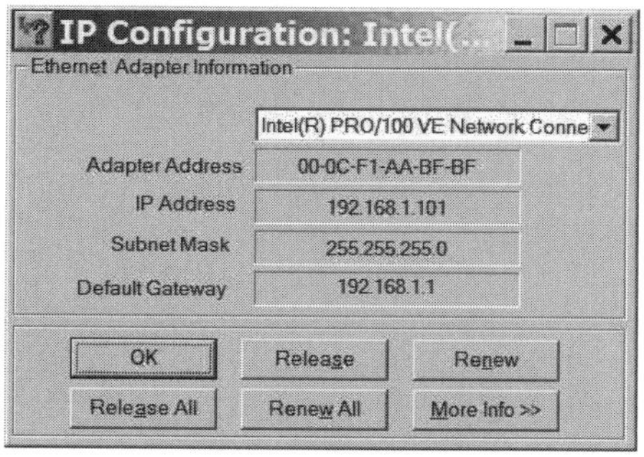

Figure 13-2: The IP address of this computer is 192.168.1.101.

In addition to the IP address, the IP Configuration tool displays several other important addresses:

Adapter address

The *adapter address* is a unique identification number assigned to the computer's network interface adapter at the factory. It's also known as the *Media Access Control (MAC) address.* Some wireless networks restrict access to network adapters with specific MAC addresses.

Subnet mask

> The *subnet mask* tells the network which number in the numeric address provides a unique identity for each device on the local network. The other numbers are the same for all devices. In Figure 13-2, the unique addresses use the last number (the 0).

Default gateway

> The *default gateway* is the address of the computer or router that connects the local network to the Internet.

If your computer connects to the Internet through a dial-up telephone connection or directly to a cable or DSL modem, the IP address is assigned by the ISP's wide area network (WAN). If the computer is part of a network, the network hub assigns the IP address. Some ISPs provide a dedicated IP address to each customer (known as a *static IP address*), while others automatically assign an address when you connect to the network (*dynamic IP address*). When you set up your account, your ISP will advise you about which IP address to use, or it will show you how to accept an automatic assignment.

The Local Network Hub or Router

If your computer shares its Internet connection with other machines by way of a local network, the network uses a *router*—a device that transfers inbound and outbound data between the local network and the shared Internet connection. The router presents its own IP address to the Internet and manages the addresses of all the other devices on the local network. The router's address is the IP address assigned by the ISP.

The local router uses two sets of addresses: one for the local network and one for its connection to your ISP. The user guide or other instructions for your network router should include the local address. (If you don't have a user guide for your router, check the manufacturer's website.) Your ISP will assign an address for your Internet connection.

The ISP's Gateway

Your computer is connected to your ISP's WAN through a telephone line, a cable TV system, or another wired or wireless link. At the ISP's control center, you and the other subscribers on the same WAN connect to the Internet through yet another router, which connects to the Internet through a *gateway*. Figure 13-3 shows the flow of data from your computer, through your local network to your ISP, and on to the Internet. Your ISP should have provided the address of its gateway to you, along with other configuration information when you set up your account. If you don't have the address, call your ISP and ask for it.

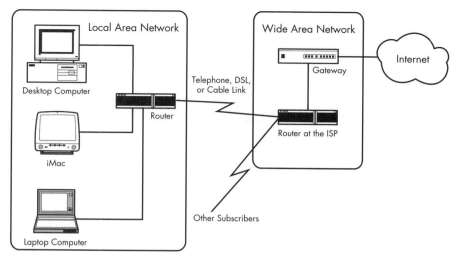

Figure 13-3: Your computer connects to the Internet through a local area network and your ISP's gateway.

Tracing the Network

Now that you know the IP addresses of your own computer, your network router, and your ISP's gateway to the Internet, you can trace the network connection all the way from your desktop to the Internet. If you can connect to a particular point in the series of addresses, but not beyond that point, the device that fails to respond is probably the source of your problem.

To view a detailed list of the computers and other devices in a network connection, use a *traceroute* program that shows the IP address of each device between your computer and a specified destination, along with the amount of time it took to receive a response and the name assigned to each device.

Most of the information in a traceroute display is more valuable to network administrators—who want to follow signals through the Internet—than to individual users, but the first three or four lines of a typical report show the path through the local network and the ISP's WAN. If the path stops after one of the local devices, look for a problem in the device that should be next on the list. Traceroute probably won't show the names of the local devices, but the IP addresses should be enough to identify each local device.

Windows XP includes a command-line traceroute program, as shown in Figure 13-4. To run a trace, open a command window (**Start ▶ Programs ▶ Accessories ▶ Command Prompt**), and type **tracert** *destination*, using the domain name (the Internet address) in place of *destination*. For example, to trace a route to No Starch Press, enter **tracert nostarch.com**.

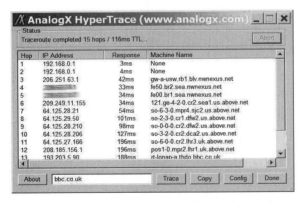

```
Command Prompt                                          _ □ X

C:\Documents and Settings\John Ross.DESKTOP.000>tracert bbc.co.uk

Tracing route to bbc.co.uk [212.58.224.131]
over a maximum of 30 hops:

  1     4 ms     3 ms     3 ms  192.168.0.1
  2     3 ms     3 ms     3 ms  192.168.0.1
  3    44 ms    49 ms    50 ms  gw-a-usw.rb1.blv.nwnexus.net [206.251.63.1]
  4    34 ms    34 ms    34 ms  fe50.br2.sea.nwnexus.net [            ]
  5    36 ms    36 ms    36 ms  fe00.br1.sea.nwnexus.net [            ]
  6    37 ms    35 ms    35 ms  121.ge-4-2-0.cr2.sea1.us.above.net [209.249.11.1
55]
  7    54 ms    59 ms    53 ms  so-6-3-0.mpr4.sjc2.us.above.net [64.125.28.21]
  8   100 ms    98 ms    98 ms  so-2-3-0.cr1.dfw2.us.above.net [64.125.29.50]
  9    99 ms    98 ms    98 ms  so-0-0-0.cr2.dfw2.us.above.net [64.125.28.210]
 10   126 ms   126 ms   126 ms  so-3-2-0.cr2.dca2.us.above.net [64.125.28.206]
 11   198 ms   199 ms   198 ms  so-6-0-0.cr2.lhr3.uk.above.net [64.125.27.166]
 12   197 ms   196 ms   198 ms  pos1-0.mpr2.lhr1.uk.above.net [208.185.156.1]
 13   193 ms   194 ms   191 ms  rt-lonap-a.thdo.bbc.co.uk [193.203.5.90]
 14   193 ms   190 ms   189 ms  212.58.238.153
 15   189 ms   188 ms   189 ms  rdirwww-vip.thdo.bbc.co.uk [212.58.224.131]

Trace complete.

C:\Documents and Settings\John Ross.DESKTOP.000>
```

Figure 13-4: The command-line traceroute program supplied with Windows shows a connection path in a text window.

If you prefer, you can use one of several free programs that convert the traceroute data to a graphic display. One of the best is HyperTrace from AnalogX (www.analogx.com/contents/download/network/htrace.htm), shown in Figure 13-5. Others include 3D Traceroute (www.d3tr.de), Visual Trace Route (www.itlights.com/traceroute.html), PingPlotter (www.pingplotter.com), and WinMTR (http://winmtr.sourceforge.net).

```
AnalogX HyperTrace (www.analogx.com)  _ □ X
┌─ Status ──────────────────────────────────────┐
│ Traceroute completed 15 hops / 116ms TTL..     Abort │
└────────────────────────────────────────────────┘
Hop  IP Address      Response  Machine Name
1    192.168.0.1     3ms       None
2    192.168.0.1     4ms       None
3    206.251.63.1    42ms      gw-a-usw.rb1.blv.nwnexus.net
4                    33ms      fe50.br2.sea.nwnexus.net
5                    34ms      fe00.br1.sea.nwnexus.net
6    209.249.11.155  34ms      121.ge-4-2-0.cr2.sea1.us.above.net
7    64.125.28.21    54ms      so-6-3-0.mpr4.sjc2.us.above.net
8    64.125.29.50    101ms     so-2-3-0.cr1.dfw2.us.above.net
9    64.125.28.210   98ms      so-0-0-0.cr2.dfw2.us.above.net
10   64.125.28.206   127ms     so-3-2-0.cr2.dca2.us.above.net
11   64.125.27.166   196ms     so-6-0-0.cr2.lhr3.us.above.net
12   208.185.156.1   196ms     pos1-0.mpr2.lhr1.us.above.net
13   193.203.5.90    188ms     rt-lonap-a.thdo.bbc.co.uk
About   bbc.co.uk           Trace   Copy   Config   Done
```

Figure 13-5: HyperTrace uses a graphic window to show the same information as the Windows command-line program.

In these examples, the first two hops pass through the local router with IP address 192.168.0.1. From there it moves through the ISP's Internet gateway at 206.251.63.1 (not the real address) and on to the ISP's network. The next two IP addresses are hidden for security reasons, but after that, the connection moves out to the Internet on the way to the BBC's website in London.

If the trace fails to show the local devices, the problem is in your local network. Check the Network Properties settings in Windows to confirm that all of the addresses and other values are correct (see the next sections of this chapter for details). If the trace makes it through the local network but stops at the ISP, call your ISP's support center and ask for assistance.

My Computer Can't Find the Internet

Whenever you try to use a program that connects to another computer through the Internet, you should make the connection without any unusual interruptions. You might have to enter a password to gain access to your Internet account, but after you have convinced your own ISP that it knows who you are, everything else should be automatic. But sometimes you might see an error message that is a variation of "unable to connect." Depending on the program and the type of connection, this message could be text in an Internet Explorer (or another browser) window or in a separate error window in another program.

Several things can cause a failure to make an Internet connection:

- Your computer's network configuration settings are wrong or missing.
- A firewall or other security software is blocking the connection.
- The modem that dials the ISP is improperly configured.
- Someone else is using the telephone line connected to your dial-up modem.
- The local network router is improperly configured.
- The ISP's network server has a problem.
- The server you are trying to reach is offline.

Does Your ISP Provide Its Own Software?

Many large ISPs, including AOL, MSN, and EarthLink, supply their own proprietary software that automatically configures Internet access through their networks and installs an additional layer of software that may or may not add value to a generic Internet connection. If you are using one of these services, it may not be possible to connect to the Internet or change your configuration without using the ISP's software.

For example, if you are an AOL subscriber, you should use the America Online Setup window shown in Figure 13-6 to change your configuration, rather than using the Windows settings described in the rest of this chapter.

If you are working with an ISP's proprietary software, don't try to second-guess the configuration by making changes to the Windows Network Configuration settings. If you can't find a solution to the problem within the ISP's own software, call their support center for help.

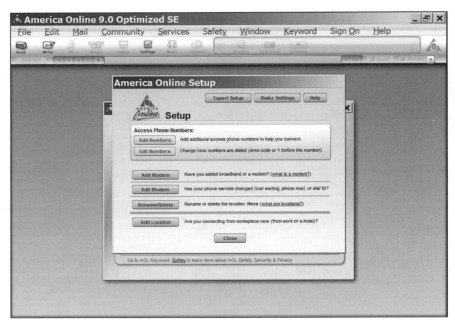

Figure 13-6: AOL uses a Setup dialog box to set connection options.

Network Configuration Settings

The configuration settings that you entered when you set up your computer to connect to the Internet should not change unless somebody or something changes them. But if any of the settings do change, the computer won't connect, so it's important to know where to find them and how to correct them.

Your ISP has probably given you an information card or sheet with a list of IP addresses, telephone numbers, passwords, and other information that you should use to set up your account. Some large ISPs, including America Online, MSN, and EarthLink, also provide a CD with their proprietary software that might configure your system for you. This is important information to keep around. You should store the information and the CD (if there is one) with your other computer manuals.

Here are the essential addresses you must use to set up an Internet connection:

- The computer's IP address.
- The subnet mask (probably 255.255.255.0).
- The default gateway that provides the interface between your ISP's wide area network (WAN) and the Internet.
- One or more domain name service servers (DNS servers) that the ISP uses to convert domain names (such as nostarch.com) to numeric IP addresses (such as 64.49.240.173). If you don't specify a DNS server, the Internet won't recognize your request to connect to a domain name.

Some systems assign these addresses automatically, while others use the same addresses for every connection. Your ISP will tell you which options apply to your account.

If you are using just one computer with a direct Internet connection, either through a dial-up telephone line or a broadband modem, the computer will use the addresses supplied by the ISP. If your computer is part of a local network, the router uses the addresses assigned by the ISP, and the computer uses addresses assigned by the router. In other words, each device—computer or router—sends its addresses back to the next device up the line. Look in your router's user manual or quick setup guide to find the configuration settings for both the router and the computers connected to it. If you can't find them, check with the router's maker; their tech support people get these questions a lot.

To view your current network settings and change them if they are not correct, follow these steps:

1. From the Start menu, select **Control Panel ▸ Network Connections** (in the Windows XP menu) or **Settings ▸ Network Connection** (in the Classic Start menu).

2. Right-click the icon for the connection profile that you want to open.

3. Choose **Properties** from the pop-up menu.

4. If you're looking at a dial-up connection, choose the **Networking** tab. If you are using a LAN or broadband connection, choose the **General** tab.

5. Select the **Internet Protocol (TCP/IP)** item from the list of services, and click the **Properties** button. You might have to scroll down the list to find the Internet Protocol item.

The Internet Protocol (TCP/IP) Properties window includes spaces for the IP addresses assigned to this computer and the domain name service (DNS) servers.

Troubleshooting a Dial-up Connection

The Properties window for a dial-up connection includes tabs that control the telephone number of the ISP's host and the IP addresses that the system will use to establish your Internet connection.

The General tab (shown in Figure 13-7) sets the telephone number and offers a link to the Modem Configuration window. If your ISP changes its telephone number, you can enter the new number here. Many ISPs have more than one local telephone number to spread the load among several trunk lines. Your ISP's support center can give you a complete list of local numbers if it was not included with your startup package or if it wasn't on the setup CD.

If you add an alternate telephone number, you can also instruct Windows to dial that number if the main number is busy. To add additional numbers, click the **Alternates** button.

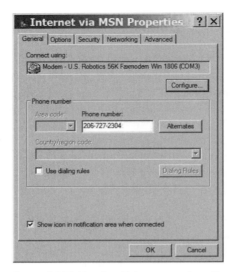

Figure 13-7: Use the dial-up networking Properties window to set the ISP's telephone number.

The Networking tab controls the network protocols that connect your computer to the Internet. Once again, your ISP's support center can tell you exactly how to configure these options.

Troubleshooting a Connection Through a Local Network

DSL, cable, and other broadband Internet services are always connected to the ISP, so it's not necessary to dial a telephone number when you want to use the Internet. However, you do have to configure the modem and router that transfer data between your computer (or local network) and the ISP's WAN. The first places to look when you're troubleshooting a broadband connection are the Network Properties window for the local area connection and the setup windows for your router and your modem.

Just like every other device on your local network, the router and the modem have their own numeric IP addresses. The manuals for each device will include the default address for that device, and most devices allow you to change the address to a value that isn't known to everyone who has a copy of the manual.

Your broadband modem probably uses a graphic configuration utility that you can reach through your web browser, but some older routers might use a command-line utility that exchanges commands and data with your computer through a serial port. To find the specific routine for your own equipment, look in the manual for each device or ask your ISP's support center for help.

Wireless base stations (access points) are similar to routers for the purpose of this discussion: If they're not integrated with a router or a modem, they just add one more layer to the system.

To use the graphic configuration utility for your modem or router, open your web browser and type the device's numeric address in the address field.

The configuration utility uses an access port on the router or modem that can only be reached from the local network, so it's not possible for outsiders to change your configuration through the Internet.

Most configuration utilities require a password; you can find the default password in the manual, or you can obtain it from the manufacturer's website or tech support center. You might need to use a computer connected to a different network or use a modem connection to reach the website, if the router is not working. Every other user on your network can also find those default passwords, including people who have no business changing the device's settings. Unless you trust everybody on the network to leave things alone (including your children if it's a home network), you should change the default password.

Figure 13-8 shows the configuration utility for a Linksys router. Other manufacturers organize their utility screens differently, but they all contain the same basic information.

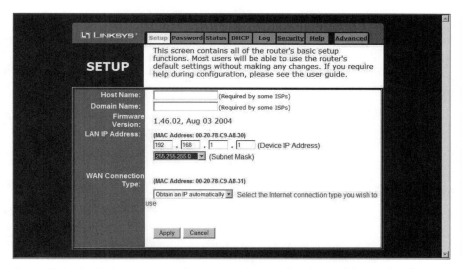

Figure 13-8: This Linksys router configuration utility specifies the IP addresses that the router uses to connect to both the Internet and the local network.

Confirm that the router's settings match the settings for the individual computers on the LAN side and the settings assigned by the ISP or the next upstream device (such as a modem) on the WAN side. If any of these settings are incorrect, you won't be able to connect to the Internet.

The Computer Can't Find a Particular Website

When you enter an address into your web browser, you expect a page to appear on your screen. If the network returns some kind of "unable to connect" message instead of the information you wanted, there's a problem somewhere in the chain of devices between your computer and the server that contains that web page.

The most likely causes of a connection failure include:

1. The address is not correct. Confirm that the name you typed into the Address field is correct and that all words are spelled correctly. Make sure that all punctuation marks or symbols (such as & signs or underscores) are correct.

2. The site you requested does not exist. Websites appear and disappear without warning, so it's entirely possible that the one you wanted has closed down. If you're attempting to reach the site through a Google search, you can often find a copy by choosing the **Cached** link in the item description.

3. The web server that contains the page you wanted is offline or over-loaded (because a lot of people are trying to reach it at the same time), or it has some other problem. If a traceroute (described earlier in this chapter) breaks off before the actual site you want, that's a good indication that the server is offline.

If you can reach other websites (or other Internet services) but not the one you want, the problem is located at the distant system rather than your own computer or network. When that happens, there's not much you can do to fix the problem other than notify the owners of the site by telephone or by some other method that does not involve using the Internet (if their web-server is down, they might not have working e-mail either). If you can't find an alternative site that can supply the same information, your only other option is to wait until the problem is solved.

Computer Connects When You Don't Want It to Connect

The opposite problem—a web page that you did not request spontaneously appears on your screen—is probably the result of either a scheduled task in a program that automatically searches for updates, or a hijack program that is misdirecting your browser.

The first category—a page related to a program, such as an antivirus utility—is generally a valuable service that you should allow to continue. But a hijack program that opens an unwanted web page is definitely something to eliminate. If scanning your computer with an antispyware program doesn't get rid of the problem, run a web search on the name of the program or unwanted site as it appears in the title bar at the top of your web browser window. Within the first two pages of matching sites, you should find at least one website devoted to killing and removing the spyware that is causing the problem. In most cases, following that advice will solve your problem.

The Internet Disappears

Sometimes your Internet connection suddenly seems to stop working without any notice, or it doesn't work after you have turned on the computer for the day. If you're not able to open any web pages or download any files, check all of the cables between your computer (or your wireless access point) and the wall outlet that carries your telephone line, DSL connection, or cable modem signal. If you're using a dial-up modem connection, make sure nobody else is using the same telephone line. Make sure the modem and router (and any other device between the computer and your Internet connection) are turned on and that the power cables are plugged into their respective outlets. If none of the cables have come loose and everything is turned on, turn off your computer and the modem or router, wait 30 seconds, and turn everything back on again. Sometimes that's all you will need to get the computer back online again; it's amazing how often some kind of completely random "bit rot" mysteriously changes a critical setting.

If it's not a local hardware problem, telephone your ISP's support center and ask whether there has been a wider failure. Their technicians will either know about the problem already, or they will tell you how to run some tests to help them identify the cause.

Firewalls and Gateway Servers

Firewalls (which might be either hardware or software) are designed to thwart outside intruders' attempts to introduce unwanted commands into a computer, and their attempts to possibly take control of it or steal data. They accomplish this by limiting access to software ports on your computer that are commonly used for standard applications like e-mail and web browsers. Firewall design is a compromise between convenience and security, so some firewall programs are more aggressive than others.

Some firewalls won't allow any program to connect to the Internet unless it's on a list of acceptable programs. Well-behaved firewalls display a message asking if it's okay to connect when you try to use an unknown program, but others simply block the connection without any notice. Therefore, it's possible that a connection failure is nothing more than the firewall doing its job.

Each firewall is different, but most of them offer an easy way to temporarily turn off their blocking functions. If you suspect that your firewall is keeping another program from connecting, turn off the firewall and try to connect again. If the connection works without the firewall, look in the firewall's manual or online help for instructions about adding the blocked program to the list of accepted connections. Don't forget to turn the firewall back on when you're done.

Don't be intimidated by an Internet problem just because it's the Internet. Like electricity, water, telephone service, and other public utilities, the Internet works reliably almost all the time. When it doesn't work, the problem is almost always limited to a small portion of the system. The Internet may be big and complicated, but it follows a set of well-defined rules that make troubleshooting relatively easy. If you apply a logical approach to locating the cause of a problem, you can almost always find a way to fix it.

14

LOCAL NETWORK PROBLEMS

Any time two or more computers and their related devices are under the same roof, they should probably connect to one another through a network. Networking allows users to share files and printers and to share access to the Internet through a common modem or broadband connection.

Windows XP includes tools and wizards that make it relatively simple to set up a network, but a network is always more complicated than an isolated, stand-alone computer. Network problems don't often interfere with the performance of your own computer, but they can be a source of serious aggravation when you need to open a file located someplace else on the network or use the network to print a document. Like any other type of computer troubleshooting, however, fixing a network is usually a matter of examining each element and returning the configuration back to the correct settings.

The sources of most network problems are either configuration settings on one or more network devices, or firewalls and other Internet security software that block access to the other devices on the network. Of course, the complexity of a network increases with the number of devices connected to it, so troubleshooting a large network can be a long and tedious process.

Big, sophisticated networks can have their own set of problems separate from those of the individual computers connected to them. Network trouble-shooting often requires a specialized set of tools and skills, but the general principles are relatively simple: check the connections and configuration of every device connected to the network, including all the computers, switches, gateways, modems, routers, and all of the interconnecting circuits.

In a corporate network, it's entirely possible that some of the computers connected to it have been cranking along without any attention for many years. If your network develops a problem, the first step in solving it is often to identify all the devices connected to the network. During the Great Y2K Panic, when businesses were trying to update the software in all of their computers to prevent them from breaking down on January 1, 2000, some network managers discovered long-forgotten servers that had been operating for a decade or more. Those old faithful machines weren't causing any problems, but they did add to the overall complexity of their networks.

Even a small household network with just two or three computers connected to it can develop problems, often without any apparent warning. And unlike problems in a big corporate network, you can't just hand them off to a network specialist. You'll have to examine the network and identify the problems yourself.

This chapter describes many of the most common network glitches, and it offers guidelines for dealing with them.

I Can't See Other Computers on the LAN

You know there are other computers on your network; you can see them and touch them. But the My Network Places window doesn't show that they exist at all. Here are some things to check:

- Confirm that the computer you want to reach is turned on and the network cable is connected firmly at both ends.

- Confirm that power is connected to the network hub or switch.

- Right-click **My Computer** on the Windows desktop, choose **Properties** from the pop-up menu, and select the **Computer Name** tab. Confirm that this computer and all the other computers on the network use the same Workgroup name. If the name is wrong, click the **Change** button next to the Rename This Computer option to open the Computer Name Changes dialog box. Change the name of the Workgroup to match the other computers on your network.

- If one or more computers appear to be offline but the others are accessible, go to each of the "missing" computers and check its network configuration settings:
  1. Open the Local Area Connection Properties window (**Start ▸ Control Panel ▸ Network Connections ▸ Local Area Connections ▸ Properties** in the Windows XP Start menu or **Start ▸ Settings ▸ Network**

Connections ▸ Local Area Connections ▸ Properties in the Classic Start menu) and select the **Client for Microsoft Networks** item, as shown in Figure 14-1.

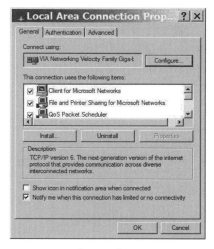

Figure 14-1: The Local Area Properties window controls the network configuration.

2. Confirm that the Client For Microsoft Networks item is active. If no check mark appears next to this item, click the name to turn it on.

3. Scroll down the list of items and confirm that the Microsoft TCP/IP Version 6 and Internet Protocol (TCP/IP) items are active. If you don't see the Version 6 item, upgrade Windows XP to Service Pack 2 or later.

• Look for a firewall or other security program on the "missing" computer. Some security programs such as Norton Internet Security or the stand-alone Norton Firewall program default to blocking access from other computers on a local network. In either Norton program, follow these steps to configure the firewall to recognize other computers on your own network:

1. From the main Norton Internet Security screen, choose **Personal Firewall**, and click the **Configure** button.

2. In the configuration window, choose the **Networking** tab.

3. Click the **Wizard** button near the bottom of the window. The Network Wizard will step through a series of screens that will configure your system to recognize other computers on the same network.

Other firewall products may require a somewhat different or more complicated routine to permit access to other computers on the same network. The basic requirement is to specify either the individual numeric IP addresses assigned to other computers on your network or a range of addresses that includes all the computers on the network. Your firewall's online help or its user manual should explain how to set these options.

To find the numeric IP address assigned to each computer running Windows XP, open a Command Prompt window (**Programs ▶ All Programs ▶ Accessories ▶ Command Prompt** or **Programs ▶ Accessories ▶ Command Prompt**), and type **ipconfig** at the prompt. The computer's IP address will appear under the Ethernet adapter Local Area Connection heading. For computers running other operating systems, enter the same **ipconfig** command at a command prompt. Repeat this process for each computer on the network.

Three of the four sections of each IP address connected to the network should be the same; the numbers in the fourth section should all be within a range. For example, the IP addresses might all be between 192.168.1.50 and 192.168.1.100. That's the range that you should instruct the firewall to accept.

After you have identified the IP addresses and instructed the firewall to recognize them, go back to the first computer, and then open My Network Places. You should now see links to the other computers and other resources connected to your network.

File Sharing Doesn't Work

Even though My Network Places tells you that a particular computer is connected to the network, you won't be able to read or alter files stored on that computer unless file sharing is active. The My Network Places window shows an icon for each computer, but there appears to be nothing inside. Or maybe you can view some of the contents of a drive, but the particular file or folder you want is missing.

The default setting for file sharing is to restrict access to the local computer. If you think about it, this is a useful feature of Windows networking rather than a flaw in the design. All of us have files that contain private information that we don't want to share with anybody else; these might include personal financial data, competitive business information, or even old photos, love letters, and blackmail notes. If another person has unlimited access to all the files on your computer, there would be nothing to stop them from reading, changing, or deleting those files. Because of these risks, Windows doesn't share your files unless you turn on file sharing. If you want to allow other people to read, change, or delete your files, you must take a couple of steps.

Each computer controls access to its own files, so you can't just turn on your own computer and automatically expect to see everything else on the network. You have to go to each computer and change that computer's configuration first.

To turn on file sharing follow these steps:

1. Run the Network Setup Wizard (**Start ▶ Network ▶ Network Setup Wizard** in the Windows XP Start menu or **Start ▶ Settings ▶ Control Panel ▶ Network Connections ▶ Network Setup Wizard** in the Classic Start menu), and step through each wizard screen.

2. When you reach the File And Printer Sharing screen shown in Figure 14-2, choose the Turn On File And Printer Sharing option.

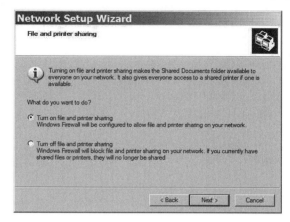

Figure 14-2: Use the Network Setup Wizard to turn on file sharing.

3. Continue through the wizard to the end.

You're not done yet. Turning on file sharing is only part of the process. You must also change the individual file sharing settings for each drive or folder:

1. From the Windows desktop, open My Computer.
2. Right-click the name of the drive or folder you want to share.
3. From the pop-up menu, choose **Sharing And Security**. The Properties window in Figure 14-3 will appear.

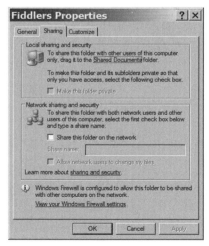

Figure 14-3: The Sharing tab of the Properties window turns file sharing on and off.

4. To allow other users to view the contents of this drive or folder, turn on the **Share This Folder** option in the Network Sharing And Security box. If you allow sharing on a drive or a folder, all of the folders and files within that drive or folder will be shared as well. To permit other users to edit or delete the contents of files or folders within the drive or folder, turn on the **Allow Network Users To Change My Files** option.

When sharing is active for a folder or an entire drive, the icon for that object appears in My Computer and Windows Explorer with an open hand "serving" the icon, as shown in Figure 14-4.

Figure 14-4: The hand under an icon indicates that sharing is active for this item.

If other computers on the network can't open a folder or another shared resource, even though file sharing is turned on and sharing is active, reset file sharing for that item:

1. Open **My Computer** from the Windows desktop.
2. Right-click the icon for the drive that you can't open, or open the drive that contains the folder that won't open.
3. Select **Sharing And Security** from the pop-up menu.
4. In the Properties window, remove the check mark from the Share This Folder option near the middle of the window.
5. Click the **Apply** button. Windows will change the setting and remove the serving hand from the icon.
6. Now click **Share This Folder** again to restore the check mark, and click the **Apply** button. After Windows has reconfigured the setting, the drive or folder should be visible to the network.

I Can't Edit a File

If you can read, view, or play the contents of a file through your network, but the computer won't allow you to edit or delete the file, check the Read-only status of the file and the folders in which it is stored. Also, check the Allow Network Users option in the Properties window described in the previous section (it's directly under the Share This Folder option in Figure 14-3). When Read-only is active, Windows will not allow any user to make any changes to the contents. This is not really a network problem, because it doesn't matter if you're trying to change a shared network file or one stored on your own computer: any read-only file or folder is protected.

To check the Read-only status of a folder or file, open My Computer or the file share window that contains the file or folder, and right-click the icon. Choose the **Properties** item from the pop-up menu. The Read-only status appears near the bottom of the window (shown in Figure 14-5).

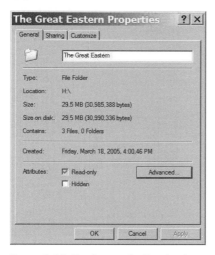

Figure 14-5: To change the Read-only status of a file or folder, open the Properties window.

At first blush, a local network for home computers might seem like a toy for geeks and gamers rather than something that the rest of us would ever need. But like the computer and the Internet, a home network can rapidly become an essential tool. Once you start using it, the network will become one of those things that you expect to find when you turn on a computer. When the network doesn't work the way you expect it to work, you should know enough about troubleshooting to solve the most common problems and restore your connections.

15

DEALING WITH HARDWARE PROBLEMS

Not every computer failure is caused by a software issue. Many problems that appear to be related to Windows are actually caused by some kind of hardware malfunction or by a conflict between two or more incompatible hardware components inside the computer. This chapter describes many of the most common problems that you might encounter when you try to add, move, or change a component inside your computer. Most of these problems have relatively easy solutions if you know where to look.

Finding and fixing hardware problems requires a different set of troubleshooting tools and techniques from the methods we've been using to deal with Windows and other software. When you're dealing with physical devices and components, it's almost always possible to either physically examine the suspect part or swap it out with another piece.

Sometimes a hardware failure is easy to spot because there's some kind of clear physical evidence that a component has gone bad. Clear signs that the apparent problem was caused by hardware, not software, include a connector that has become unplugged and a blackened area on a printed circuit board (caused by burned insulation). But just as often, the difference between a software problem and a hardware failure is not that easy to identify. For example, if an audio player or a video image fails, the problem could be caused by either a device driver (software) or a damaged controller card or other hardware.

If a problem has no obvious cause (such as a melted component on a printed circuit board or a plug or jumper in the wrong place), it's good practice to eliminate a possible software glitch as the source of the problem. First try updating or reinstalling the device driver software before you replace any hardware.

Problems with New Hardware

It's a unique feeling when you install a drive, memory module, or motherboard, connect up all the cables, and turn on the computer . . . and the computer just sits there, doing nothing. Adding, moving, or replacing a major hardware component in your computer can provide several opportunities for trouble.

Most new-hardware problems are relatively easy to fix. Most often, either the cables or jumpers are set incorrectly, or an electrical short circuit is causing the device to fail, or a new component is not compatible with the rest of the equipment inside the computer. Or of course, it's always possible that the new device is DOA—dead on arrival—right out of the box because of a defective electronic component or faulty assembly, but you probably won't discover that until you eliminate the usual installation errors.

Hardware Troubleshooting

A hardware failure might present itself as a complete failure, or it could appear as reduced performance. For example, a video monitor might not display any image at all, it could lose one or more of the separate colors that it blends to create full-color images, or it might compress the image on the screen into a small horizontal band at the center of the screen. When a network component such as a modem or a router breaks down, your computer could completely fail to exchange data with the Internet or your local network, or it might reduce the data transfer rate to a fraction of its original speed.

The best way to identify a hardware problem is to isolate the problem to a single component, cable, module, or connection. When you evaluate a possible hardware problem in a peripheral device, try to identify and examine each component separately. For example, if your monitor goes dark, check the video card or controller inside the computer, the cable from the computer to the monitor, and the monitor itself. If you don't hear any sound coming from the speakers, look for trouble in the sound card, the cables, and each of the speakers.

Formal troubleshooting methods include replacing individual components, testing suspect devices on another computer, and dividing a circuit or a signal path into smaller segments. However, just about every experienced service technician also follows another important rule: *Look for a cheap and simple solution first.*

Look for a Simple Fix

Before you pull out the test equipment and start replacing circuit cards or other components, make sure the problem was not caused by something you can fix easily, like a power switch that is turned off or an unplugged cable. You should try this kind of repair first for two reasons: if it solves the problem, you can be back to work in just a few minutes, and you won't have to waste time with more complicated troubleshooting that doesn't accomplish anything.

Here are some of the easy-to-solve problems that you should check before moving on to a more formal troubleshooting routine:

- Is the computer turned on? How about the other devices?
- Is power connected? Is the AC power plugged in? Are the batteries dead?
- Are all the other cables securely connected? Check all the cable connectors plugged into the computer's case, all the internal cables connected to the motherboard, and all the other devices inside the case.
- Are the controller cards and other expansion boards firmly in place? Are all the cable connectors and jumpers in the right places?
- Is there a loose screw or other part rattling round inside the case? Pick up each device and gently shake it to make sure. A screw or other metal part could create a short circuit that causes an electrical device to fail.
- Is an adjustment, such as a volume control or brightness control, turned all the way down?
- If a problem appears to be in one of the PCI cards mounted onto the motherboard, try moving the card to a different PCI socket.
- Is there a software control that has disabled the device? For sound, check the Mute options and levels in the Volume Control window; for video, look in **Display Properties ▸ Settings** to make sure the display is active. On all devices, look in the Device Manager (**Start ▸ Run ▸ devmgmt.msc**) for a yellow question mark (?) or a red exclamation point (!) next to the name of a device.

Replace and Test Each Component

If you have a spare cable, video card, or other component, try removing the one that might have failed and installing the spare. If the problem disappears, you can be pretty certain that the old part was causing it. If the problem remains, replace the original part and try a different component.

NOTE   *Be sure the replacement is similar to the original. For example, don't try to install an SATA drive if your computer's motherboard only uses IDE drives. Don't try to force a video card designed for a PCI socket into an AGP slot. If you're replacing an IDE drive (whether it's a hard drive, CD drive, or some other type), make sure the jumper settings (master or slave) are identical to the settings on the original device.*

For each component you want to test, the process should include these steps:

1. Turn off the computer and all the devices connected to the computer, and then remove the suspect device or part.
2. Install a replacement for the part you removed in Step 1.
3. Turn on the computer and the other devices, and check whether the original problem is still there.

If the problem remains, replace the component, remove another component, and test the computer again.

It's important to replace and test components one at a time, rather than simply throwing a complete set of spares into the broken computer all at once. If you don't check each component separately, you might restore the computer's functions, but you will never know which of the components you removed was the source of the problem. In other words, all of the pieces you replaced will be suspect, which means that you will either end up returning one or more broken components to your collection of spares, or you will have thrown away one or more perfectly good parts.

Move the Device to Another Computer

Sometimes it's easier to connect a suspect component to a working computer rather than replacing the item on the broken machine. This approach is particularly useful when you're testing relatively large devices like keyboards, monitors, and modems that connect to the computer, and the computer's motherboard, through external cables. For example, if your keyboard stops working even after you turn the computer off and back on again, try conecting it to another computer. If the keyboard works on the second computer, you can eliminate that keyboard as the source of the problem. If it still doesn't work on the second computer, you can usually deduce that the keyboard was faulty.

When you test something on a second computer, however, make sure you check the obvious settings: if there's a power switch, confirm that it is turned on; if the device uses external power, be sure that it is plugged in to a working AC outlet; and if the device requires a device driver, install the driver on the second machine before you assume that the device itself is broken.

Divide the Circuit

Dividing the circuit is an old telephone technician's method for finding a defective component in a communications circuit as quickly and efficiently as possible. In certain situations, such as troubleshooting a LAN, it can also be helpful for finding computer problems. In simple terms, you divide a system into two segments and test each half. One segment will work properly, and the other will not. Divide the defective segment again, and test each of *those* segments. Repeat until you have isolated the problem to a single component.

For example, a broadband DSL connection to the Internet looks like Figure 15-1. Your computer connects through a LAN router to a DSL modem, which uses a telephone line to connect to the telephone company's nearest central office. At the central office, the line connects to a device called the *digital subscriber line access multiplexer (DSLAM)* that passes the signal onward to the Internet.

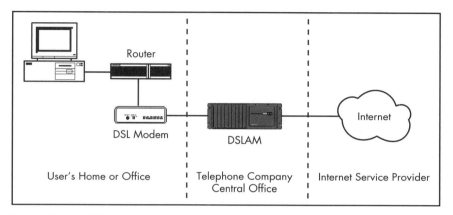

Figure 15-1: A DSL connection passes through several links between your computer and the Internet.

If the connection fails, a service technician might start troubleshooting the line by sending you a series of test signals that move through the entire circuit, from the Internet all the way to your computer. If you don't receive them, the next step could be to try sending tests from the ISP to the central office and from the central office to your computer. If you don't receive the test from the central office, the technician will tell you to watch the lights on your DSL modem as another test comes through. If the lights don't flash, the modem didn't receive a signal, so you have isolated the problem to the link between the central office and the modem.

To apply this technique to a computer problem, start by making a list of all the components in the chain between the apparent failure and the computer's motherboard. The analogy to a communications circuit may not always be perfect, but it can often help you isolate the problem.

For example, if your computer stops playing music or other sounds, the list might look like this:

- Speakers
- Cables from speakers to sound card (if they're not permanently attached to the speakers)
- Sound card
- Motherboard

To split the chain, unplug the speaker cable from the back panel of the computer, and plug it into a different computer. If the speakers still don't work, you now know that the problem is either in the speakers or the cable. Now try the same speakers with a different cable. If they work this time, you have isolated the problem to the cable.

If the speakers and the cable work on the second computer, you can make an educated guess that the problem is in either the sound card or the motherboard.

Here's another example: When you turn on the computer, an error message tells you that the computer can't find your C: drive. In this case, there are several components in the chain: the motherboard, the BIOS (which is software that controls hardware), the cable from the motherboard to the hard drive, and the drive itself. You can assume that the motherboard is okay because it is able to display the error message, so the problem could be the BIOS, the cable, or the drive. You can't test the drive without a cable, so you should carefully examine the cable and replace it if you can't find an obvious problem (like a connector that has come loose or a plug that is not aligned properly with the pins on the motherboard). If the same error message appears after you replace the cable, you have isolated the problem to either the BIOS or the drive. In this case, the problem might be either hardware or software—if the BIOS does not automatically detect the drive, check the BIOS settings first, and then examine the drive.

Repair or Replace?

Isolating the problem to a single component is important, but it's only the first step in fixing it. Now you must decide whether it makes more sense to repair the broken device or simply install a replacement. The choice depends on the amount of time it will take to perform the repair and the cost of the new part.

Sometimes, the choice is obvious: If you discover that a connector has shaken loose from a socket, it will take just a few seconds to plug it back in and restart the computer. But if a power surge has fried a dozen resistors and integrated circuits on your video card, it's easier to install a new card. As a rule of thumb, if a repair requires a soldering iron, or if you see signs of burned components on a printed circuit board, you're better off replacing the part.

If a device or a component is still covered by the manufacturer's warranty, the choice is obvious: remove it and send it back to the factory. Look in the user manual or the manufacturer's website for information about obtaining warranty service; most companies require a return authorization before they'll accept a broken device for service. When they receive your shipment, they'll either repair the original item or send you a new one, usually within a few days. For small and inexpensive parts, you might not even have to return the broken part—when you telephone or e-mail the manufacturer's support center, they'll just send it to you right away.

For relatively cheap parts, it's just not worth the time and trouble to repair them. You have better things to do with your life than spending an hour to repair a $3 cable or a $15 keyboard, especially if you have to buy $35 worth of tools to perform the repair.

If you can't fix a part yourself, check the cost of a replacement before you commit to a repair. Unfortunately, the cost of repairing a more expensive device, like a video monitor or a motherboard, can often be more than the price of a new one.

At some point, the cost of repairing or replacing individual parts can be as much or more than simply buying a whole new computer, especially if you can move your existing video monitor to the new system. Obviously, this isn't always true, but it's something to consider before you spend a lot of money on an expensive new video controller card or some other major component—or, worse, replacing several parts at the same time. If your computer is more than two or three years old, even a relatively inexpensive new computer will probably give you better performance than the old one could, even after you replace a bunch of individual components.

Microsoft's Product Activation: Not a Big Deal

Beginning with Windows XP, Microsoft has introduced an anti-piracy scheme that requires every Windows user to contact the mother corporation within the first 30 days after installation, and again *whenever a major hardware change occurs.* This is intended to prevent people from installing the same copy of Windows on more than one computer. Windows Product Activation only applies to copies of Windows sold at retail and some versions that come pre-installed on new computers. If your company has a volume licensing agreement, or if you bought your computer from a major manufacturer such as Dell or IBM, you won't have to worry about activation unless you add or replace several major hardware components, such as a hard drive or a motherboard.

At best, activation is a minor nuisance that allows Microsoft to protect their intellectual property; at worst, it provides an opportunity for the world's largest and most profitable software company to inspect the contents of your computer and track the way you're using their products and those of their competitors.

Either way, Microsoft has a legitimate gripe against people who try to install Windows without paying for it. Without some kind of authentication, it would be easy enough to buy a single copy of Windows (or any other program) and install it on two or more computers.

The fine print (which almost everybody accepts without reading) limits the use of the software to a single computer, but Bill Gates has enough money already, doesn't he? Well, maybe, but the fact remains that Microsoft has both a legal and an ethical right to restrict the use of a single copy of Windows XP to just one computer. They spent a lot of time and money to create Windows, and they can decide how they want it used. With Windows Product Activation, Microsoft has an effective way to enforce that restriction.

Like it or not, you really don't have any choice about activation. If you want to use Windows XP, you'll have to activate it. And you can't buy just one copy of the Windows upgrade package and install it on all of your home computers, your laptop, and the one in your office.

It is possible to buy up to three additional Windows licenses at a slight discount. Each license has a different Product Key, and each license allows you to install Windows on one additional computer. In other words, you'll pay about 85 percent of the original price for a code that allows you to load the same copy of Windows on another machine. For more information about additional licenses, take a look at www.microsoft.com/windowsxp/pro/howtobuy/addlic.asp.

If you have five or more computers, you might qualify for a volume license at a significant discount. You can find information about volume licenses at www.microsoft.com/licensing.

How Product Activation Works

Each retail copy of Windows XP comes with a unique Product Key printed on a sticker in the package that contains the CD. You will enter the Product Key during Windows installation. Microsoft will also ask for the Product Key when you request technical support. During product activation, Windows uses the Product Key to create a product ID code and a "hardware hash" code that contains information about eleven different hardware characteristics:

- The display adapter
- The SCSI adapter (if any)
- The IDE adapter
- The MAC address of the network adapter
- The amount of RAM memory
- The type of processor
- The processor's serial number
- The type of hard drive
- The hard drive's volume serial number
- The CD or DVD drive
- Whether the computer uses a docking station or PCMCIA socket

There are two ways to submit product activation information: through the Internet as digital data, or by talking with a Microsoft customer service representative by telephone. The Internet option is a lot easier and faster, but it's not always practical.

Windows will ask if you want to run activation during Windows Setup, but you probably won't be able to establish an Internet connection until setup is complete unless you're upgrading an existing system. So it's often best to skip activation until after you have configured your network link or set up your dial-up Internet account on this computer. Remember, you have thirty days to complete activation, so waiting an hour or two won't make any difference.

When you do connect to the Product Activation server through the Internet, Windows will send a string of digital data from your computer to Microsoft, and it will receive a confirmation packet in the form of a digital certificate. The whole process is automatic and takes no more than a minute or two.

If you don't have a way to connect the computer to the Internet, you can activate by telephone. The telephone activation option in the Activation Wizard will display a list of countries and provide a telephone number for the country you select. When you call that number, a customer service representative will ask for the Product Key and the 50-digit installation ID code that Windows provides in the Activation Wizard. Windows divides both the installation ID code and the confirmation code into short segments, so you won't have to worry about mangling an outrageously long code number. After the representative confirms that the code is valid, he or she will give you a 42-digit confirmation code to type into your computer.

If Microsoft receives an activation request for a product ID code that has already been activated, it will compare the information in the hardware hash to the earlier activation. If all the hardware is the same, there's no problem, and the activation goes through. But if the hardware hash shows that four or more elements have changed, the activation system won't return a confirmation because it assumes you're trying to use the same copy of Windows on more than one machine.

What Happens If I Upgrade My Hardware?

When Windows Product Activation detects one, two, or three hardware changes, it accepts the changes and reactivates your system, just as if there had been no changes. So you can add more memory or a bigger hard drive to your computer, or replace the video card and go on with your life without any interference from Microsoft.

But if you try to change too many components at the same time, or if you try to install an existing copy of Windows on a new computer after the old one was destroyed or stolen, the online activation system will reject your request. In most computers, it takes four or more changes before Windows refuses to activate. However, the Windows activation system will automatically accept major changes (four or more of the items that trigger reactivation) through the Internet up to four times a year.

If online activation rejects your request, Windows will display a telephone number and ask you to call and explain. The customer service people who answer those calls are pretty good about accepting reasonable stories, so a major hardware update (such as installing a new motherboard, a new processor, more memory, and a new hard drive at the same time, or loading Windows on a replacement for a stolen laptop) should not be a problem. But if you try to activate the same Product Key on two or three (or a dozen) completely different machines within a short period of time, you're probably out of luck.

Is This a License to Snoop?

If Microsoft is sending information about your processor and hard drive to their product activation center, are they also poking around the contents of your hard drive and reading your personal information? Is product activation an invasion of your privacy?

Probably not.

The information in the hardware hash is stuff like the serial numbers of your hard drive and processor and the type of video card and IDE adapter inside your computer. Even if you register as a Windows user at the same time you activate Windows, none of this information is related to your personal identity.

Officially, Microsoft says, "At no time is personally identifiable information secretly gathered or submitted to Microsoft as part of activation. Product Activation is completely anonymous." Several people have tried to disprove this claim, but none have been successful, so it's probably best to accept the whole product activation scheme at face value. As far as anybody outside of Microsoft has been able to determine, they don't collect any personal information from your computer. There's no evidence that product activation does anything that isn't described in Microsoft's technical bulletins and marketing documents (www.microsoft.com/piracy/basics/activation). Its only purpose is to force everyone who wants to use Windows to pay for the software, and maybe to gather some statistical information about how many users are using different types of hardware.

The only thing Microsoft wants from you is money for separate copies of Windows on every computer you install and use. If that's not acceptable to you, switch to Linux or some other operating system.

What About Registration?

It's easy to confuse activation and registration, but they're not the same thing. They're not even related. Activation is a required part of installing Windows XP that was designed to protect Microsoft from users who don't want to pay for every copy of Windows that they use; registration is an optional process that supplies information about you and your computer to Microsoft's sales, marketing, and technical support departments.

The most important thing to know about registering Windows is that you don't have to do it. If you do, you will send Microsoft your name, address, and telephone number; some information about how you use Windows; and if you choose, an inventory of the equipment inside your computer. This information could actually be useful if you ever ask Microsoft to help solve a problem, but Microsoft can also use it to support their market research and to send you advertising from Microsoft and other companies.

It's your choice. Windows won't stop working if you don't register, and you might reduce the amount of junk mail you receive. But it's probably harmless. If you want Microsoft to send you new product announcements and other sales offers, or if you think the information you send will help improve the next generation of Microsoft products, go ahead and fill out the Registration Wizard. The rest of us will skip it, and we'll be none the worse for it.

16

TROUBLESHOOTING AND REPLACING HARD DRIVES

Hard drives are a special case. On a cost-per-bit basis, drives are cheap and getting cheaper all the time. When a drive fails, the cost of replacing the physical device is relatively small, but the data stored on the old drive is often irreplaceable. So you shouldn't throw away an apparently broken drive until you have done everything possible to recover the data, and you shouldn't do anything to the drive that might erase or damage any more data.

When your boot drive (almost always the C: drive) fails, you have two related problems: the first is to get the computer working again, and the second is to recover as much of the data from the broken drive as possible. If a secondary drive fails, the computer will probably continue to load and run Windows, but you still have to find a way to recover the data from the broken drive.

Therefore, you should treat the two objectives separately. First get the computer and Windows running again, and then worry about the data on the damaged drive. If you're going to do this yourself, you'll have to open up the computer case and install a new drive. Bear with me on this; it's not that difficult and it will save you a lot of money if you do the job yourself.

But if you're absolutely convinced that you can't do this repair on your own, at least read the section "What to Tell the Service Guy" on page 191.

NOTE   *Of course, if you have been careful about making regular backups of your data, a drive failure is little more than a minor nuisance. You can install a new drive, load Windows from the Microsoft CD, install new copies of your application programs and utilities, and restore your data files from the backup media. No big deal, right? Well, yes, but making backups is one of those things that we all know we're supposed to do every few days, but most of us don't bother. If you do have an up-to-date backup handy, you have my permission to feel superior to the rest of us. If not, put down this book right now and go make backups of all your data.*

Restoring the Computer to Useful Operation

When Windows won't load because of a hard drive problem, your first priority should be to remove the damaged drive from your computer and install a new C: drive. After you have Windows working again, you can worry about recovering the old data.

Reinstalling Windows from scratch on a new or different drive is a time-consuming process, but it's the only way to be sure that you don't lose data on your damaged drive. You will probably kill at least half a day messing with the computer before you get it back to its state before the drive failed. If you have never done it before, removing and installing the drive itself, formatting the drive, installing and updating Windows, downloading and reinstalling drivers, reinstalling and updating security software (such as antivirus and firewall programs), reinstalling and updating software, and tweaking your personalized settings can easily consume a full day or more.

If the damaged hard drive is the only one inside your computer, you will need to buy and install a new drive. If you have more than one drive, you can use the other drive as the boot drive, but considering the low cost of new drives, you might just as well buy a new one instead. You will need at least two gigabytes of free space for the Windows XP software alone, plus space for all of the programs and data that were stored on the damaged drive.

You can buy a new hard drive at most places that sell computer supplies, including most computer retailers, mail-order and online merchants, and office supply stores. The best prices are probably at the big national chains, where there's almost always one brand or another on sale with a mail-in rebate offer. Look for the best combination of drive size and price, but make sure the new drive is at least as big as the old one.

We're assuming that the damaged hard drive uses an Integrated Data Electronics (IDE) connection to the computer's motherboard. If it's a Small Computer System Interface (SCSI) drive or a Serial Advanced Technology Attachment (SATA) drive, you will want to replace it with a new drive of the same type. (See the section "SATA Drives" on page 181.)

To remove the old drive, follow these steps:

1. Turn off the computer. If there's a power switch on the back of the case, turn that switch off.

2. Unplug the AC power cable from the computer case.

3. Disconnect all of the other cables from the computer's back panel.

4. Remove the outer cover from the computer. This probably involves removing two or more hex-head screws or thumbscrews to separate the cover from the case.

5. Find the hard drive. It's probably located directly behind the front panel of the computer, but it might be someplace else inside the case.

6. The drive is connected to the rest of the computer through two cables: one for power and the other for data. Carefully disconnect both cable connectors from the back of the drive. Don't unplug the data cable from the motherboard.

7. If there are screws holding the drive to the case, remove them and slide the drive out of the case. If the case uses tracks or some other method to mount the drive, remove the drive from the case. If your computer has more than one IDE hard drive, remove both of the drives connected to the IDE1 connector on the motherboard.

The computer uses tiny jumpers on the back of the drive to identify each drive as either a master or a slave drive. Look on the top of each drive or in the documentation supplied with the drive for one or more diagrams that show the correct jumper locations. Figure 16-1 shows the location of the jumpers on a typical drive.

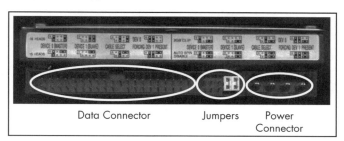

Figure 16-1: The position of the jumpers on a hard drive sets the drive as either a master or a slave.

If you have removed only one drive, put it aside in a safe place until you have installed the new drive. If you have more than one drive, find the drive with the jumpers in the master position and put that drive aside. Replace the other drive, with the jumpers in the slave position, back inside the computer.

Installing a New Hard Drive

You might want to add a new hard drive to your computer because the one already in place isn't big enough to hold all of your files (especially if you want to store a lot of large video or audio files), or because the installed drive has failed. If you're just adding more storage capacity, you can generally leave the old drive in place (unless you're dealing with a laptop computer that has space for just one drive).

NOTE *It's not essential, but many computer retailers and mail-order or online places sell inexpensive round IDE cables that replace the flat ribbon cables supplied with most drives and motherboards. The round cables are more flexible than the flat ones, so they're easier to handle inside the computer case. When you buy your new drive, think about getting a round IDE cable at the same time.*

Mounting the Drive

The first thing you must do is to open up the case and find a place to put the new drive. Most desktop and tower cases have spaces for several drives, but the exact location varies from one case to the next. You can usually find a place for an additional drive directly above or below the existing hard drive, or behind an unused panel on the front of the cabinet.

NOTE *Even if you're planning to replace the existing drive, it's a good idea to leave the old one in place until you can copy your data files to a new drive. See "Recovering Your Data" on page 183 for information about retrieving data from a damaged drive.*

It seems as though every computer case uses a unique mounting arrangement for hard drives and other storage devices. CD and DVD players might slide in from the front of the case, or they could move forward from the inside. Some use removable tracks, racks, or sliders, and others bolt the drives directly to the framework of the case. Hard drives might fit behind removable faceplates or be buried deep inside the case. The only certain thing is that there *is* a way to install the drives; it's a safe bet that the person who assembled the computer didn't build all the sheet metal racks around the drives.

Laptop computers are no better. On some machines, you can simply lift up the keyboard to get to the hard drive, but others force you to remove several layers of other components before you reach it. Too many laptops seem to be products of the Trash Compactor School of Industrial Design; that's the method that lays everything out on a big work table and then squeezes it all into a tiny enclosure. Reversing the process is a lot more difficult.

If you can find an instruction manual that explains how to disassemble your computer, that's the place to start. Even it it's just one of those exploded diagrams with screws and washers flying off in all directions, it will probably tell you what the designer had in mind, and where to find that last critical screw that holds everything together.

If you don't have a manual (and you can't find one on the manufacturer's website), you'll have to spend some time staring at the drive to figure out exactly how to remove it. On a more positive note, once you figure out how to remove a drive from a particular case, it's a safe bet that other drives use the same mounting technique. Fortunately, all of the drive manufacturers place the mounting screw holes in the same locations, so replacing one brand of drive with another will not present any new mounting problems.

The physical mounting arrangements are the same, but each drive manufacturer uses a slightly different system to configure and format the drives, so it's essential to follow the specific instructions supplied with each drive. That's fine in theory, but some retailers buy drives in case lots and resell them without manuals or other documents. If you don't have a manual, download a manual and installation software from the manufacturer's website before you try to install the drive.

NOTE   *In some computer cabinets, it's very difficult to reach the tiny machine screws that hold the drives to the frame. A #1 Phillips screwdriver with a shaft at least three inches long can often make it easier to insert or remove the screws. While you're at it, make sure that you don't use a magnetized screwdriver around your computer; the magnetic field could erase or damage the data on your hard drives and floppy disks.*

Before you mount the drive, look for the labels that identify its make and model number, along with several other important characteristics. Note these values:

- Name of the manufacturer
- Model number
- Capacity
- Number of cylinders
- Number of heads
- Landing zone
- Number of sectors

If the BIOS does not detect them automatically, you will need to type these values into your computer later. If you copy them now, you won't have to remove the drive again later to read them. If all of these values are not printed on the label, the computer's BIOS will probably detect them. If not, use the make and model number of the drive to look for the drive's specifications on the manufacturer's website.

To use an existing drive as the new primary drive, move the jumper on the back of it from the slave to the master position, replace the drive in the computer, and connect the cables to the drive.

Changing the BIOS Setting

After you reassemble the computer, connect the power cable and turn it on. Immediately press the key that opens the BIOS setting menu (usually F2 or DELETE) and go to the screen that shows the hard drive settings. If the BIOS does not automatically detect the drive as the IDE1 Primary drive, move the cursor to that menu item, and press the ENTER key to run the autodetect function.

Formatting the Drive

Before you can use a new hard drive (or a floppy disk, for that matter), it's necessary to format the drive. Formatting creates a file system on the drive, along with one or more partitions, each of which appears to Windows as a separate "logical" drive with its own drive letter and file allocation table. The drive letters you see in the My Computer window are the names of logical drives. If you want to assign more than one drive letter to portions of the same physical hard drive, you can partition the physical drive into two or more smaller logical drives.

Even if a drive has a very large physical capacity, the actual amount of storage on the drive is determined by the computer's BIOS. In many computers, the BIOS has a maximum drive capacity limit that was much bigger than the designers expected to need at the time the computer was built. That limit might be 4GB, 8.4GB, or about 130GB. Every time the BIOS people raised the limit, it seems as if the drive manufacturers introduced a new line of even bigger hard drives. If your drive's capacity is greater than the limit of your BIOS, you must use special software (included with Windows XP or supplied with the drive) to bypass the capacity limit.

NOTE *Don't be surprised if the BIOS or the formatting tool shows a slightly smaller capacity than the one on the drive package—some drive makers show capacity in decimal kilobytes (equal to 1,000 bytes), while Windows and the BIOS makers use binary kilobytes (equal to 1,024 bytes), so Windows will report the capacity of a 200GB (decimal) drive as a little over 180GB (binary).*

If you are using the new drive as your boot drive, at this point the BIOS startup sequence will display a disk-error message because the new drive does not contain any boot files. If the new drive is not the boot drive, the boot sequence will run and Windows will start, but Windows Explorer (My Computer) won't show the new drive.

There's a formatting utility included on the Windows XP CD. If you're installing a new drive as the C: drive, you can format the drive as part of the process of installing Windows:

1. Place the Windows XP software CD in the computer's drive.

2. Restart the computer. The computer should start to install Windows from the CD. If the computer can't find the CD, open the BIOS Setup Utility and change the Boot Device Sequence to place the CD drive ahead of the hard drive.

3. Shortly after the Windows Setup routine loads the initial programs to the computer's memory, it will offer to format and partition your drive. The Windows formatting tool bypasses the BIOS capacity, so you should be able to reach the full capacity of the drive.

If you're installing a new drive into a computer that already has a boot drive, start the computer and run the formatting and partitioning program supplied with the drive after Windows loads. The package that contains the new drive should also include a CD—and possibly a floppy disk—with the formatting tools for the drive. If not, download the software from the drive manufacturer's website (look for a link to "support" or "downloads"). Follow the instructions on the website to create a CD or a floppy disk from the downloaded software.

In most cases, the formatting program on either the Windows CD or the disk supplied with the drive will format and partition the drive without any trouble. But some drive makers require an alternate jumper setting or some other obscure configuration to bypass the capacity limit; if you don't know the secret handshake, you may spend hours beating your head against the table as you try to get the @#$%! thing to format properly. If your drive won't format itself with a capacity close to the size shown on the drive label (but don't forget about the difference between binary and decimal kilobytes and megabytes), look for instructions in the manual supplied with your drive or in the Support section of the drive manufacturer's website.

When Windows is up and running on a new boot (C:) drive, install all the extra drivers and other software necessary to activate your video controller, network interface, sound card, and other peripheral devices and services. Don't forget to load the latest Windows patches, updates and service pack, and your antivirus and antispyware software. To link to the Windows Update website, open Internet Explorer, and select **Tools ▸ Windows Update**.

SATA Drives

Within a few years, Serial ATA (SATA) will become the standard interface for hard drives, CD and DVD drives, and other storage media. SATA drives produce less heat than IDE drives, they are easier to install and replace because they don't require jumpers, and the connectors are easier to handle. The smaller cables (shown in Figure 16-2) also improve the flow of air and the cooling inside the computer case. In the future, SATA will also allow faster data transfer than the older IDE drives.

Most computers and motherboards made in the last couple of years support SATA drives, even if they came with older-style IDE drives. However, you should confirm that your own system can support SATA before you buy a new drive. If you can't find the information you need in the manual, consult the tech support center for your computer or motherboard by telephone or e-mail.

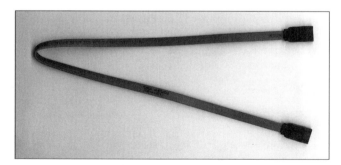

Figure 16-2: SATA data cables are smaller and easier to handle than IDE cables.

If your computer's power supply does not include a SATA power connector, you will need an adapter like the one shown in Figure 16-3 to connect power to the drive. These adapters are often included with SATA drives.

Figure 16-3: Use a power adapter to connect an SATA drive to an older power supply.

Installing an SATA drive is easier than installing an IDE drive because it doesn't require any jumpers, and the computer's BIOS can automatically detect multiple SATA drives. If your BIOS does not detect an SATA drive after you install it, confirm that the data-cable connectors are firmly seated in the mating connectors on the drive and the motherboard, and the power cable connector is seated in the drive. If you're using an adapter cable between the power supply and the drive, make sure it's connected to a cable from the power supply.

Replacing a Drive in a Laptop Computer

Hard drives in laptop computers have smaller dimensions than the ones in desktop computers. Each maker has its own system for opening up the case and mounting the drive, so it's much more difficult to offer general instructions for replacing a drive. On some models, it's just a matter of releasing the keyboard and lifting it out of the way, but on others, it's a form of major surgery.

If you're not comfortable working inside a laptop computer, don't try to learn how to do it now—it's more important to recover the data on your drive than to develop skills as a hardware technician. After your data is secure, you can either pay somebody to install a new drive or ask the laptop maker's technical support center for instructions on doing it yourself.

To recover the data, connect the laptop computer to another computer through a network, and follow the instructions in the next section of this chapter.

What About USB Drives?

USB and FireWire hard drives and other storage media (such as pocket-size flash drives) are separate devices that plug directly into a USB port or some other kind of input/output socket. Because it's easy to connect and disconnect these drives, they are extremely convenient for backing up data, storing data offline, and moving data from one computer to another.

Windows XP should automatically detect a USB, FireWire, or flash drive as soon as you connect the drive to the computer. If nothing happens when you plug in the drive, try restarting the computer. If that doesn't work, make sure your computer has Windows XP Service Pack 2 installed. If you're using a flash drive, download and install the Microsoft USB Flash Drive Manager program (UFDSetupWizard.msi) from www.windowsmarketplace.com/ prices.aspx?itemId=1744677.

Recovering Your Data

Unless the physical platters inside the drive are severely damaged, it's probably possible to recover the data from a bad drive. In extreme cases, you might need to send the drive to a very expensive recovery service that will take the drive apart in a clean room environment and replace the damaged parts, but it can be done. Before you spend that money, try the techniques in this section to read your files with special recovery software. The most important thing to remember when a drive appears to fail is *don't panic.*

At least, not yet. One way or another, you can probably get your files back.

NOTE *Once again, remember that you will not have to recover as much data from a damaged drive if you make regular and frequent backups.*

It's often easy to confuse a software failure on a hard drive in which Windows can't read data because of damage to the File Allocation Table (FAT), the boot sector, or other sectors, with a hardware failure caused by a physical or mechanical problem in the drive itself. These problems may include damage to the drive's motor, circuit board, or to the magnetic platters that actually hold the data. Fortunately, software failures are a lot more common, and it's a lot less difficult (and a lot less expensive) to recover the data from a disk with software problems.

If the drive is making grinding or scraping noises, or if you see signs of burned components on the drive's circuit board, don't try to recover the data yourself. *Turn the computer off immediately and remove the drive.* Any attempt to read data on a physically damaged drive could do even more harm, and it could reduce the chances of reading the surviving data. Retrieving the data from a drive with physical damage is a job for a commercial recovery service.

On the other hand, if your computer still recognizes the drive, there's a very good chance that you can use a specialized data recovery program to copy your files to another drive.

If you decide to try using a recovery program, you must connect the damaged drive to the computer running that program. In most cases, you can simply set the jumper on the drive to make it a slave (if there's an existing slave, disconnect it first), and plug in the power and data cables without fitting the drive into a mounting frame inside the computer's case. Depending on the exact location, you might want to place the drive on top of a small box or a couple of books next to the computer.

Follow these steps to connect the drive to your computer:

1. Turn off the computer, and unplug the AC power cable from the case.
2. Remove the cover from the case.
3. If there's a spare IDE connector on the computer's motherboard (or an SATA connector if you're connecting a SATA drive), connect a cable from the drive to the motherboard. Set the jumper on the drive to the master position.
4. If both IDE connectors on the motherboard are in use, disconnect the data cable on the CD or DVD drive, and plug that connector into the damaged hard drive. Set the jumper on the hard drive to the same setting (master or slave) as the setting on the CD or DVD drive.
5. Connect a spare four-pin power connector to the drive.
6. Reconnect the AC power plug to the computer case.
7. Turn on the computer and immediately enter the BIOS setting menu. On most computers, you can open the BIOS menu by pressing the DELETE key or the F2 key. You should see an instruction on the screen at the beginning of the POST that tells you which key to use.
8. Go to the BIOS menu that lists the CMOS settings for your drives. Select the drive you just connected to the computer, and use the autodetect feature to configure the settings.
9. If the BIOS does not detect the drive, check the jumper settings. If they are correct but the BIOS still can't find the drive, close the BIOS utility, turn off the computer, and then remove the drive. You'll have to send the drive to a recovery service to retrieve your files.
10. If the BIOS detects the drive, save the BIOS settings and let the computer restart Windows.

Data recovery software is available from several sources. I've had very good luck with GetDataBack from Runtime Software (www.runtime.org), but a Google search on "data recovery software" shows several other products that may do the job as well or better. GetDataBack is available as a free download that can examine your drive and open individual files, but it requires a one-time payment to create and store copies of the files from the damaged drive on a second hard drive.

GetDataBack offers separate versions for drives that use FAT and NTFS file systems. To learn which system your damaged drive used, open either version of the program and let it scan your system. The screen shown in Figure 16-4 identifies the file system used by each drive. In this example, all of the drives use NTFS, but the program is GetDataBack for FAT. To read files on these drives, it will be necessary to download and install GetDataBack for NTFS.

A good data recovery program can often perform miracles on a drive that appeared to be a lost cause, but it's not perfect. Some files on a damaged drive may indeed be completely lost, with no hope of recovery.

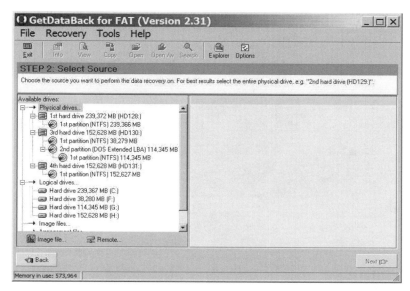

Figure 16-4: GetDataBack shows the file type for each hard drive in a computer.

If the data recovery program can create a complete or partial image of the damaged drive, you can use that image to restore your data. If the recovery is successful, it might be possible to reformat the old drive and reuse it, but that's generally not a good idea. It's safer to throw away the damaged drive and use a new one instead because there's a danger that the same problem that caused the original failure could still exist on the drive.

Recovering Data from a Laptop Drive

If the drive in your laptop computer fails, you will almost always have to replace it with a new drive because there's only enough space inside the computer for a single drive. The best approach is to install the new drive, load Windows from the CD, and then copy your data files from the old drive onto the new one.

If you have a backup copy of your data, it's easy to restore it to the new drive, but if you must retrieve it from the damaged drive, things become more complicated. Because the connectors on a 2.5-inch laptop drive are not the same as the ones on a standard 3.5-inch IDE drive, you will need an adapter like the one shown in Figure 16-5 to mount the drive in a desktop or tower case, or a kit that converts the drive to a USB device. These adapters and converters are available at large computer retailers or through the Internet.

NOTE   *It's even more important to make regular backups of the data stored on your laptop computer than on the computer that stays in your office or at home. In addition to the usual hazards of damaged and unreadable hard drives, you will also lose your data if your laptop is lost or stolen. Losing your computer is bad enough, but losing irreplaceable data can turn an expensive nuisance into a major disaster.*

Figure 16-5: Using a 2.5-inch hard drive with a standard IDE cable requires a special adapter.

If Windows can't read the contents of the damaged drive, try one of the data recovery programs or other methods described earlier in this chapter. After you restore the data, copy it to the new drive in your laptop through a network or by using a flash drive or a CD to physically move the data from one computer to the other.

Troubleshooting Hard Drives

If the computer does not recognize your hard drive during startup (before Windows loads), it's likely that one of these settings is not correct:

- Jumper settings on the drive
- Cable connections to the motherboard
- BIOS settings

Jumpers on ATA Drives

The most common type of hard drive in modern computers uses the IDE or ATA interface with the computer's motherboard. Both ATA and IDE describe the same type of connection. An IDE interface can support hard drives, CD and DVD drives, and other types of storage media. Other drives might use a SCSI or a SATA interface.

Motherboards that use the ATA interface system usually have two IDE connectors, each of which can support two drives. The two connectors may be marked as IDE0 and IDE1, or IDE1 and IDE2, but the BIOS identifies them as the primary channel and secondary channel, or as IDE channel 1 and IDE channel 2.

The standard IDE cable has connectors for two drives. The two drives connected to each IDE channel are known as the master and the slave. If only one drive is connected to a channel, it's the master (unless it's a Western Digital drive, in which case it's a "single" drive). You can have a master with no slave, but you can't have a slave without a master. (This is a technical definition only. We leave the philosophical implications of that sentence to you.)

If the boot disk—the one that contains the boot sector and the Windows XP operating system files—is an IDE drive, it should be the master drive on the primary channel (IDE channel 1). You can use the other channels for either hard drives or other storage media.

NOTE *Western Digital drives use a slightly different jumper system from all of the other manufacturers; they require different jumper settings for a master drive with a slave on the same channel, and for a single drive. If you're adding a slave to a channel with an existing Western Digital drive, you must move the jumper on the old drive from the single position to the master position.*

To set a drive as either a master or a slave, move the jumpers located on the back of the drive (next to the data and power connectors) to the position shown on the diagram on top of the drive and in the user manual. If you can't find a diagram, try one of the links from www.ontrack.com/jumperviewer. Depending on the physical location of the drive, you might have to remove the drive from the frame to change a jumper setting.

If the BIOS does not detect your new drive, double-check the jumper settings on the drive to make sure that the jumper is connecting the correct pair of pins. If the new drive is set as a master, confirm that the other drive connected to the same data cable is the slave. If the new drive is the slave, confirm that the other drive is the master.

Cable Connections

The cables that connect drives to the computer's motherboard are another possible source of trouble. If the data and power connectors aren't firmly attached to the drive, or if a cable has one or more broken wires, the drive won't work correctly.

ATA Drives

Confirm that the plugs on the cables that connect the drive to the computer's motherboard (or a driver card plugged into the motherboard) are firmly seated into the mating connectors at both ends. The connectors have molded shells that only allow the connectors to fit in one position, but if there's a problem, it won't hurt to make sure that the connector wasn't forced into the socket incorrectly.

If the jumper settings on both IDE drives are correct and the cables are connected properly, but the BIOS still refuses to detect any of the drives connected to an IDE port, it's possible that the cable is damaged or defective. Turn off the computer and replace the cable. Most new drives come with new cables, so there's almost certainly at least one spare cable in your accumulation of odd computer parts.

SATA Drives

If your BIOS does not detect an SATA drive after you install it, confirm that the data-cable connectors are firmly seated in the mating connectors on the drive and the motherboard, and the power cable connector is seated in the drive. If you're using an adapter cable between the power supply and the drive, make sure it's connected to a cable from the power supply.

SCSI Drives

SCSI drives are less common in computers running Windows XP than IDE or SATA drives, but they are often used in network servers and other critical applications. The SCSI interface supports faster data exchange than IDE, but the difference is not always significant, especially on a home computer or one used in a small business.

Unlike IDE devices that connect directly to a connector (called a *port*) on the motherboard (or a plug-in IDE controller card), SCSI devices connect to the controller through a series of daisy-chained cables that might connect several devices in series to a single port (a SCSI bus). Each SCSI port can support either eight or sixteen separate devices on a common channel—or bus—depending on the SCSI version. One of those devices is the SCSI controller, so the true maximum is either seven or fifteen devices per port.

Because the same input/output port supports several devices, each device must have a unique ID number. If the same number is assigned to more than one device on the same bus, none of the devices on that bus will work. Some drives and other devices use jumpers to set the ID number, and others use a thumbwheel or some other type of switch. The documentation supplied with each drive, or the manufacturer's website should tell you exactly how to set the ID number.

At the end of each SCSI bus, the last item in the chain must be a resistor circuit called a terminator. The terminator can be a TERM switch setting on a SCSI device, or a separate plug that connects to the second SCSI connector on the last device in the chain. Again, the drive manual or manufacturer's website should contain specific instructions for terminating the SCSI bus.

The two common causes of problems with a SCSI drive are conflicting ID numbers and an unterminated SCSI bus. If your BIOS fails to detect one or more SCSI drives, confirm that each drive (and the SCSI controller) has a different ID number. At the same time, look at the last device in the chain to confirm that the chain is terminated.

BIOS Settings

Before Windows can exchange data with a hard drive, the computer's BIOS must detect the drive and identify the drive's characteristics. The BIOS can automatically recognize the characteristics of almost any drive that you're likely to install (unless it's more than six years old), but you do have to instruct the BIOS to go looking for the drive. If the BIOS settings and the drive values don't match, the computer will either display a (possibly fatal) error message during startup, or it will ignore the drive.

To instruct the BIOS to detect the drive, follow these steps:

1. Install the new drive. Make sure the power cable and the data cable are both connected, and the jumper setting (described in the previous section) is correct.

2. Turn on the computer and immediately press the key that opens the BIOS Setup Utility.

3. Move to the screen that includes the IDE and other drive options. This might be in the main menu, in a submenu called Standard CMOS Features, or someplace else in the Setup Utility. Look for a section of the menu that lists either primary and secondary masters and slaves (like the one in Figure 16-6), or two or more IDE channel numbers with masters and slaves (Figure 16-7).

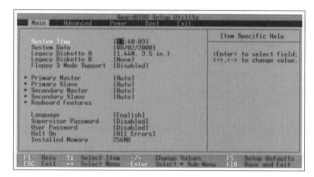

Figure 16-6: The BIOS Setup Utility might show the hard drive configuration options as primary and secondary masters and slaves . . .

Figure 16-7: . . . or as numbered IDE channels.

4. To set the options for a drive, select that drive from the list and open the submenu. You will see a list of options like the one in Figure 16-8.

5. Follow the instructions on the screen to automatically detect the drive's characteristics, including the data capacity, the number of cylinders and heads, and other values. In this example, press the ENTER key. Don't worry if the utility does not show the correct capacity for your new drive. You will fix this when you format the drive.

Figure 16-8: The submenu for each IDE device shows that drive's characteristics.

6. In most cases, the BIOS will obtain the correct values directly from the drive and display them in the submenu. If the autodetect function does not recognize your drive, advance to each line of the menu and enter the correct values by hand (these are the values you copied before you mounted the drive in the case). If the values are not printed on the drive label, look for them on the manufacturer's website.

7. Follow the instructions on the screen (usually at the bottom or on the right side) to save your changes, and close the BIOS Setup Utility. The computer should restart and load Windows.

Moving a Hard Drive to a New Computer

Moving an old drive to a new computer is often the best way to continue using the same data after you start using the new machine. However, it's often not possible to use the old drive as the boot drive (the C: drive) on your new computer. You can't just drop the old drive into the new box and use the Windows software that you installed on the old computer. Unless the old and new computers are exactly the same make and model or they use exactly the same motherboard and drive controllers, many of the listings in the Windows registry will not apply to the new computer. Rather than loading Windows, the computer will probably display a Blue Screen.

In almost all cases, the best method is to set up the new computer and install Windows XP on the drive that came with that computer and treat the old drive as a D or subsequent drive. It might be possible to change the critical registry entries, but making these changes to the registry can sometimes create more problems than it solves. Article No. 3140082 in the Microsoft Windows Knowledge Base contains more information about moving a system disk.

Even if you don't try to use it as the C: drive in the new computer, you still might want to install the old drive, both to read the data stored on that drive and to increase the storage capacity on your new computer. If Windows won't detect a drive after you move it from one machine to another, consider these questions:

- Are the jumpers on all the hard drives and other IDE devices set correctly? Remember that each IDE channel can have just one master and one slave.

- Has the BIOS detected the drive? Restart the computer and run the BIOS Settings Utility to add the drive. See "BIOS Settings" on page 188 for detailed instructions.

On the other hand, if the old drive is more than about five or six years old, it's probably close to the end of its useful life—a hard drive is a mechanical device, and eventually all hard drives do wear out or break down. And that ancient drive's capacity is probably just a fraction of your new one, so it's best to just copy the data files from the old drive and then discard it.

NOTE *Remember that your drive probably contains personal data files that you won't want strangers to see. Before you dispose of an old drive, use a data shredder program such as BPS Data Shredder (www.shareup.com/BPS_Data_Shredder-download-13608.html) to destroy the data on the drive, or physically destroy the drive by removing the circuit board, opening the case, and scratching or bending the disks inside.*

What to Tell the Service Guy

If the thought of opening up your computer and adding or removing a hard drive seems as unlikely as removing your own gall bladder, it's okay to let somebody else do the job. Either a computer service shop or your cousin who builds computers for fun should be able to do the job for you. But it's important to explain exactly what you want done.

If you have to take the computer to a repair shop, bring your Windows CD in the package that contains the Product Key. The technician will need your key code to reinstall Windows on the new drive. If you can find the driver CDs that came with the computer or motherboard, the video controller, and other devices inside the computer, bring them too. If you don't have those disks, though, the technician can download the drivers through the Internet.

If the drive is scraping, grinding, or making other unpleasant noises, ask the technician to remove the damaged drive and install a new one. Otherwise, explain that you want to install a new drive and try to use recovery software to create an image of the damaged drive on the new one.

First, explain that the C: (or whichever) drive is damaged, and you want to try to recover the data. Emphasize that you do *not* want to run Check Disk or defragment the damaged drive. Tell the service person that you want to install a new C: drive and set the broken drive as a slave. Ask the technician to load Windows XP and the latest patches and service pack on the new C: drive, along with the drivers for your video controller, network interface, and other peripheral devices.

After the new C: drive is in place and Windows XP is up and running again, ask your technician to run GetDataBack or another data recovery program to create an image of the damaged drive on the new drive. If the people in the shop are not familiar with the data recovery software, show them the information in this chapter.

After the data recovery is complete, or if the technician discovers that the drive is damaged beyond the ability of the recovery software to create an image, ask the tech to remove the damaged drive from the computer and return it to you. Even if you don't send the drive to a recovery service, you don't want a stranger (or even a relative) to keep a drive that contains your personal data.

Problems with Other Storage Devices

CD drives, DVD drives, and most other storage devices use the same IDE, SCSI, or SATA interfaces used by hard drives. Therefore, many of the same problems can occur with these drives—loose connectors, incorrect jumper settings on IDE drives, and mechanical failures.

If Windows does not detect a newly installed drive, check the cables and the jumper settings, and run the BIOS settings utility. If the autodetect feature in the BIOS tool does not identify the new drive automatically, try changing the individual settings for that drive.

If the BIOS won't recognize a new drive, it's possible that the drive was introduced more recently than the BIOS version running on your system. Check with the manufacturer of your computer or motherboard for information about obtaining and installing an update to the BIOS software.

If a drive stops working after it has been in use, the cause is most likely either a damaged driver file or a mechanical failure of the drive itself. Try reinstalling the driver software first; the device manufacturer's website should offer downloads of the most recent driver release.

If the drive itself stops working rather than the formatting or file structure on the drive, it's almost always faster and easier to simply replace it with a new one than to try to repair a broken mechanism or circuit board. To be blunt, most of these devices were designed to be disposable. If your computer (or a drive installed later) is still under warranty, call or e-mail the manufacturer for a replacement. If it's out of warranty, just pull the old unit out of the computer and install a replacement.

A Few Last Words About Drives

When a drive fails and you can't use the software tools and techniques in Chapter 3 to fix it, you should have two objectives: first, saving and recovering the data files on the damaged drive, and second, restoring the computer to normal operation by installing Windows on a different drive (if the damaged drive was the old system drive). If you treat these two separately, you will reduce the impact of a damaged drive to a minimum.

17

TROUBLESHOOTING AND REPLACING OTHER HARDWARE

Hard drives aren't the only parts of a computer that can fail. Memory modules, the central processor, the motherboard, the power supply, and all of the peripheral devices that allow the computer to exchange data with the rest of the world can stop working properly. Obviously, troubleshooting a memory module is very different from trying to fix a mouse or a keyboard, so this chapter contains specific advice about fixing many of the most common devices and components in and around your computer.

Memory Problems

Working with memory in older computers was easy: If the memory modules fit into the motherboard sockets, you could generally expect that the computer would successfully recognize and use them. Even if some of the modules were not identical to the others, the system would default to the slowest one and continue working.

But today, as computer processors and motherboards have become faster and more complex, adding more memory to your computer has also become more complicated. If all of the memory modules in the computer are not exactly the same, the system can become unstable and crash.

Memory problems fall into several general categories: one or more of the physical memory chips mounted on a memory module might not be working properly, the memory modules installed in the computer could have different ratings, or the memory modules might not be compatible with the CPU or other components on the motherboard.

NOTE   *You will have to open your computer and add or remove memory modules to identify a damaged or defective memory module by swapping them and changing sockets. If you're not happy about working inside the box, you can still run the Memtest86 diagnostic tests described in the following section to determine whether there's a memory problem. If Memtest86 identifies a problem, let somebody with more experience repeat the Memtest scan and perform the physical repairs.*

Identifying Memory Problems

The POST runs a quick memory test every time you turn on the computer. If the POST shows less memory than the amount installed in your computer, there's at least one bad module in place.

If you don't know how much memory is installed in your computer, look in the General tab of the System Properties window (**Start ▶ Settings ▶ Control Panel ▶ System**), as shown in Figure 17-1. The amount of memory appears at the bottom of the list of system details.

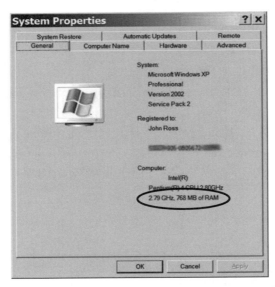

Figure 17-1: The speed of the CPU and the amount of memory available to Windows appears at the bottom of the list of system details.

To find the bad module, turn off the computer, remove all but one module from the motherboard, and turn the computer back on. If the POST shows the correct amount of memory on the remaining module, repeat the test with a different module until you find the one that does not pass the POST.

If the POST does not identify a problem, but you get a Blue Screen with a "memory error" code or a Stop message after Windows starts, the problem could be either a bad module or a conflict between modules with different ratings.

For a more extensive memory test, download and run the Memtest86 diagnostic program from www.memtest86.com. Memtest86 creates a startup diskette or CD that automatically runs a series of detailed memory test scans to search for bad memory.

If Memtest86 does not find any problems, then the memory modules are good, but a conflict between the memory and something else on the motherboard might be present. Try these methods one at a time to find and fix the problem:

- Confirm that you are using the latest version of the drivers that control the motherboard. Go to the websites maintained by the manufacturer of your computer or motherboard to find and download the latest motherboard drivers. Look for a new video controller driver at the video card maker's website.

- Update the BIOS to the most recent version available at the computer or motherboard manufacturer's website. The same website should also offer a software tool for performing the update.

- Choose the default BIOS setting command (or Optimized Defaults settings), and save the new settings.

- If the computer has more than one memory module installed, try running the computer with just a single memory module in place. If the computer appears to be stable, remove that module and try another until you have tested each module. If one module causes the computer to be unstable, that module is almost certainly the source of the problem. If you have more than two modules, replace all the others and test the computer again.

- If you have more than one memory module, try swapping sockets. Put the second module in the first socket and the first module in the second socket, and so forth.

- If all of the modules work separately, but not when they're all in place, it's possible that they have different speeds or different latency ratings (as reported by Memtest86), or the power supply is not compatible with your motherboard. If the modules have different ratings, try replacing them with modules that have identical speeds and ratings, or buy and install a single new module that has at least the same number of megabytes as the total of all the old modules. For example, if the computer has two 256MB modules, you could remove both of them and use one new 512MB or 1024MB (1GB) module.

- When you have confirmed that all of the memory modules in the computer have identical speeds and latency ratings, open the BIOS Settings menu and look for the settings (usually in the Advanced Chipset section) for CAS latency, tRCD (RAS-to-CAS delay), tRP (RAS Precharge), and tRAS (minimum Active-to-Precharge delay). All four of these settings should match the ratings for your memory modules, as reported by Memtest86. Don't worry about understanding what these settings mean—the important thing is that they match. Mismatched modules are supposed to default to the slowest setting, but sometimes they can produce Blue Screens in Windows.
- Find the BIOS setting for SRAM Frequency and confirm that it matches the speed rating of your memory modules. The speed rating is usually marked on each module and is reported by the Memtest86 diagnostic tool.

NOTE *Latency is the amount of time that it takes a memory circuit to respond to different kinds of commands, expressed in clock cycles. The latency rating of a memory module shows the amount of delay for three or four command types, so a typical rating might be "2.5-3-3-7" or "4-4-4." Lower latency rating numbers indicate better performance.*

If you can identify a specific memory module as the source of your problem, remove it from your motherboard. If it's the only module in the system, replace it with a new one with at least the same number of megabytes (MB). Look in the user manual for the computer or the motherboard, or the manufacturer's website for information about the type of memory your system needs. You can also find tools that specify the right memory type for specific computers at these memory manufacturers' websites:

www.corsairmemory.com/corsair/configurator_search.html

www.crucial.com

www.kingston.com

www.mushkin.com/doc/products/advisor.asp

www.pny.com/configurator

www.buffalotech/products/memory-configurator.php

If you have less than 512MB of memory in the computer, this is probably a good time to add more. Installing more memory (to bring the total up to a gigabyte or more) is the single least expensive way to improve your computer's performance. Make sure the speed and latency ratings of your new modules are exactly the same as the ratings of the modules already in place.

Also, try not to mix and match memory speeds, even if they are brand names. In theory, you should be able to do this, but I have had ugly Blue Screens caused by mismatched modules.

If you discover that your memory problem was caused by mismatched modules, don't throw away the modules that you remove from your computer. You might find a use for them in another computer some time in the future.

NOTE
Look for a brand name (such as Kingston, Crucial, Corsair, Viking, PNY, or Mushkin, among others) on the module that caused the problem and use Google or another search tool to find the manufacturer's website. Most quality memory module suppliers offer lifetime warranties, so you might be able to obtain a free replacement from the product support center. If your memory module is a "no-name" product, or if there's a brand name on the label but you can't find a website, it was probably cheaper than a brand-name unit because it didn't include a warranty. As that old TV commercial for auto parts said, "You can pay me now or pay me later."

Replacing the Motherboard

Installing a new motherboard is the computer equivalent of a brain transplant. It's major surgery that replaces the central components that control everything the computer does. Obviously, you won't perform a motherboard swap very often, but if you are a truly dedicated hardware geek and you're not afraid to tear the whole computer apart, it can be done. Just follow the instructions that come with motherboard, take your time, and double-check all the little details. As long as you pay attention to what you are doing, it isn't that difficult.

Every other component in the computer connects to the motherboard, so there are plenty of opportunities for something to go wrong. If the computer does not work at all after you install a new motherboard, look for these possible reasons:

- Is the power supply turned on? Is the AC power connected?

- Are all of the power cables plugged into the motherboard?

- Are all of the data cables and control cables plugged into the correct outlets and pin connectors? Are all the external components (mouse, keyboard, video monitor) plugged in?

- Are the central processor chip and the memory modules properly mounted?

- Are there any loose screws or other small parts rattling around inside the case? To remove them, pick up the case, turn it upside down, and shake it.

- Is the bottom of the motherboard grounded to the case? Most motherboards allow enough space for the screws and washers to keep away from the printed circuit, but sometimes they do touch part of the electrical path. Try placing an insulating fiber washer between the motherboard and each of the brass spacers that support the board inside the case, as shown in Figure 17-2. If you have trouble keeping the washers in place while you insert the screws, use a tiny dab of rubber cement to hold each washer to the bottom of the motherboard.

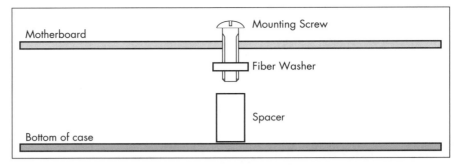

Figure 17-2: Use fiber washers to insulate the motherboard from the bottom of the computer's case.

Power Supply Problems

The computer's power supply converts 110V AC (or 220V outside North America and a few other places) "house current" to the lower DC voltages used by the computer's electronic components, motors in the drives, and fans. Power supply problems can take several forms:

- No AC input. If the AC power cable isn't connected, or if the on/off switch on the back of the power supply is turned off, or if an internal fuse has blown, then the power supply won't have any power to convert to DC.

- No DC outputs. With no power, the computer won't start, the fans won't spin, and all of the lights will remain dark. If you suspect a power supply failure, check the fans on the side of the power supply and the fans on the heat sink on top of the central processor chip.

- Incorrect voltages. If the voltages are too low, the electronic circuits won't work, or if they do work, the computer restarts at random or Windows produces Blue Screens. If the voltages are too high, some components could be damaged.

- Fan malfunctions. If the fans aren't turning, or if you see other symptoms of a power supply problem, use a meter or a power supply tester like the one described in Chapter 1 to check the power supply's output voltages. If the voltages are correct, replace the fan.

Some cheap power supplies might provide all the correct voltages, but their internal components can generate radio signals that can interfere with other electronic equipment, including radios, telephones (both wired and cordless), TV sets, computer displays, and even heart pacemakers and other medical devices. If you hear a buzz on a radio or telephone when you turn on the computer, or if you see a series of horizontal lines moving across a video display, try turning your computer off and back on again. If the interference goes away when the computer is off and it comes back when it's turned on, replace the power supply.

It might be possible to repair a broken or noisy power supply by replacing one or more of the internal components, but it's almost never worth the time and trouble. Replacement power supplies are not expensive, and they're likely to be more reliable than a repaired unit. When you buy a new power supply, look for one with at least the same number of watts as the old one. You can find the power rating on the label attached to the power supply's case.

To replace a power supply, follow these steps:

1. Turn off the computer.
2. Disconnect the power plug from the computer.
3. Remove the cover from the computer's case.
4. Disconnect all of the power cables leading from the power supply to the motherboard, the hard drives, other storage devices, and components.
5. Remove the screws that hold the power supply to the case.
6. Lift the power supply out of the computer.
7. Place the new power supply in the location where you removed the old one, and replace the screws.
8. Connect the power cables to the motherboard, the drives, and the other components.
9. Plug the AC power cable into the back of the computer.

Mouse Problems

Mice and other pointing devices use a variety of technologies to transmit motion from your hand to the computer. Some are purely mechanical, with a small ball that rotates as the mouse moves, while others use a light beam or laser to track mouse motion. If the driver software is working properly, the most common cause of mouse problems is dirt.

Cleaning a Mechanical Mouse

A clean mechanical mouse uses a rubber ball to rotate three cylinders that translate motion across a flat surface (such as a table or a mouse pad) to three numeric values that the computer uses to place a cursor on the screen. As the mouse passes along the surface, it can pick up grease and dirt that can interfere with the motion of the ball and the rollers, causing them to rotate less reliably.

To clean a mechanical mouse, follow these steps:

1. Turn the mouse over, and rotate the small retaining plate that holds the ball inside the housing. If it's a trackball with the ball on top, just turn it over or turn the retaining plate.
2. Remove the ball.
3. Use a soft, moist cloth to clean the ball.

4. Look into the space that held the ball to find the three rollers. If they are not immediately visible, use a flashlight. There is probably a vertical line of dirt and other crud across each roller. Use a sharp knife (an X-Acto knife or the small blade of a Swiss Army knife work well) to scrape the dirt away from each roller. Use compressed air to remove any loose dust from inside the cavity.

5. Replace the ball and reassemble the mouse.

Cleaning an Optical Mouse

There are no moving parts in an optical mouse, so cleaning it is easier than cleaning a mechanical unit. Use a soft, damp cloth to remove all the accumulated dirt and gunk from the bottom of the mouse, and make sure there is nothing obstructing the light or the reflective surface.

Keyboard Problems

A computer keyboard is a mechanical device that sends electrical signals to the computer. Each key on the keyboard produces a different signal, which the computer interprets as the letter or other symbol printed on the key cap. Most keyboards are cheaply constructed assemblies that use a membrane under the plastic keys to make contact with a printed circuit board when you press a key. Some more expensive keyboards use individual switches for each key.

Unless you are using an expensive ergonomic or wireless keyboard, it's generally not worth the effort involved in trying to repair a keyboard. You should be able to find a better-quality keyboard than the ones supplied with most computers for less than $20. For a little more, you can splurge on a fancier keyboard with special features for more comfortable operation and extra keys that automate certain frequently used commands.

However, there are some things you can try before you throw away your old keyboard and buy a new one. If a single key or a small group of keys stops working, the problem could be dirt between the membrane and the circuit board. Try shaking the keyboard or rapping the edge of the keyboard gently against a tabletop to dislodge the dirt.

If the keys become sticky, or if somebody drops or spills food crumbs, coffee, soda, or some other form of goop into the keyboard, it's often possible to clean it. For minor spills, a cotton swab can sometimes fit between the keys, or try using compressed air or a vacuum cleaner with a small nozzle to dislodge the stuff under the keys. For cleaning the tops and sides of the keys, the 3M No. 674 Keyboard Cleaner Kit shown in Figure 17-3 works well, but you might accomplish the same thing with a damp cloth.

For a more complete job, you can remove the character keys, use a vacuum cleaner or air hose to clean the tray, and wash the loose keys in warm soapy water. It's possible to remove the keys by gently prying upward with a screwdriver, but it's a lot easier with a tool like the one shown in Figure 17-4 that fits around the side of a key (available from Design Components, http://members.aol.com/capsoff). Don't try to remove the space bar, the ENTER key, or any of the other large keys; they're extremely difficult to reinstall.

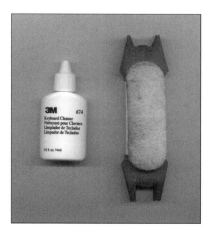

Figure 17-3: The 3M Keyboard Cleaner Kit includes cleaning fluid and a special tool for reaching the sides of individual keys.

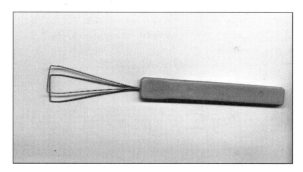

Figure 17-4: To remove a key cap with a tool like this one, fit the wires around the key and lift.

To replace each key, place it over the shaft and push down. Be sure to replace each key in the right place. For reference, Figure 17-5 shows the standard American English keyboard layout. For keyboards used in other countries, look at the Windows Keyboard Layouts web page at www.microsoft .com/globaldev/reference/keyboards.mspx.

Figure 17-5: Use the standard keyboard layout when you replace the keys after cleaning them.

USB and FireWire Problems

If you assembled your own computer, or if you bought the computer from a screwdriver shop that built it out of standard parts, you might be using a case that has more USB or FireWire sockets on the front and back of the case than the motherboard can support. When you try to install a new USB or FireWire device several months after you built the box, it's possible that you will try to plug into to a socket that isn't connected to the motherboard.

If Windows fails to detect a USB or FireWire device when you connect it to the computer, try using a different socket. If the first socket you tried was on the front, try one on the back. If that doesn't work, open the case and confirm that there are cables connecting the sockets on the case to sockets on the motherboard. If Windows still can't find the device, try reinstalling the USB or FireWire driver supplied with the motherboard.

Printer Problems

Printers are mechanical devices controlled by computers, so they can suffer from the worst of both worlds: mechanical failures and bad data. When a printer fails to produce the document you expect, or the document doesn't look the way you expected it to look, you should look for both types of problems.

Restart the Printer

Sometimes the printer's options and configuration settings will return to the correct values after you turn off the printer and then turn it back on again. This is a very quick and easy fix, so it's worth trying first, before you spend a lot of time looking for something more complicated.

No Lights

If *none* of the lights or LED indicators on the printer is on, the printer probably has an electrical problem. Confirm that the power switch is turned on, and the power cable is plugged into both the printer and a live AC outlet. If the printer is plugged into a power strip, make sure the power switch on the strip is also on.

If the printer is turned on and receiving power, look for a fuse in the printer, most often located next to the power cable or power connector. If the fuse blows again, take the printer to a service center.

No Response

If the lights are on, but the printer does not respond when you send it a command from the computer, there can be several possible causes.

Cable

Confirm that the printer cable is connected to both the computer and the printer. If the printer requires a bidirectional cable, confirm that you are not using an older parallel cable. The printer manual will tell you what type of cable you should be using.

Is there any other device between the computer and the printer, such as a switch, a buffer, or a network server? Is the intermediary device turned on and working properly? Is the switch set to the right position to connect your computer to the printer? Are all of the cables connected?

Printer Error

If the printer has a digital display or a set of LED indicators, look for an error code or an error message. The printer manual should include explanations of all the codes and message that your printer can produce. If not, look for them on the manufacturer's website.

If Windows or an application program displays an error message on your monitor, follow the instructions in that message to clear the problem. For example, if you see an "out of paper" message, add more paper to the printer.

On Line

Confirm that the printer's On Line indicator light is on. If it is dark, push the button or operate the switch to set the printer's setting to On Line.

Printer Driver

Try reinstalling the correct printer driver. Look for the most recent driver software on the printer manufacturer's website.

Properties and Preferences

From the Windows XP Start menu, choose **Printers And Faxes**, or from the Classic Windows Start menu, choose **Settings ▸ Printers And Faxes**, and select the printer you are trying to use. When the printer window opens, choose the **Printer** menu and then the **Properties** and **Printing Preferences** commands. The Properties and Preferences windows, which are unique for each make and model of printer, contain the specific settings and options that apply to that printer. Confirm that all of the settings are correct.

When you enter the Print command from an application program, make sure the Select Printer option in the Print window (shown in Figure 17-6) is set to the correct printer.

Ink and Paper

Check the printer's ink, toner, or ribbon. If there is none left, replace or refill the supply. Confirm that the printer has enough paper to handle the current job.

If the printer has more than one paper path (such as a laser printer with a fold-down tray), make sure the pages are not using the alternate path.

If the printer seems to be printing, but nothing appears on the paper, check the ribbon or the ink or toner supply.

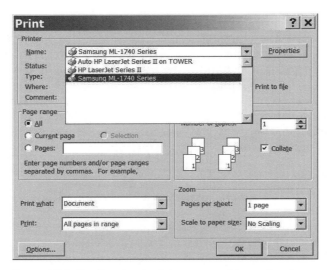

Figure 17-6: Confirm that the Print command is sending the document to the right printer.

Paper Jam

If the printer reports a paper jam, open up the printer and remove all sheets of paper from the paper path. Then close the printer and make sure the On Line indicator is on.

Not Enough Memory

If the printer stops printing a page that includes one or more complex graphic images before the page is complete, the printer does not have enough internal memory to handle the job. Either reduce the size or definition (in dots per inch) of the image, or install more memory in the printer. If you are trying to print two or more images on the same page, reformat the document to place each picture on a separate page.

Wrong Font

If the document prints with gibberish characters, or if it the text appears in the wrong typeface, make sure your printer recognizes the font used by your application program. Confirm that the font is installed in your computer by opening **Start ▶ Settings ▶ Control Panel ▶ Fonts**. If you can't find the name of the font shown in the application program, either choose a different font in the application, or install the font from the application CD.

Double-check the connectors plugged into both the printer and the computer to make sure they are firmly seated into their sockets.

Make sure the application that is using the printer is not set to "draft output" or another draft setting.

Wrong Colors

If some or all of the text or image is in the wrong color, it's possible that one or more of the ink or toner color cartridges may be empty, or the ink in a cartridge may be clogging an ink jet. To solve the problem, try removing and shaking each cartridge. If that doesn't work, replace the cartridge that contains the color of ink or toner that does not print.

Wrong Size

If the text or image runs off the edge of the paper, confirm that the Printer Settings are configured for the right paper size and image size, and that you have selected the correct printer. If both of these settings are correct, look for updates to the printer driver and the application program.

Try Printing Some Test Pages

Most printers have a diagnostic feature that will print a test page when you press the right combination of buttons or switches. Your printer manual (or the printer manufacturer's website) will tell you exactly how to run a test page on your particular printer.

When the printer does not respond to a print command from the computer, try printing a test page. If the test is successful, the printer itself is working correctly, so you should direct your troubleshooting efforts to the cable and the computer. Don't forget to return the printer to its On Line state.

Windows also includes a Print Test Page function that can test the link between the computer and the printer. To print a test page from the Windows XP menu, open **Start ▶ Printers And Faxes**; from the Classic Windows menu, open **Start ▶ Settings ▶ Printers And Faxes**. Then right-click the name of the printer, select **Properties** from the pop-up menu, and click the **Print Test Page** button at the bottom of the General tab. If this test is successful, then the problem is probably in the application program that produced the print command rather than with Windows.

Try a Different Program

After you confirm that the printer itself is working properly and that the Windows printer driver is also working, try a different program to print your document or image. If you can save the document or image that you want to print and open it in some other program, you can sometimes print the document from the second program.

If printing from a different program is successful, look in the original program for options or settings that control printing. It's possible that one or more of these settings are directing the document to the wrong place.

Printing to a File

Almost all programs that include a print command offer the option of sending the formatted document to a file rather than sending it directly to a printer. This makes it possible to take the stored file to another computer on a floppy disk, a recordable CD, another form of portable media, or through the Internet. At the distant computer, the recipient can print the document, even if the original program is not installed on that computer. This can be useful in a household with several computers in different rooms but no network connections between the computers.

If nothing happens when you try to print a document directly from a program, make sure the Print To File option in the Print Setup dialog box is not turned on.

Printing Through a Network

If your printer is connected to your computer through a network, a printing problem can be located in your own computer, in the network, in the print server, or in the printer itself. If none of the troubleshooting methods in this section solve the problem, talk to your network support person, if you have one. If you don't have a network support person, look for a problem in a switch or router, in a network interface at either the print server or the printer itself, or with a bad address or another incorrect network setting. On a large network, it's also possible that too many users have tried to order print jobs at the same time, overloading the buffer.

Monitor Problems

Whether the display monitor connected to your computer is a flat panel or an old-technology cathode ray tube (CRT), most of the troubleshooting methods are similar. When a monitor does break down, there's not a lot that you can do to fix it without a well-equipped electronics test bench. And that's just as well, because some of the capacitors inside a CRT monitor can hold an electric charge strong enough to injure or kill you, even if the power cord is not plugged into a live outlet.

Unlike the rest of your computer, the monitor does not contain any modules or other parts that you can remove and replace, so it's best to either retire a sick monitor or take it to a qualified repair shop. The price of CRT monitors has dropped so much that it's almost always less expensive to buy a new one instead of sending the old one out for repair.

Not every display problem indicates a dead monitor. If you have access to a second monitor, try disconnecting the one with a problem and connecting the spare. If the replacement displays the same symptoms, the problem is almost certainly in the video card inside the computer rather than the monitor. You can also try connecting the suspect monitor to a different computer; if the problem is still visible, then the trouble is in the monitor.

The following are some common symptoms and fixes.

Screen Is Completely Dark (No Image)

If you don't see any image at all, check these connections and settings:

- Is the monitor's AC power cord plugged in at both ends?
- Is the power switch on the monitor turned on?
- Is the signal cable connected to a video adapter in the computer?
- Is a screen saver or an energy-saving program running? Press the space-bar on your keyboard to restore an image.
- Is the brightness control on the monitor turned all the way down?

If none of these tests solve the problem, the monitor's internal power supply has probably failed. It's time to repair or replace the monitor.

The Image Is Squashed

If the image is compressed either vertically or horizontally toward the middle of the screen, try using the controls on the monitor or the on-screen adjustments to restore the image. This might solve the problem for a short time, but it's a warning that the monitor's vertical or horizontal output is failing. If you can't restore the image, or if the image is reduced to a very narrow vertical or horizontal line through the center of the screen, replace the monitor or send it for repairs.

The Shape of the Image Is Distorted

A distorted image is probably caused by physical damage to the deflection coils around the CRT. Try using the controls on the monitor to adjust the Pincushion or Geometry settings. If that doesn't help, replace the monitor.

Color Is Wrong

A color video display uses three separate image scans to display a mixture of different colors. If one of the color scans fails, the colors in the on-screen display will look peculiar because the red, green, or blue scan is missing. If this happens, replace or repair the monitor.

Missing Pixels

On a flat-panel screen, each point (a "picture element," or *pixel*) in the display receives an electric charge controlled by a separate transistor within an integrated circuit in the monitor's control circuit. If a transistor fails, the corresponding pixel either goes dark or remains a bright solid color all the time. Either way, the bad pixel appears as a tiny dot that does not change color when you view an image.

Many monitor manufacturers consider a very small number of dead pixels to be acceptable, but if you discover bad pixels on a new monitor or laptop display, return it for a replacement as soon as possible. If your monitor develops bad pixels after the warranty expires, there's not a lot you can do about it. Some people have had good luck using a soft cloth wrapped around a finger to rub the screen very gently around the bad pixel, but that doesn't always work.

Audio Problems

The most common problem in a computer's audio system is complete silence when you are trying to play a sound file, or when you are listening to streaming audio from the Internet. Look for one of these causes:

- Are the speakers plugged into the computer's sound card?
- Is the speaker's power unit connected to the speakers? Is it plugged into an AC outlet?
- Is the volume control knob on the speaker turned all the way down?
- Are any of the software volume controls turned all the way down? Check the application program that is playing the sound file (such as Real-Player or Windows Media Player), the control program that works with your sound card, the Windows Volume Control, and the Sounds and Audio Devices Properties window (open the Properties window from the Windows Control Panel).
- Is the Mute option turned on in any of the programs that control the sound? Again, check the application program, the control program, the Windows Volume Control, and the Sounds and Audio Devices Properties window.

If the speakers still don't work, or if the sound is distorted, the speakers or the amplifier that controls them have probably developed a problem. This could occur because you have been playing the speakers too loudly or because of a wiring problem. If turning down the volume on the speakers doesn't solve the problem, it's time to replace them. When shopping for new speakers, look for a set that can comfortably handle the volume level you expect to play without distorting the sound.

In general, the solutions to hardware problems are likely to be more obvious, or at least easier to understand, than the ones produced by obscure wrinkles in software code. If none of the specific techniques in this chapter help you find a problem, take a break for a cup of coffee (or whatever it takes for you to relax for a few minutes), and then go back to the general trouble-shooting methods at the beginning of the chapter. Take a closer look at the symptoms and the individual components that are not working properly. In most cases, a calm examination of the problem will take you most of the way toward a solution.

18

IF ALL ELSE FAILS . . . CALL TECH SUPPORT

You've tried all the troubleshooting techniques in this book, but nothing seems to solve your particular problem. The computer still displays an unhelpful error message every time you turn the thing on, and you have replaced everything except the screws that hold the case together. There's nothing about this problem in the user manual or the online Knowledge Base, and a Google search only produces pleas from other people who are facing the same problem.

Now what?

It's time to ask for help from a living, breathing expert.

Asking an expert offers at least two important benefits. First, if you have already spent several hours or more trying to solve a problem, a second brain can provide a fresh view of the situation and possibly discover symptoms and solutions that you have overlooked. And second, a bona fide expert might have seen the same or similar problems before and know what it takes to fix them.

We mentioned some of these sources of assistance in Chapter 1. In this chapter, we'll describe the various types of technical support in more detail and offer some advice about getting the most out of them.

Warranty Service

When you bought your computer, it probably came with a warranty that provides prepaid repair service for at least a year after the purchase date. If your computer is still under warranty, the manufacturer's support center is the first place to call for help. If your computer was made by a major manufacturer—such as Dell, Lenovo (formerly IBM), or Hewlett-Packard, among others—the support center has an extensive set of information about symptoms and solutions, and it also has direct access to the Microsoft Knowledge Base. And depending on the specific terms of your warranty, the support center can sometimes authorize a local service technician to come to your home or office to repair a hardware problem *at the company's expense.* And of course, the manufacturer is the expert on any proprietary software that was supplied with the computer.

The big computer companies all ship their computers with customized versions of Windows that include features that are slightly different from the generic operating system. As part of their contract with Microsoft, the companies that provide custom versions of Windows are also obligated to provide technical support for their own customers (that's you).

Even if your computer came from a "white box" supplier that assembled the system from parts, the supplier included some kind of warranty with the computer and the software. You paid for that warranty support, so you should use it. You might have to take the computer back to the store or to a local service center, but that's often better than packing up the whole system and shipping it halfway across the continent.

Try Your Help Desk First (If You Have One)

Many of us don't have the luxury of access to a formal help desk. Those of us who use the computer at home or in a small business generally don't have a full-time, in-house support center available to us. In many cases, we *are* the help desk for many of our friends, relatives, and coworkers.

If you do have access to a help desk or other in-house computer support center, or if you subscribe to a commercial computer support service, that's the first place to call. The people who work in those centers probably know exactly which components and software are in your computer, and they will be among the first to learn about localized problems (like virus infections) that are going around the office and your local network. If somebody else within your company or organization has faced a similar problem, the help desk might already know exactly what you have to do to fix it. And they have access to administrator privileges, diagnostic tools, and other resources that you can't always reach as a lowly user.

If your company has support contracts with Microsoft or the maker of your computer, and with other hardware and software companies, your help desk often has a direct line (or a list of private telephone numbers and e-mail addresses) to support specialists who are assigned to your company's account. Those specialists often have more experience and skill than the people who take calls from the general run of users. Because your local help desk staff members talk to these people all the time, they can often cut through a lot of bureaucracy and wasted time. If you have access to a help desk, you should call the help desk instead of going directly to an outside support center. Even if the computer is still under warranty, let the help desk handle the problem.

In a business with more than three or four computers, there's almost always somebody responsible for keeping them working properly. They may not have a title that identifies that part of their job, but that person probably fills the niche of your local help desk.

Depending on the size of your organization, the help desk might be one or two people in the same office where you work, an entire department halfway across the continent, or even an independent group that provides computer support under contract. Some help desks prefer to receive requests for assistance by telephone, and others want you to make your initial contact by e-mail. If you're having a problem with a laptop or other portable computer, they might even accept walk-ins.

It's always a good idea to know who to call and how to call them *before* your computer fills your office with orange smoke (or smoke of any other color, for that matter). These same people are probably responsible for things like maintaining your security programs and installing timely software updates and upgrades. And if they have time, you might convince them to come around and show you how to perform preventive maintenance and optimize your computer's performance.

When you talk to the help desk under non-panic conditions, be sure to let them know that it's not an emergency, and that they should take care of more immediate problems before they handle your request. The support folks will appreciate this, and the next time you have a real computer crisis, they'll know that you're serious. They might even move you to the top of their list ahead of the chronic complainers. It never hurts to have your support people think you're one of the good guys.

Before the computer breaks down, ask your help desk or support center how they prefer to receive trouble reports. Is there a special telephone number or e-mail address? Are there different people to contact for hardware and software problems? Do they need some specific information about your account or your computer's location or network address? The more you know about how the help desk wants to work, the more you can help them solve your problem for you.

In-Laws and Other Informal Tech Support

For those of us who can't call a formal help desk, a friend or relative who is "good with computers" can sometimes provide useful advice and assistance. Don't expect your nephew to have all the tools that a full-time support center can use, but often an experienced user with a slightly different perspective from your own is all that's necessary to find and fix a problem.

However, it's important to be aware that some self-defined "computer experts" don't know much more than you do. You have to trust your own instincts about this, but there are a few common warning signs. For example, if your adviser ignores the text of a Blue Screen error message and immediately suggests some kind of major repair, such as reformatting the hard drive or replacing the motherboard, *before* they try any less destructive methods, or if they somehow seem too enthusiastic about opening up the computer without a good reason, you should look for a second opinion before you allow them to perform any potentially destructive "repairs." Thank your "expert" politely for their help, and take the computer back before they can make the problem more serious than it is already.

Remember that you're asking your friend or cousin for valuable advice and help. If possible, give them something in return—mow their lawn or invite them to a nice dinner or something. And have some sympathy if your source of free support works on computers for a living; you're asking him or her to take on extra work on their own time.

Finally, keep in mind that not everyone who works with computers is a Windows guru; someone who is an expert Macintosh or Unix user might never lay hands on a Windows computer. The world's greatest expert on highly complex structured databases or Java programming is not necessarily the person who can help you recover data from a hard drive with a damaged boot loader. If your cousin or your neighbor tells you that he or she really doesn't know much about Windows, it's probably true.

Dealing with Microsoft Tech Support

If you can't find a solution to a Windows problem in the built-in Help system or the documents in Microsoft's online Product Solution Centers, you may want to ask Microsoft for one-on-one assistance.

Microsoft offers technical support services by telephone, e-mail, and live online one-to-one text messaging. The first couple of support calls for Windows XP are free, but after that, there's a flat $35-per-request fee, regardless of the method you use to communicate with them. Other Microsoft products have their own price structures for support services. The two free calls are enough for most people to solve installation and setup problems, but the $35 charge is enough to discourage most users from calling for support when the solution is available from another source, such as the online Knowledge Base or the Help screens built into Windows.

Prepaid support contracts and other alternatives to per-call support are also available from Microsoft, but those services are usually more appropriate for large businesses than for smaller organizations and home users. For instructions on reaching tech support for XP and other Microsoft products, go to http://support.microsoft.com.

That $35 fee probably means that you won't call (or e-mail) Microsoft until you have tried everything else you can think of. And that's how Microsoft wants you to treat their support services: as a last resort. If nothing else can solve a problem, their technicians are ready and waiting to help you.

Some people believe that Microsoft and other companies should provide support at no charge; after all, we wouldn't need to call for help if the products weren't so flaky. Maybe so, maybe not, but the vast majority of support calls are questions whose relatively simple answers are in the installation guide or the online Help included with the product. It costs companies money to maintain call centers and pay the support people, so it does make business sense to discourage people from treating them as the first place to go for help rather than the last resort. If the call centers can't solve the problem, or if you can convince the support people that the problem was caused by a bug in the software, you can often convince them to refund the service request fee.

NOTE   *If your copy of Windows was supplied with your computer, Microsoft doesn't want to talk to you. Your first point of contact should be the computer manufacturer's tech support center or website. Some are better than others, but the support centers at major manufacturers like Dell, IBM (now Lenovo), and Hewlett-Packard all have access to the same information resources as the support people at Microsoft, and they should also have detailed information about your computer's hardware that might make the troubleshooting process go more quickly. In practice, some manufacturers are a lot worse than others about providing truly helpful software support. If you reach a support center that can't or won't help you with a Windows problem, your best bet is probably to post your question on one of the Microsoft support bulletin boards described in Chapter 6.*

When you telephone the Microsoft support center, the first person you reach will be a call screener. Call screeners know how to direct your call to the right specialist, and how to take your name and product ID number, but they can't help solve your technical problem. Be nice to these people; they have the power to direct your call to a hotshot support specialist at Microsoft headquarters in Redmond or a bored contractor in Bangalore. And like that unfortunate incident with the goldfish in the second grade, if you acquire a reputation as an abusive or overly demanding caller, it goes onto your Permanent Record—a warning about you will appear at the call center every time you request support on any Microsoft product.

The quality of Microsoft's support varies wildly, depending on the experience of the support technician assigned to your case. Many Microsoft support people are helpful, friendly, and knowledgeable. They will know exactly where to find answers to your questions, or if they don't, they'll take it as a challenge to work with you until a solution emerges. Most of the time, Microsoft's support folks will spend as much time with you as necessary to solve your problem, even if it's a matter of several hours or more.

However, others never move away from the standard scripts they learned during their training. And now that Microsoft has shifted much of their support operation to South Asia, it can sometimes be extremely difficult to cut through very heavy accents and noisy telephone lines to understand exactly what the support people are telling you to do. Support technicians in Asia are often as knowledgeable and helpful as their colleagues in North America and Europe, but the combination of an unfamiliar accent and a bad connection can create an impenetrable barrier. It can be almost painful to try to obtain help by telephone from technicians whose heavily accented English forces you to ask them to repeat almost every sentence.

NOTE   *The people who run many offshore call centers want you to feel comfortable with their support people, so they instruct them to use "Western" names, such as "Richard" instead of Rajeesh or "Irene" instead of Indira. They also instruct them to drop references to American sports into the conversation. It's almost never successful. If someone asks you about a basketball or baseball game, I recommend shifting the conversation to last week's cricket match.*

The cost is the same for all three types of support—telephone, e-mail, and text chat—so you can choose the one that seems most comfortable to you. E-mail and text offer the advantage of a printed record of the information provided by the support representative, but voice calls can often go more quickly because you don't have to wait as long for answers to your questions. The time lag between responses in e-mail and chat often gives the impression that the same technician is handling several conversations at the same time.

When you telephone or exchange messages with Microsoft (or any other product support center), it's important to know how to make the system work to your advantage. Here are some things to remember:

- Before you call, gather all the information the support person might need, including the version of Windows, the latest service pack you have installed, and the Product ID number of your copy of Windows (right-click **My Computer**, and choose **Properties** from the pop-up menu to see the ID number in the General tab of the System Properties window). If you can't get far enough in Windows to view the Product ID number, you will need the Product Key printed on the original plastic case or paper sleeve that contained the Windows CD.

- Make a list of all the things you have already tried and the numbers of any Knowledge Base articles that seem to apply to this problem.

- As soon as you're connected to a support person (not the call screener who answers your call), ask for their full name, e-mail address, and a direct telephone number. You won't always get all three (many support people won't give out their full names to protect their privacy), but if you explain that you want to know how to reach them if the telephone or messaging system drops your call, most people will give you their contact information. Keep a copy of this information on paper. If you talk to anybody else during your call, remember to get the same information for each of them.

- Ask for your case number or "trouble ticket number." If you have to talk to another technician, the case number gives them a way to read the previous tech's notes on your problem.

- If you become convinced that the person taking your call can't help you, ask to "escalate" the call to the next level. If the first support person won't do it, insist that they transfer your call to a supervisor. This won't happen often, but it can sometimes be useful. If the technician puts you on hold several times to ask somebody else about your problem, ask to talk to that person.

- Be nice. If a support call has lasted an hour or more with no end in sight, ask the technician if you're going past his or her quitting time, and if so, offer to let them either call you back the next day or pass you to somebody else, so they can go home. Remember that the people you're calling might be in a different time zone, continent, or country, or be working an odd shift, so it might be going-home time for them when it's early afternoon on your time.

There is another way to reach Microsoft support staff without paying for a support request. Many product support specialists and experienced users monitor the Microsoft newsgroups (described in Chapter 6), and often post replies to questions almost as soon as they are posted.

NOTE *As an alternative to Microsoft's support services, you can request help from a third-party "Microsoft Partner" support center that charges by the minute for telephone support. To find links to a list of these support service providers, go to http://support. microsoft.com/oas/default.aspx and follow the links to your version of Windows XP. Look for the "Partners" section with links to support services that have been approved by Microsoft. One such service is www.ingenio.com/documents/partner/microsoft/support/ getadvice.asp. These time-based services are often a better deal than Microsoft's flat-rate service for questions with simple answers, but if you have a complicated or particularly obscure problem that will take more than just a few minutes to solve, it's probably better to call Microsoft.*

Other Vendors' Tech Support

Most of the same methods for getting the most out of Microsoft technical support will also work with other companies. Just about every supplier of computer hardware and software provides some kind of support for their products. Some offer toll-free telephone lines and their own knowledge bases, online bulletins, or discussion boards, but many companies don't supply any kind of free telephone support. They will only accept questions by e-mail. As a general rule, the number of tech support options increases along with the price of the product.

If you're calling a tech support center that charges by the hour (or by the minute) for the time you spend talking to a technician, do everything you can to save time before you place the call. Gather all the paperwork related to the product, and note the version number, release number, and serial number. If it's a hardware problem, remove the screws from the case so you can lift it off without wasting a lot of time.

One sign that a tech support center is overloaded is a very long wait to reach a live person. If you have to listen to bad music and "your call is important to us" announcements for more than about five minutes, try using another way to ask for help such as e-mail or an online forum. You can also try calling back at another time of day; late morning and early afternoon are often the best times. If the company offers round-the-clock support, it's often much easier to get through late at night. Monday mornings and the days after holidays are the worst times to call, especially for consumer products that have a habit of breaking over the weekend.

Many companies have moved their support centers overseas; your call to a California area code might reach somebody in India or the Philippines. This is not always a bad thing; tech support gigs often pay very well by local standards, so they attract smart people with strong computer skills. The quality of an offshore support center can be every bit as good as one in North America.

Wherever they are located, good tech support people are worth every penny (or Rupee) their employers pay them. They are calm and friendly, they know the product inside and out, and they will stay with you until the problem has been solved. But too many support centers measure their success by the number of calls each agent handles during a shift rather than the number of problems actually solved, so the agents are under intense pressure to get rid of each caller within just a few minutes. When you're talking to one of those sweatshops disguised as support centers, you will probably receive an all-purpose answer intended to make you go away, unless your question is on their list of common problems (and it won't be, if you have done some research before calling).

Here are some of the most common "go away and stop bothering me" answers provided by incompetent support centers:

- Install the software again.
- Check all the cables.
- You're using an obsolete version; install the new release.
- Reinstall Windows.
- Nobody has ever had that problem before. *It must be your fault.*
- Oh, they all do that. We'll fix it in the next release. *It's not a bug, it's a feature.*
- We don't support that; it's Microsoft's fault. I can't help you.
- (If you're talking to a software company.) It's not our fault. It's a hardware problem. I can't help you.

- (If you're talking to a hardware company.) It's not our fault. It's a software problem. I can't help you.

- (Without running any kind of diagnostic test.) It's a bad drive (or video card, or motherboard, or some other component). Give me a credit card number, and we'll send you a new one.

- Reboot the computer. *You never know; maybe the problem will go away.*

Of course, any of these might be a legitimate answer to your question. You should have tried some of them, like restarting the computer and checking the cables before you made the call. But if you sense that the support person seems to be giving you an all-purpose answer, it's time to insist that they escalate the call to someone who can give you some real help.

If it becomes obvious that the first-line support person can't help you, explain that you understand that they are expected to get rid of each caller as quickly as possible, but you want a real solution to your problem. Ask them to transfer your call to somebody who has more experience with the product. And make it absolutely clear that you will not go away or allow them to end the call until the problem has been fixed. If you can politely keep control of the call, your chances of receiving real help are a lot better.

Working in a bad support center is a high-stress job. The support agents don't always receive adequate training, and their supervisors are constantly pushing them to turn over calls as fast as possible. And most of the callers are upset because their computers have died, they've been waiting too long for somebody to answer, they don't really understand what has gone wrong, and first two places they called told them to call somebody else. Too many callers are rude, arrogant, or both, or they blame the support person for causing the problem in the first place.

So it's better to treat the people taking your calls with sympathy rather than abuse. You want the technician to think he's on your side so he will concentrate on solving your problem instead of making you go away. Let him (or her, as the case may be) feel that the two of you are a team, facing the evil problem together. Your call should be the one call that day that the support person actually enjoyed, because she had to analyze an interesting problem and maybe even learned something new in the process.

Don't Be Afraid to Escalate

In the last section, I talked about escalating a service call. This is an important word and concept; it pays to learn how to use it.

In almost every support center, the people who take incoming calls are at the bottom of a pyramid that might have two, three, or even more higher levels. The people at each level have more experience and more knowledge about the products they support than the levels below them. As a result, your chances of reaching somebody who can actually provide help should increase as you move up the line.

Give the first-tier person a chance to solve your problem before you give up on him or her. But if it's clear that you have gotten as much as you can from that person, politely ask to escalate the problem to the next level. In most call centers, a support agent must honor a request to escalate. If yours refuses, or tells you that they can't do that, ask for a supervisor. Remember, you want to keep control of the call, rather than letting the technician run the show.

When you reach the next level, don't assume that the new person has been listening to your earlier conversation. There's probably a written summary on the computer screen in front of the second-tier person, but it's entirely possible that the person who originally took your call did not understand your problem well enough to describe it in the incident summary. You should offer to start over from the beginning, and describe all of your symptoms and unsuccessful attempts to solve the problem.

When you get to the second or third level, it's likely that you're talking to somebody who actually knows how the product in question works, and how to fix (or work around) most of the known problems. At this level, the easy problems have already been solved, so the job is generally more challenging (and more interesting) than talking to people who don't know how to use the CTRL key or open a Windows menu. If you are dealing with an obscure problem, these are the people who will know how to fix it; if you have discovered a new and exciting bug in the product that nobody has reported before, these folks honestly want to know about it.

Wait! The Last Person Told Me Something Different

Don't be surprised if you receive contradictory information from different people. It's possible that the first person you reach (or the first two or three people) has never seen the problem before, and it's not written up in any of their reference material, so they're telling you to try some generic solutions hoping that one of them will work. The next person up the chain has a different favorite all-purpose technique, so they'll tell you to try that one. When you finally get to somebody with more experience with the product in question, that person might know about an approach that has not been revealed to the rest of the tech support staff.

All of the same rules apply when you talk to second- or third-tier support people: keep careful notes about your conversations, explain the symptoms and what you've already tried, and treat the technician as a partner in your battle against the computer. With their help, you should eventually find a solution to the problem.

E-mail, Bulletin Boards, and Other Ways to Avoid Talking to You

Many computer hardware and software manufacturers *hate* providing live technical support to their customers. Dedicated staff, special telephone lines, live message centers, and internal information resources all increase the cost of a product without producing any apparent compensating revenue. Even if a manufacturer charges for support requests, it's never more than a break-even deal.

So the big companies all spend money and other resources to create alternatives to those expensive one-on-one telephone call centers. Some of them provide detailed manuals and other documentation. Others, including Microsoft, have publishing departments that sell separate manuals that really should come with the product. Many companies have created online FAQ lists and knowledge bases that allow the product staff to write about known problems just once and supply the information to an unlimited number of users without the need for individual hand-holding. And as yet another way to save money, they also establish online forums or bulletin boards that encourage their users to provide free support to "other members of the WhizBang 901 community." If you have been reading this book from front to back, you already know about these services (if you're reading the book from back to front, hang on; you'll get to that information soon).

Even e-mail, which allows a single person (or a small group of people) to handle many queries at one time, is a lot more efficient and cost-effective for the support center than voice telephone calls. It's true that e-mail at some companies can be a black hole where questions go in, but nothing ever comes out, but I'm trying to be optimistic—you should expect to receive an answer to your first e-mail within 24 hours or less (except on weekends).

As long as the manufacturers offer those alternative support channels, you might as well take advantage of them. If you can solve a problem using information you find in FAQs, e-mail, or bulletin boards, go ahead and do it.

Making Tech Support Work for You

In a perfect world, no one would ever need to call for support. The computer would work perfectly every time you turn it on. But this world is far from perfect, so every computer user should know how to get the most out of a support center. For that matter, the same methods also apply to other forms of customer support; feel free to use them when your refrigerator stops making ice.

Whenever you call for help, remember these important points:

- Your objective is to solve a specific problem. The support representative's objective might be to get you to go away quickly. Don't give up control of the call.

- Keep track of the time and date of your call, and the name of each person you talk to.

- Note the length of time you waited for somebody to answer the telephone, and how long you were placed on hold. This can be useful if you have to complain later.

- Remember to ask for an incident or case number. This will speed things up the next time you call about the same problem.

- You have paid for support, either as part of the cost of the product, or on a per-incident or a per-minute basis. Don't let the support representative off the hook until your problem has been solved.

- Be nice to everybody you talk to. Don't blame the support people. They didn't cause the problem.

- If the person handling your call can't help you, escalate to the next level.

- Keep careful notes. If you see the same problem again on another computer, you shouldn't have to place a second call to solve it.

- If you receive particularly awful service, write a letter to the head of the department, or write to the president of the company. Make sure to include all the horrible details, including the time and date of the call and the names of the people involved.

- On the other hand, if you receive very good service, write a letter to the company that provided the service, letting them know that you appreciate their excellent service and support. Be sure to include the names of the people who provided the great service; this will make them look good to their bosses. Writing a positive letter will remind the company that somebody does notice when they provide quality service and support. Remember that an actual letter, on paper, will attract more attention than either a telephone call or an e-mail message. You can probably find the company's address on their website; send the letter to the corporate office or directly to the head of the company, and let them pass it along to the right department (possibly with their own "attaboy" note attached).

- Keep your sense of humor. Don't let bad service get under your skin.

- Remember your experience—good or bad—when you're ready to buy a new widget or a new software product. Reward good service with your repeat business.

19

CUTTING YOUR LOSSES: WHAT TO DO WHEN NOTHING ELSE WORKS

As painful as it might be to admit, some Windows problems just won't go away. In spite of everything you have tried, everything suggested by local computer experts, the manufacturer's technical support center, and the combined wisdom of the Internet, your computer continues to display symptoms of a serious problem. Neither the Windows Knowledge Base nor any of the advice in this book contains anything that does much good.

At some point in the process of troubleshooting, the amount of wasted time and aggravation you expend on the whole mess is greater than the value of the solution. When you feel like you've been beating your head against a brick wall, it's often best to admit defeat and resort to extreme measures.

Ultimately, you must shift your goal from identifying and repairing the problem that caused your computer to crash to restoring the computer to normal operation. It's quite possible that you will never know exactly what caused the original problem, but it's more important to get back to work than to find an elegant solution to a problem.

When you have eliminated a hardware failure as the cause of the problem and nothing else restores your computer to normal operation, the next-to-last thing to try is reinstalling Windows. You can try a "repair" installation, but because that preserves many of the existing registry settings and support for all of the programs installed on the computer, it won't always fix a truly monumental Windows disaster.

If you do try the Repair option, but it does not solve your problem, a full Windows installation that replaces the whole operating system with a new copy of the software probably will. However, this creates a completely new registry, so you will also have to reinstall all the other programs installed on the computer.

And if *that* doesn't work, it's likely that your system is infected with one or more particularly ugly viruses or spyware that your security programs don't know how to eliminate, or something else has severely corrupted the files on your hard drive. At this point, if you can't get rid of the problem, your only remaining choice is to reformat your C: drive (the boot drive), install Windows from scratch, and then rebuild your entire file system.

Don't take any of these steps unless they're absolutely necessary, and don't jump into them until you have done as much as you can to preserve your data and program files. Reinstalling Windows from scratch will destroy all of the system configuration settings, including your Internet Explorer bookmarks, the icons and shortcuts on the Windows desktop, and all of the other customized settings that define the look and feel of Windows on your computer. It will also destroy the registry entries for all of the programs and utilities that had been installed on the computer. Reformatting the drive is even more serious—you will lose absolutely everything on that drive unless you have a backup.

Before you start this process, be sure you have enough time to complete it. Between reloading and activating Windows, installing the latest Windows service pack, and installing the drivers for your network adapter, your sound and video controllers, all your other peripheral devices, and all of the utilities and application programs that you want to run on this computer, you can easily spend four or five hours (at the very least) before you get the computer back to normal. If you have a project that requires your immediate attention, it's often best to move to a different computer to complete the job *before* you try to deal with restoring the original machine.

Preserving Your Data

Before you reload Windows or reformat the C: drive, do what you can to save the files stored on that drive. If possible, copy the important files from that hard drive to one of these destinations:

- A second physical drive in the same computer
- An external hard drive temporarily connected to the same computer through a USB port or a FireWire port
- A hard drive located on a different computer or on a network server
- A tape drive, a CD or DVD drive, or other removable media drive

- An online backup service. These services connect to your computer through the Internet and store your data in a secure location. The companies charge a monthly or annual fee that varies with the amount of data and the specific services each company provides. Online backup services are generally intended for regular periodic backups rather than one-time emergency use.

  Major online backup services include:

@backup	http://backup.com
BackUp Solutions	http://www.backuphelp.com
Data Protection Services	http://www.dataprotection.com
Data Protector	http://onlinebackup.connected.com
IBackup	http://ibackup.com
Xdrive	http://www.xdrive.com

The method you should use to copy your files will depend on the nature of the problem that is affecting your computer:

- If Windows is running normally, either use a backup program or simply drag and drop the folders and files that you want to copy from one drive to another. You can also transfer files from one computer to another through your network.

- If Windows is not running normally, try starting the computer in Safe Mode (see Chapter 1 for instructions). When Safe Mode runs, drag and drop the folders and files you want to copy.

- If Windows won't run at all, use a file recovery program such as Get-DataBack to copy the files. See Chapter 15 for more about using GetDataBack.

NOTE   *If the original problem was caused by a virus or spyware program, it's possible that copying program and configuration files will transfer the infection to the destination drive or computer. Rather than copying everything on the old drive, select text and data files only. Don't copy any files whose names end with .exe, .com, or .dll. Immediately after you copy the files, run up-to-date virus and spyware scans on the computer that contains the copied files.*

If your computer will load Windows, you can use the Files And Settings Transfer Wizard to copy the configuration settings from your existing Windows setup, including Internet Explorer, Outlook Express, the desktop, and the display settings. After you install a new drive, use the Transfer Wizard to quickly configure the system to the same settings you were using before the original problem occurred.

Follow these steps to run the Files And Settings Transfer Wizard:

1. From the Start menu, open **All Programs** (or **Programs** in the Classic menu) ‣ **Accessories** ‣ **System Tools** ‣ **Files And Settings Transfer Wizard**.

2. Click **Next** to move to the Which Computer Is This? window shown in Figure 19-1.

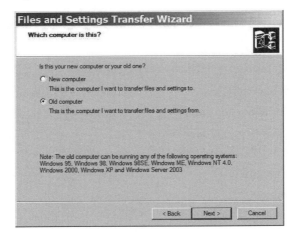

Figure 19-1: Choose the Old Computer option to back up your Windows settings.

3. Choose the **Old Computer** option, and then click **Next**. After the wizard processes your request, it will display the Select A Transfer Method window shown in Figure 19-2.

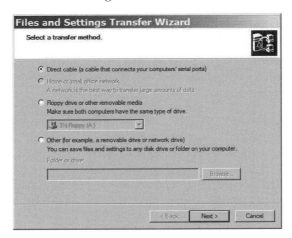

Figure 19-2: Choose the location where you want to store the backup files and settings.

4. Choose the media or network destination where you want to store the backup information. Click **Next** to move on to the next window.

5. The What Do You Want To Save? window offers the choice of saving settings only, files only, or both. If you choose the Custom option, you can choose the specific settings, folders, and file types that you want the wizard to save. To save space on your backup media, consider removing file

types you don't need from the list. If you have already backed up your data files, you can remove all of the file types and just save the Settings and Folders.

6. Click **Next** to collect and copy the files and settings you want to save.

When you are ready to restore the settings, run the wizard again and choose the New Computer option in the Which Computer Is This? screen.

You will also want a written copy of the computer's network settings. Follow these steps to find these settings:

1. From the Windows XP Start menu, choose **Connect To** ▶ **Show All Connections** and select **Local Area Connection**; if you use the Classic menu, choose **Start** ▶ **Settings** ▶ **Network Connections** ▶ **Local Area Connection**.

2. When the Status window appears, choose the **Support** tab.

3. Note all four of the Connection Status settings: Address Type, IP Address, Subnet Mask, and Default Gateway.

4. Click **Details**. The Network Connection Details window shown in Figure 19-3 will appear.

Figure 19-3: Make a written copy of the Network Connection Details before you reinstall Windows.

5. Add the addresses of the DHCP server and the DNS Servers to the list you made in Step 3.

Reinstall Windows

To reinstall Windows, you will need your original Windows XP CD and the Product Key code supplied with the CD.

If Windows was supplied with your computer, you might have a recovery CD instead of the full Windows XP disk. See the section on recovery disks later in this chapter for instructions on using a recovery disk.

Assuming you have either the full Windows XP CD or an upgrade disk, follow these steps to reinstall Windows:

1. Turn on the computer and place the Windows XP CD in your CD drive.

2. Restart the computer. If Windows is running, use **Start ▸ Turn Off Computer ▸ Restart**. If Windows did not load, press the CTRL, ALT, and DELETE keys at the same time.

3. Watch the text messages that appear during startup, before Windows loads. If you see the Press Any Key To Boot From CD message, press the spacebar.

4. If you don't see that message, and the computer does not automatically start loading Windows from the CD, then restart the computer again, open the BIOS Settings utility, and then change the Boot Sequence setting to move your CD drive to the No. 1 position. Save the new BIOS settings, and let the computer start.

5. Windows setup will run from the CD. At first, it will display a solid blue screen with a gray text line across the bottom. When the Welcome to Setup screen appears, press the ENTER key to choose the Set Up Windows XP Now option.

6. After you accept the Licensing Agreement, Setup will offer to either repair the existing Windows installation, or install a fresh copy. To repair the existing Windows installation, press the R key. To load a completely new copy of Windows, press the ESC key to choose the fresh copy option.

7. Setup will spend another half hour or more installing the rest of Windows XP. When the program asks for the Product Key and your network settings, enter the appropriate information.

8. After the Windows installation is complete and the computer displays a generic Windows desktop, it might automatically detect and install one or more device driver or drivers. If the driver was not included in the Windows disk, use the driver disk supplied with each device, or download new drivers from each manufacturer's website (see Chapter 5 for a list of Internet links to sources for device driver software).

9. If your computer or motherboard came with a driver disk, place it in the drive, and use the installation software on the disk to load these drivers.

10. If you have a copy of the latest Windows XP Service Pack on a CD, place the disk in the drive and install the service pack.

11. Use the Windows Update command in the Start menu (**Start ▸ All Programs ▸ Windows Update**) to download and install updates through the Internet. If you don't have a CD, Windows Update will also load the latest Service Pack.

12. After Windows restarts for the last time, run Windows Update again to confirm that you have loaded all available updates. Choose the **Custom** option to see a list of nonessential but useful updates, including the latest versions of utilities, new add-on programs, and updated device drivers.

13. Allow the Automatic Updates function to find and install all of the patches, security updates, new drivers, and other updated software as it becomes available. You can specify either an automatic download or a request for a manual download.

14. Install your antivirus and antispyware utilities. If you don't already have programs on disks, you can download a free Windows antispyware program from www.microsoft.com/downloads. Free antivirus programs (for non-commercial home users only) are available from http://free.grisoft.com, www.free-av.com, www.avast.com/eng/avast_4_home.html, and www.clamwin.com.

15. If you used the Files And Settings Transfer Wizard to save your configuration, run it again now to restore your old settings.

16. If you didn't use the Transfer Wizard in Step 15, open the Control Panel from the Start menu and set the properties for your mouse, printer, scanner, sounds and audio devices, and other peripheral devices. Each of these shortcuts opens a Properties window that shows all of the options and settings for a specific type of device.

17. If you didn't use the Files And Settings Transfer Wizard, open the Taskbar and Start menu Properties window from the Control Panel to customize your Start menu. Open the Display shortcut to customize the appearance of your desktop.

18. If you are running a full Windows installation from scratch, install your other utilities and application programs.

Using a Windows Recovery CD or a Hidden Partition

Many major computer manufacturers supply a recovery disk instead of a full copy of Windows XP with their products. Unlike the full Microsoft Windows package, a recovery disk can restore the version of Windows that was on the computer when it was shipped from the factory, including all of the proprietary programs and tweaks supplied by the manufacturer (whether you want them or not). Still others place the compressed "recovery" or "rescue" files on either a hidden partition on the computer's hard drive or a folder called I386, with a special program that opens the files and restores the operating system to the C: drive.

If the recovery files are stored on the computer's drive, the manufacturer expects you to create your own set of recovery CDs or DVDs. The instructions for making those disks are included somewhere in the printed matter supplied with the computer, but many people ignore those instructions until Windows has already crashed.

Most recovery disks don't offer the choice of a partial repair installation. When you run the recovery program, it completely overwrites the existing Windows installation, including all the updates and service packs, and everything in the registry. If you were able to run the File And Settings Transfer Wizard (described earlier in this chapter), you can use same program to restore your old settings after the recovery program has done its work.

To restore Windows from a recovery disk, place the CD (or DVD) in the drive, and restart the computer. The recovery program should automatically run from the CD and display instructions on your monitor screen for reloading Windows. Once Windows is up and running, remember to run Windows Update and install your security programs before you do anything else.

Computers that use a hidden partition or a rescue folder to recover from a Windows crash don't do much good when solving a disk drive problem that requires either a full reformat or a complete replacement of the drive that contained the recovery files. If you didn't create a set of recovery CDs or DVDs before the system broke down, your only choice is to telephone or e-mail your computer manufacturer's support center and ask for help. Make that call *before* you buy a new drive someplace else. If you have a Dell or a Sony computer, they might send you a new copy of Windows on a CD, or even a whole new hard drive with their version of Windows already installed. Most other manufacturers won't replace the drive unless the computer is still under warranty, but they will provide a true recovery CD upon request, sometimes for a nominal charge. When you call, have as much of the original paperwork (and the CDs) that came with the computer within reach as possible. You may need an invoice or a serial number to convince the support center that your computer is still under warranty. If it's out of warranty, the support center still might want some kind of proof that you're asking about one of its company's products.

Reformatting the Drive

Short of dumping the whole computer or replacing major components, the most extreme form of computer repair is to completely wipe out everything on the C: drive and start over from square one. Reformatting the drive should only be done as a last resort, but if you continue to see the same problems *after* you run a full Windows reinstallation, you can eliminate those problems—along with everything else on the drive—with a reformat.

If the drive you want to format is the only drive in your computer, your best bet is to use your drive manufacturer's installation software. Each manufacturer supplies an installation CD with new drives, and they also make them available online for free download. Most computer manufacturers, however, don't supply hard disk driver CDs, so you will want to download the driver files directly from the disk manufacturer. Even if you have an installation CD, go ahead and download the most recent version, which might include features (such as drivers for the latest Windows service pack) that were not available when the CD was shipped.

To find the name of the drive manufacturer and a web address from which you can download driver files, open the computer case and read the label on the drive.

Use the following steps to use installation software to format your drive:

1. Back up the data from the drive you want to reformat to another storage media, if possible.

2. Use another computer to connect to the drive manufacturer's website. Link to the Support section, and then download the installation software and any other programs or drivers related to Windows XP (or the operating system you plan to install on this drive).

3. Follow the instructions supplied with the installation software to create an installation CD or floppy disk.

4. Place the CD or floppy disk in the appropriate drive, and then restart the computer. The computer should load and start the installation software from the CD or floppy disk.

5. Follow the instructions on the screen to partition and format the drive. In most cases, you will want to accept and use the default settings for the number of partitions and other options.

6. When the installation program is complete and the computer restarts, place your Windows XP CD (or restore CD) in the drive, and restart the computer one more time to load and install Windows on the newly formatted C: drive.

If you have two or more hard drives in your computer, you can use the Windows Drive Management tools to reformat a drive that is not the system drive:

1. Choose **Start ▶ Run**, and type **diskmgmt.msc** in the Open field. The Disk Management window shown in Figure 19-4 will open.

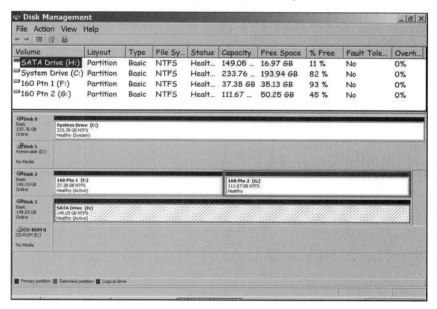

Figure 19-4: Use the Disk Management program to format a nonsystem drive

2. Select the name of the drive you want to format from the graphic display. Don't use the list of physical drives on the left side of the window. The drive you select should be shaded, like Disk 3 in Figure 19-4.

3. If the drive you want to format has two or more one partitions (like Disk 2 in the sample), select one of the partitions and choose **Action ▸ All Tasks ▸ Delete Partition**. If necessary, repeat until the drive has only one partition left.

4. Confirm that the shaded drive is the one you want to format, and choose **Action ▸ All Tasks ▸ Format**.

5. Follow the instructions on the screen to complete the formatting routine.

6. When the formatting program asks if you want to use File Allocation Table (FAT) or NT file system (NTFS) volumes, choose NTFS. FAT formatting is required for some older Windows versions, but NTFS will give you better performance with Windows NT or Windows XP.

7. After formatting is complete, you can either continue to use the newly formatted drive as a nonsystem drive, or you can change the jumper settings on the physical drive to make it the primary master drive and use the procedure earlier in this chapter to install a new copy of Windows from the Microsoft CD or the computer manufacturer's restore CD.

Reformatting a hard drive is a big deal because it destroys all the files on that drive. Running a full reinstall of Windows can be only a little less destructive. But sometimes one or the other is a better approach to problem-solving than trying to examine and repair every file on the drive, one file at a time. If none of the less brutal methods accomplish what you need to do, go ahead and reinstall or reformat, especially if you can salvage your data files first.

Remember, your real objective is to get the computer working again; if you can do that without losing any data, that's fine. The tools and methods in this book will help you fix things most of the time. But when they don't you have better things to do with your life than chasing down a problem that doesn't want to be found.

20

THINGS TO DO NOW, BEFORE YOUR COMPUTER CRASHES

Maintaining your computer is just like any other complex piece of equipment: There are a handful of tedious tasks that you should do on a regular schedule to keep the machine running properly and to avoid major problems. You should change the oil in your car several times a year and replace the filter in your furnace every couple of months, or they won't continue to perform as well as they should. It's the same with a computer. If you don't make backup copies of your data, defragment the hard drive, and run some other preventive maintenance on your computer, its performance will gradually slow down. Eventually, some crucial component may break, taking all your information with it.

You should either perform these preventive maintenance tasks on an automated schedule, or remember to run them manually. Like changing the oil in your car, there's no immediate satisfaction to these tasks, but you know that they need to be done. As those people who sell the expensive sneakers keep saying, "Just Do It"; in the long run, the potential cost of *not* making backups or defragmenting your drive is a lot greater.

Back Up Your Data

It may not happen today or tomorrow, but eventually your hard drive will stop working. Either a mechanical part will wear out, or an electronic component will die, or your computer will be exposed to a massive electric surge, or something else will cause it to fail. Hard drives do not last forever. If you have a laptop or other portable computer, there's still another risk: somebody will steal your computer.

When that happens, you will have one of two reactions: either you will experience a horrible sinking feeling in the pit of your stomach as you try to resuscitate the thing, because it contains all the details of your entire life, all of your business and financial records, and all the work you've done for the last six months; or you will curse briefly, and then go to the place where you stored a backup copy of your data, load the data onto another drive, and get on with your life. There's an obvious lesson here: that lesson is "Back up your data."

There are programs that can read files on damaged drives (see Chapter 16 for more information about those programs) and commercial services that can recover data from almost any dead drive (unless the physical disk platter inside the drive is damaged), but those programs don't always work, and the services often charge hundreds of dollars just to look at the drive and let you know if the data can be saved. The actual recovery can run into several thousand dollars or more. It's a lot easier and safer to keep backup copies of anything you don't want to lose.

There's a lot more information about disaster recovery in Chapter 16. But there's no question that making backups every day or two is the absolute best way to avoid losing data. Even so, most people don't bother unless they work in a place where the boss insists on it; not until they have already suffered through a catastrophic.

People who are serious about backups often make two sets of copies; a daily backup that stays near the computer for convenient access, and a separate weekly set that goes someplace where it will be safe after a major disaster such as a flood or a fire. You might want to store the off-site backups in your safe-deposit box, or maybe in a storage box at the home of a relative or good friend across town.

As you plan your system for making backup copies, you should ask several questions:

- What data should I back up?
- How often should I back up my data?
- What kind of media should I use to store the backup copies?
- What method should I use to make the copies?

What Should I Back Up?

It's almost never necessary to back up absolutely everything on your hard drive. You already have copies of both Windows and the application programs that run on your computer on the CDs and diskettes that were used to distribute the software. When you have to replace a drive, it's almost always easier to reinstall the software from scratch, rather than trying to restore it from a backup. You might have to spend some time changing the configuration settings and options, and downloading patches and updates through the Internet, but in most cases that's not a particularly big deal.

Of course, this assumes that all of the software on your computer came in colorful boxes from commercial sources. It's likely that you're also using some programs and utilities that you downloaded through the Internet and stored on your hard drive. You might even have some programs that you created yourself. If your only copy of a program is on your hard drive, you should either create a set of copies on CDs or other removable media, or make a list of the programs and the web addresses where you can download another copy of each one. You can almost always find the web address for downloadable programs by opening the **File** menu and choosing **About**. Print a couple of copies of the list of downloaded programs, and store them with the backups of your data files.

Data files are much more difficult (if not impossible) to restore from other sources. If the only copy of your novel, your company's accounts, your digital photos and videos, or any other work is on a hard drive, and that drive dies, you're out of luck. The data, and the time it took to create that data, is lost. You should definitely make backups of those files.

Some programs store the data that they create in subfolders within the program folder. For example, your e-mail program probably keeps copies of all the messages that you have sent and received in files and folders stored in the same folder as the software that controls the program itself. So you can't ignore the subfolders that Windows stores within the Program Files folder when you're backing up your system. You should look at each program folder and make sure there aren't data files inside. Most backup programs include a list of all the files on each drive, and a method for selecting individual files and complete folders for the backup. When you're ready to make your backup, you should step through the list of folders and files and choose the ones you want to copy.

Your rule of thumb should be, "When in doubt, back it up." It's a lot better to have a backup copy of a file you never use than to skip a file that turns out to have been essential after your drive has failed.

And don't forget your laptop computer. For many of us, the laptop has replaced the notebook or the yellow legal pad as the place where we store notes, memos, and other essential information. Because laptop computers are attractive targets for thieves, you should back up your data as frequently as it is practical to do so. Maybe not every day, but whenever you come home from a trip or an important meeting. If you're on the road, think about sending copies of important documents, notes, and files to yourself via e-mail on a regular schedule.

How Often Should I Back Up My Data?

How many days of data can you afford to lose? Your backup schedule will depend on how important you consider your data and other files to be. If the files are absolutely essential to the conduct of your business, you should make backups at the end of every business day, or even more frequently. On the other hand, if the drive contains data that you can reconstruct from other sources, it could be safe to make backups only once every week—or even less often than that.

And of course, there's no rule that says you have to create your backups on a formal schedule. If you're working on an important project such as a thesis or the manuscript of a book, or if you have just uploaded some irreplaceable photographs from your digital camera, you should make a backup at the end of each work day.

What Kind of Media?

It doesn't really matter what type of storage media you use to hold your backed-up files, as long as you have a convenient way to read those files. If your computer has a CD or a DVD drive that can record onto blank disks, that's an excellent choice—recordable CDs and DVDs are cheap, easy to read, and they have a relatively large capacity. Other recordable media, such as Zip disks or tape, will also work, but the devices required to read them are less common, and the storage media are more expensive. Remember, you're preparing for a worst-case disaster in which your own computer has been stolen or damaged beyond repair, so you shouldn't choose media that use an obscure storage type that will be difficult or impossible to read when you have to retrieve your data.

An external drive that connects to the computer through a USB or FireWire port is another practical storage alternative. Tape drives, hard drives, and recordable CDs are all available in external packages with USB and FireWire connections.

Storing your backup data on another computer is still another alternative. Making copies from one computer to another through a network can be fast and convenient, but remember that you're making the backups to protect against a major disaster. If the backup computer is in the same building as the original, it's possible that a fire, earthquake, or lightning strike would destroy both machines at the same time. And a burglar who discovers two computers in the same room will probably take both of them.

What Backup Method?

The least complicated way to back up your data is simply to use Windows Explorer to copy them from the hard drive to the backup storage media. It may be easy, but it's also tedious: you'll have to copy each folder and file separately. This process consumes a lot of time, and they take a lot of space on the storage media because the backed-up files and folders aren't compressed.

A dedicated backup program, or a program that creates an image of the whole drive, is the better approach. Microsoft has included a backup utility with Windows XP, but if you're using an earlier version, you'll have to find one from another source. Symantec's Norton Ghost product is widely distributed through retail software channels, and several other backup programs are available as try-before-you-buy shareware. The Tucows website (www.tucows.com/downloads/Windows/IS-IT/FileManagement/BackupRestore/) offers links and ratings for a long list of these programs.

To use the Backup Utility in Windows XP, follow these steps:

1. From the Windows desktop, open **My Computer**.

2. Right-click the icon for the drive you want to back up, and choose **Properties** from the pop-up menu.

3. Open the **Tools** tab and click the **Backup Now** button. The Backup Utility will open.

4. Open the Backup tab to open the window shown in Figure 20-1.

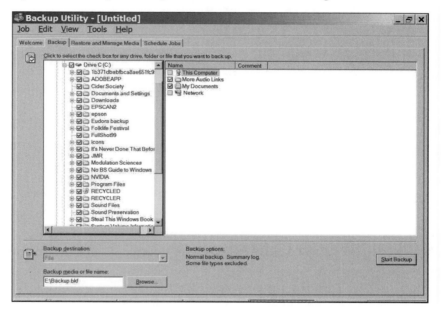

Figure 20-1: Use the Backup Utility to back up your hard drive in Windows XP.

5. Use the tree structure to find and select each of the files and folders that you want to include in this backup. Click the + symbol next to each drive or folder name to expand the list of its contents.

6. Use the **Browse** button at the bottom of the window to choose a location where you want to store the backup file.

7. Click the **Start Backup** button at the lower-right corner of the window. The program will copy your files to the location that you have specified.

8. When the backup is complete, remove the storage media that holds the backup, and place it in a secure location.

To restore the backed-up data, open the Backup Utility and follow these steps:

1. Connect or load the media that holds the backed-up data to your computer.

2. Open the Backup Utility, and select the **Restore And Manage Media** tab shown in Figure 20-2.

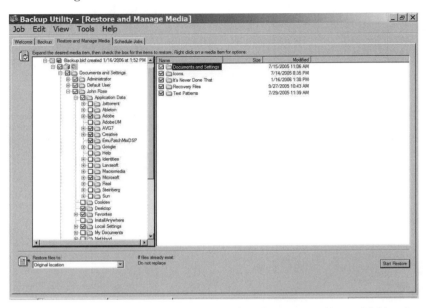

Figure 20-2: Use the Restore And Manage Media tab to recover files and folders from your backup.

3. Expand the backup tree structure to find and select the file or folder you want to restore.

4. Use the drop-down Restore Files To menu to choose the location where you want the place the restored data.

5. Click the **Start Restore** button.

Defragment Your Hard Drives

To understand why you must defragment your hard drives, it's useful to know something about how a hard drive stores information. When you write a string of data onto a disk, Windows finds space on the disk that doesn't already contain data. On a new drive, most of the disk is empty, so it's easy to write a large file or other string of data in a blank area on the disk. But when you delete a file, the drive returns the space that the file had occupied to its "bank" of space available for new files.

However, the next file that you try to store might be bigger than the amount of space available in any single block. So the computer breaks the file into smaller pieces, called *fragments*, and stores each fragment in a different location on the disk. This is known as *fragmentation*. On a severely fragmented drive, a single file might be split into a dozen or more pieces. When the computer retrieves a fragmented file, it must reassemble the pieces before it can load the file into a program, so a fragmented file can take a lot longer to load than a file that's all in one place on the drive.

Keep in mind that Windows is constantly reading and writing temporary files and other data to the hard drive, so your computer will gradually become more and more fragmented, even if you don't ever delete a permanent file. Over time, a drive that was zipping along when it was new will seem to take longer and longer to store and retrieve data, and your computer's overall performance will become sluggish. Depending on the size of your drive and the amount of activity, you might not notice a difference for six months or more—but it's happening, and you should take steps to prevent it.

A defragmenting program reassembles each file into a single block, and it creates the largest possible blocks of free space to allow room for new files without splitting them into fragments. Some more sophisticated defragmenters also position the programs on the drives that are used most often close to the inside part of the disk. This allows the drive to find them more quickly than other files that you don't use as often.

Windows includes a perfectly adequate defragmentation program, but several other software vendors offer programs that do the same task more quickly or efficiently. If you have one of the general-purpose utility suites such as Norton System Works, you can use the defrag program included in that package instead of the Windows utility, but if you don't have other software, the Windows program is good enough for most users. For a stand-alone defragmenter with an excellent graphic display, take a look at O&O Defrag from O&O Software (www.oo-software.com/en/products/oodefrag/). Diskeeper (www.diskeeper.com) is another well-regarded program.

Defragmenting a modern hard drive with a huge amount of space on it can take several hours or more, and it's not practical to try to do any other work on the same computer while that operation is in progress. Instead, you might want to run the program overnight, or on a day when you don't plan to use the computer for any other purpose.

If another program adds or deletes data to the drive while a defragmenter is running, the Windows defrag program might start over from the beginning of the drive. Therefore, a defragmenter running on an active drive can take forever to finish the process. You might come back after eight or ten hours and discover that only ten percent of the drive has been defragmented, just because the e-mail program has automatically checked for new mail every ten minutes. To eliminate this problem, turn off as many other programs as possible before you start the defragmenter—use the CTRL-ALT-DELETE command to bring up the Windows Task Manager and shut down all the programs currently running in both foreground and background. If that doesn't solve the problem, shut down Windows and restart in Safe Mode (press the F8 key while Windows reboots and follow the instructions on the screen), and then run the defragmenter program.

To run the Windows defragmenter, follow these steps:

1. From the Windows desktop, open My Computer and right-click the drive you want to defragment.

2. Select **Properties** from the pop-up menu, and choose the **Tools** tab. A dialog box similar to the one in Figure 20-3 will appear. In older versions of Windows, the dialog box will also tell you when each tool was last run.

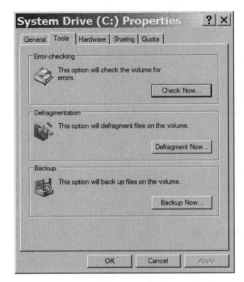

Figure 20-3: Use the Properties window for each drive to defragment that drive.

3. Click the **Defragment Now** button. The Disk Defragmenter will start. If you have installed a third-party defragmenter such as Norton Speed Disk or Diskeeper, that program will run instead of the Microsoft utility. Figure 20-4 shows the Microsoft Disk Defragmenter main screen.

4. Click the **Analyze** button. The program will examine your drive and display the current amount of fragmentation. If the disk is heavily fragmented, the program will recommend that you run the Defragment program.

5. To defragment the disk, click the **Defragment** button. The program will analyze the drive again and then start to defragment the files. This process will take a long time to complete, so you will probably want to do something else for a few hours, or you can leave it to run overnight.

If the defragmenter doesn't seem to be making any progress, confirm that everything else is turned off and try again.

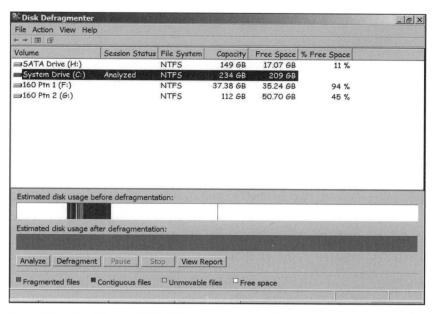

Figure 20-4: The Microsoft Disk Defragmenter shows the current state of each hard drive in your computer.

Check for Other Disk Problems

Fragmentation isn't the only problem that can occur on a hard drive. If a few crucial data bits stored on the drive become corrupted, it may no longer be possible to find or retrieve an entire file. If some *extremely* crucial bits become corrupted, the whole drive could become impossible to read. These errors are caused when Windows shuts down without properly saving open files, but it's also possible for disk errors to occur due to nonspecific bit rot. Chapter 2 of this book includes instructions for recovering from some of these problems after they occur, but you can also take some steps to prevent them.

Sometimes the drive's file system might have an incorrect setting that instructs it to assign more than one filename to data in the same location. Of course, the data at that location belongs in only one file; the second assignment is a mistake called a *cross-linked file error*.

It's also possible for data to exist on a drive, but not in the file system. If the data doesn't have a filename assigned to it, the computer can't read it without special tools. The portions of the drive that contain these orphans are known as *lost clusters* or *lost fragments*.

Modern disk drives are a lot more reliable than the drives that were provided with computers ten or fifteen years ago, but they can still suffer from file system errors. So Windows includes a utility program called Scandisk that examines all the data on a drive and identifies cross-linked files and lost clusters. When the program detects these errors, it can either correct them automatically, or display a list of errors and wait for a separate command to fix them.

Windows automatically runs Scandisk when you turn on the computer after an "improper" shutdown. You can also run it from within Windows by following these steps:

1. From the Windows desktop, double-click the **My Computer** shortcut to open Windows Explorer.
2. Right-click the icon for the drive you want to test. Choose **Properties** from the pop-up menu. The Drive Properties window will open.
3. Select the **Tools** tab in the Properties window. The System Drive Properties dialog box will appear.
4. Click the **Check Now** button in the Error-checking section of the Tools dialog box. The program will offer some options.
5. The options include automatically fixing errors and scanning for bad sectors. These options appear slightly differently in different versions of Windows, but they have the same effect. Turn on the Automatic Fix option, but don't bother scanning for bad sectors. Click the **Start** button to begin the scan.
6. A complete scan will take less than half an hour unless your drive is seriously corrupted. Don't run any other programs while the scan is in progress. Unlike the defragmenter, which you can run and ignore until the job is complete, you should check the computer for error messages every few minutes.

When the Scandisk program finds an error, it will either flag the problem and bring it to your attention, or it will automatically fix it by deleting the cross-linked file or the lost cluster and creating a new text file that contains the data that had been in the deleted file or cluster. It's a good idea to take a look at each of those files after the scan is complete to see if they contain anything you want to keep. The contents will most often be digital gibberish, which you should delete. If there's a useful string of text in one of the salvaged files, copy it to a new text file using a text editor such as WordPad and assign a name that describes its contents.

Create a Set of Utility Disks

Normally, your computer uses the files on your system drive to start Windows, but when your system drive fails (or the Windows files become corrupted), you'll have to use software from a CD, a floppy disk, or another source to start the computer. The time to make those disks is now, *before* you need them.

Make a Restore Disk

Whether you have a copy of Windows XP in the original Microsoft package or a restore CD that came with your computer, you can use the startup files on that CD to reinstall Windows. However, if your computer came with restore files in a folder or a hidden partition on the hard drive, you might have a serious problem if the drive breaks down. You must make your own restore disk *before* the hard drive fails.

When you unpacked the computer, the instructions for assembling the system and starting Windows probably included a section about making restore disks: almost nobody pays any attention. By that time, your shiny new computer was up and running, and you were exploring all the exciting new bells and whistles that came with it.

Now that you have had plenty of opportunity to ring the bells and blow the whistles, take the time to make your restore disks now. There's probably a command in the Windows menu that will start the process: if you can't find it, look for instructions in the startup guide and other manuals that came with your computer.

Make a Boot Disk

When the system drive won't load Windows, even in Safe Mode, it's often helpful to start the computer from a "boot disk" that loads a simple operating system. You can use this system to examine and evaluate the contents of your drives and possibly create copies of data files that you can use on another computer. If the computer has a floppy disk drive as well as a CD drive, you should make boot disks in both formats.

To create a simple startup diskette (a floppy disk), follow these steps:

1. Insert a floppy disk in the diskette drive.

2. Open **My Computer** from the desktop, and right-click the floppy disk drive. It's almost always the A: drive.

3. In the pop-up menu, click the **Format** command. When the Format window shown in Figure 20-5 appears, check the **Create An MS-DOS Startup Disk** option.

Figure 20-5: Use the Format tool to create an MS-DOS Startup Disk.

4. Click the **Start** button.

If your computer does not have a floppy disk drive, you will need either a boot CD or similar software on some other media that your computer can read, such as a USB flash drive. Your best approach is to find a friend or a colleague whose computer still has a floppy drive (or try the public library), and copy the contents of a boot floppy to a CD.

Windows XP does not provide an easy way to create a boot CD, so you'll have to use a utility from another source:

- Datapol (www.datapol.de/dpe/freeware) offers a free program called NTFS4dos that provides full access to the files on an NTFS drive.

- The Bootdisk.com (www.bootdisk.com) website contains links to startup software for many Windows versions and for other operating systems.

- Free PC Tech offers links to several boot disks, but they're all self-extracting files that write the software to a floppy disk. Go to http://freepctech.com/pc/002/files010.shtml and scroll down the page. After you download a program, run it on a computer with a floppy drive, and then copy the contents of the floppy to a CD.

Scan for Viruses and Spyware

As Chapter 13 discussed, every computer user must take steps to keep viruses, spyware, and other security threats out of their systems.

It's an unfortunate fact that every computer that connects to the Internet will almost certainly become a target for viruses, spyware, and other forms of malevolent software. Security experts report that an unprotected computer will start to receive probes from unwanted intruders within a few minutes after it establishes an Internet link, so it's absolutely essential to use effective tools to find and remove infections that have already installed themselves, and to keep additional nasties away from your system.

In order to keep your computer clear of these potential problems, you must use these tools:

- A firewall to keep unwanted programs and other intruders from gaining access to your computer.

- An antivirus program to inspect incoming e-mail, check file downloads, and block viruses that can destroy data files and consume memory and storage space.

- An antispyware program to detect and block programs that can hijack e-mail clients, web browsers, and other Internet services.

- All of the security patches and service packs released by Microsoft and other software vendors that apply to the programs installed on your computer.

If you don't already have a firewall, an antivirus program, and an antispyware program installed on your computer, do it now. Make sure the automatic update features are active.

Get Rid of the Dust

One more form of preventive maintenance is often overlooked. Over time, most computers are likely to accumulate dust and other crud inside the case. Unlike the dust bunnies under your sofa, the ones inside the computer are more than just an aesthetic disaster.

Excess heat is a common cause of damage to the CPU and other electronic components inside computers. The parts that produce the most heat usually have fans or other cooling devices attached to them, and the ventilation holes and fan in the case pull the hot air out and cooler outside air in. But if a blanket of accumulated dust insulates the components from the moving air, the heat might not have a way to escape. Therefore, keeping the inside of your computer clean can also extend its life.

The same intake and exhaust fans that are supposed to move a stream of air through the computer case can also pull airborne dust into the machine, so dust collects on most internal parts whenever the computer is turned on. And if you have a cat or a dog, there's probably a lot of their hair inside the computer, too.

In particular, these parts will run cooler and better when they're clean:

- The motherboard
- The heat sink and the fan on top of the CPU
- The video or graphics adapter
- The memory modules
- The fans in the case, the power supply, and any plug-in cards mounted on the motherboard
- The hard drives

There's no need to become a fanatic about dust inside the computer, but you should open it up and remove the dust several times each year. A small vacuum cleaner (or a larger one with a small hose) is the best tool for the job because it will provide a place for the dust to go, but a compressed air hose or a soft brush will also work. Be sure to turn off the computer before you start poking around inside, and don't use a metal tool that could create short circuits or damage a fragile component.

In addition to the obvious dust collectors on the motherboard and other electronic circuit boards, remember to clean the large flat surfaces on top of the hard drives and the sleeves and finger guards around all the fans.

If your computer has a tower cabinet, dust has probably settled on the floor of the case, so you should clean that area as well as the internal components. If you're using a desktop cabinet, blow a shot of compressed air into the space between the motherboard and the bottom of the case; reaching underneath the motherboard with a brush or a vacuum hose is not worth the trouble.

Some computers, including many laptop models, have metal screens or mesh filters over the ventilation holes where the air enters the case. These screens can capture airborne dust before it gets into the computer, but as the dust collects on the screen, it reduces the amount of air that can flow through the screen and into the computer. This can allow the internal components to overheat. Use a vacuum, an air hose, or a soft brush to remove the dust from each screen or filter.

Clean Your Screen

A dirty monitor screen won't break down any sooner than a clean one, but it's harder to see the information on the screen through all the crud. If your monitor has a glass screen, use a household glass cleaner spray and a soft cloth to clean it; if it has a flat-panel screen, use a soft brush or a soft dry cloth.

As I said at the start of this chapter, all of this maintenance is easy to ignore because it's tedious and time-consuming, and it doesn't provide any kind of instant gratification after you've done it. But it's worth the time and trouble; losing the contents of your hard drive to a disk failure or other disaster can ruin your entire day. Indeed, if the information stored in your computer is important enough, losing it could destroy your business.

A

DEVICE MANAGER ERROR CODES AND BIOS POST BEEP CODES

This appendix contains explanations of the numbered error codes produced by the Windows XP Device Manager and the beep codes produced by the three major BIOS manufacturers' power-on self tests (POSTs).

Windows XP Device Manager Error Codes

To view an error code, open the Device Manager (right-click **My Computer ▶ Properties ▶ Hardware** tab ▶ **Device Manager**) and double-click the name of a device with a yellow exclamation point (!) or a red X superimposed on the icon at the left of the device name.

The Properties window for each device driver includes several tabs. If an error condition applies to this device, the Device Status section of the General tab contains an Error Code and message.

The General tab also includes a Troubleshoot . . . button that opens a troubleshooter with specific information about the current device. In most cases, the specific steps listed in this appendix will solve a problem more quickly than stepping through a troubleshooter, but the troubleshooter might offer one or more alternative solutions to the problem.

Code numbers that are missing from this sequence do not apply to Windows XP. If you're using an older Windows version and you see a code number that is not included here, look at Article No. 310123 in the Microsoft Knowledge Base, or search the entire knowledge base for "Code XX," using the code number in place of the XX.

Code 1

This device is not configured correctly. (Code 1)

The drivers for this device are missing, or the configuration options are incorrect. Click the **Update Driver** button to reinstall the device driver.

Code 3

The driver for this device might be corrupted, or your system may be running low on memory or other resources. (Code 3)

Several unrelated problems can produce this error code. First, try uninstalling and reinstalling the driver:

1. Close the Properties window for this device.
2. Right-click the name of the device in the Device Manager.
3. Choose **Uninstall** from the pop-up menu.
4. When the uninstall is complete, open the **Action** menu and select **Scan For Hardware Changes**.

If reinstalling the driver doesn't solve the problem, you probably have too little memory installed in this computer. As a temporary fix, try changing the memory usage settings:

1. Open the System Properties window (**Start ▶ Settings ▶ Control Panel ▶ System**) and choose the Advanced tab.
2. In the Performance box, click the **Settings** button.
3. In the Performance Options window, choose the **Advanced** tab.
4. Change the active setting in the Memory Usage box from Programs to System Cache.
5. Click **OK** to save your changes and close all the open windows.

Adjusting the memory usage might solve the immediate problem, but you should seriously consider installing more RAM. This error code is a strong indication that you can improve the computer's overall speed and performance by adding another memory module.

Code 10

If the Windows Registry listing for this device includes a FailReasonString in its hardware key, the Device Manager will use that string as the error message. If not, the Device Manager uses this generic error message:

This device cannot start. (Code 10)

A Code 10 error occurs when the device failed to start. Try updating or reinstalling the device driver, and restart the computer.

Code 12

This device cannot find enough free resources that it can use. If you want to use this device, you will need to disable one of the other devices on this system. (Code 12)

A Code 12 error occurs when two or more devices are trying to use the same Input/Output (I/O) port, the same interrupt, or the same Direct Memory Access (DMA) channel. To identify the conflict, follow these steps:

1. In the Device Manager, open the **View** menu and select the **Resources By Connection** option.
2. Open the Direct Memory Access (DMA), Input/Output (I/O), and Interrupt Request (IRQ) listings and look for the device that produced the Code 12 error. You should see one or more additional devices in the same listing with the same DMA, I/O, or IRQ number.
3. Double-click the name of one of the conflicting devices to open a Properties window, and choose the **Resources** tab.
4. If it's not grayed out, remove the checkmark from the Use Automatic Settings option and click the **Change Setting . . .** button.
5. Change the value to a new setting that does not conflict with any other device.
6. If it's not possible to change the resource value, open the **General** tab and disable the conflicting device.

Code 14

This device cannot work properly until you restart your computer. (Code 14)

Close and save any active programs, and then restart the computer (**Start ▶ Turn Off Computer ▶ Restart**).

Code 16

Windows cannot identify all the resources this device uses. (Code 16)

Code 16 errors occur when the device configuration is not complete. To assign additional resources to this device, follow these steps:

1. Double-click the name of the device in the Device Manager, and select the **Resources** tab.
2. Look in the list of Resource Settings for a question mark next to the name of a resource.
3. Select the item with a question mark and click the **Change Setting . . .** button. If that button is grayed out, turn off the Use Automatic Settings option.

If the device that produced the error is not a plug-and-play device, you won't see an Automatic Settings option. It may be necessary to use some other method to change its configuration, and the procedure should be described in the manual supplied with the device. If the manual is not available, contact the device manufacturer's technical support center for instructions.

Code 18

Reinstall the drivers for this device. (Code 18)

Error Code 18 appears when Windows is unable to read the device driver. To solve the problem, follow these steps:

1. Right-click the name of the device in the Device Manager and choose **Uninstall** from the pop-up menu.
2. Open the **Action** menu and choose the **Scan For Hardware Changes** option to reinstall the device driver you just uninstalled.

If the same error code appears again, right-click the name of the device, and then choose **Update Driver** from the pop-up menu.

Code 19

Windows cannot start this hardware device because its configuration information (in the registry) is incomplete or damaged. To fix this problem you can first try running a Troubleshooting Wizard (see below). If that does not work, you should uninstall and then reinstall the hardware device. (Code 19)

Code 19 errors are caused by these registry problems:

- Two or more services are defined in the registry for a single device.
- The service subkey has failed to open.
- The service subkey failed to obtain the driver name.

Use the following steps to repair a Code 19 error:

1. Starting at the General Properties tab (where you see the error message), click the **Troubleshoot** button. The Troubleshooting Wizard will open.
2. Follow the instructions in the Troubleshooting Wizard.
3. If none of the Troubleshooting Wizard's suggestions solve the problem, close the Properties window and right-click the name of the device in the Device Manager list.
4. From the pop-up menu, choose the **Uninstall** option.
5. Open the **Action** menu in the Device Manager window, and select the **Scan For Hardware Changes** button. Windows will try to find and install a usable copy of the driver you just uninstalled.
6. Restart the computer and immediately press the F8 key repeatedly until the Windows Advanced Options Menu appears.
7. Use the up and down arrow keys to select the **Last Known Good Configuration** option and press the ENTER key.

8. If this procedure does not solve the problem, try to either install a new copy of the device driver from the disk supplied with the device, or download the latest version of the driver from the Internet. See "Where to Find New Drivers" on page 70 for a list of online sources for device drivers.

Code 21

Windows is removing this device. (Code 21)

Code 21 errors are short-term conflicts that occur during the brief period of time when Windows is in the process of uninstalling a device. After the uninstall is complete, the name of the device will no longer appear in the Device Manager list. If the device is still in the list, restart the computer.

Code 22

This device is disabled. (Code 22)

Error Code 22 indicates that the device was disabled by a user at some time in the past. The icon next to the name of a disabled device has a red X over the image. To enable the device, follow these steps:

1. Right-click the name of the device in the Device Manager list.
2. Choose **Enable** from the pop-up menu.

Code 24

This device is not present, is not working properly, or does not have all its drivers installed. (Code 24)

Code 24 errors appear when Windows is unable to detect a device. This can happen when a hardware device is not working properly, the power switch is turned off, the device driver software is damaged, or the device driver version doesn't match the hardware.

To solve the problem, try uninstalling and reinstalling the device. If that doesn't work, run the Troubleshoot Wizard from the General tab of the device's Properties window.

Code 28

The drivers for this device are not installed. (Code 28)

This error appears when Windows detects a device but can't find the device drivers. To install the drivers, choose the Driver tab in the device's Properties window, and click the **Update Driver** button.

Code 29

This device is disabled because the firmware of the device did not give it the required resources. (Code 29)

Some hardware devices (such as video display adapters) have *firmware* (software code stored on a read-only memory chip) that can become corrupted. If a Code 29 error appears, follow the instructions provided by the hardware manufacturer to reinstall or update the firmware. If there's nothing in the manual supplied with the device, check the manufacturer's website or call its tech support center.

Code 31

This device is not working properly because Windows cannot load the drivers required for this device. (Code 31)

A Code 31 error indicates yet another sort of problem with the device driver. Either the device driver software is not compatible with the current Windows release, or you have installed the wrong device driver.

To fix a Code 31 problem, follow these steps:

1. Download the most recent device driver version from Microsoft or directly from the device manufacturer (see "Where to Find New Drivers" on page 70 for sources).

2. Select the name of the device in the Device Manager window and select **Update Driver** from the Action menu.

3. When the Hardware Update Wizard window shown in Figure A-1 appears, select the **Install From A List Or Specific Location** option, and then click the **Next** button.

Figure A-1: To solve a Code 31 error, run the Hardware Update Wizard.

4. Use the **Browse** button to specify the location where you stored the downloaded device driver file. Click the **Next** button.

5. Continue to work through the Hardware Update Wizard to finish installing the new driver.

If the Code 31 error continues to appear, it's possible that the device in question is not compatible with Windows XP. Look in the device maker's website or the Microsoft Knowledge Base for more information.

Code 32

A driver (service) for this device has been disabled. An alternate driver may be providing this functionality. (Code 32)

This error occurs when the Start Type setting for this device driver in the Windows Registry is disabled. To restore this device, follow these steps:

1. Use one of the device driver websites listed in "Where to Find New Drivers" on page 70 to find and download the most recent Windows XP device driver file for this device.

2. Right-click the name of the device in the Device Manager and select the **Uninstall** option.

3. When the uninstall is complete, open the **Action** menu, and then choose **Scan For Hardware Changes**. Windows will find the device and reinstall the device drivers. Use the **Install From A Specific Location** option to specify the driver version that you obtained from the manufacturer's website.

Code 33

Windows cannot determine which resources are required for this device. (Code 33)

Code 33 errors are hardware problems. The translator that specifies the resources used by Windows to use the device has failed. Try uninstalling and reinstalling the device driver. If that doesn't fix the problem, confirm that the hardware configuration settings are correct, or replace the device.

Code 34

Windows cannot determine the settings for this device. Consult the documentation that came with this device and use the Resource tab to set the configuration. (Code 34)

Code 34 errors occur when a hardware device that requires manual configuration is not set correctly. Some devices use jumpers or switches, while others use on-board firmware; consult the manual supplied with the device for specific instructions.

Other devices require manual setting of the resource settings that they use to exchange commands and data with the computer's central processor. Open the device's Properties window from the Device Manager and select the Resources tab to change those settings.

Code 35

Your computer's system firmware does not include enough information to properly configure and use this device. To use this device, contact your computer manufacturer to obtain a firmware or BIOS update. (Code 35)

This error code appears when the BIOS on the computer's motherboard does not recognize the device because it is not listed in the Multiprocessor System (MPS) table within the BIOS. To solve this problem, you must update the BIOS firmware. Chapter 8 of this book explains how to obtain and install a BIOS update.

In a few rare instances, the most recent BIOS version won't recognize a very new device type. If that happens, the device won't work with that computer. Your only choices are to find a different device that does the same job, or wait for a new BIOS update.

Code 36

This device is requesting a PCI interrupt but is configured for an ISA interrupt (or vice versa). Please use the computer's system setup program to reconfigure the interrupt for this device. (Code 36)

A Code 36 error will appear when an interrupt request (IRQ) fails because the BIOS is set to recognize the wrong type of interrupt. Restart the computer and change the BIOS setting. The manual supplied with your computer or motherboard should include information about changing BIOS settings.

Code 37

Windows cannot initialize the device driver for this hardware. (Code 37)

This error occurs when the DriverEntry routine in a device driver returns a failure indication. To solve the problem, uninstall the device, and then choose **Scan For Hardware** from the Action menu in the device Properties window.

Code 38

Windows cannot load the device driver for this hardware because a previous instance of the device driver is still in memory. (Code 38)

A Code 38 error occurs when Windows fails to clear the device driver after the device has been shut down. To clear the problem, restart your computer.

Code 39

Windows cannot load the device driver for this hardware. The driver may be corrupted or missing. (Code 39)

This error code appears when Windows is unable to read a driver. To solve the problem, follow these steps:

1. Right-click the name of the driver and select **Uninstall** from the pop-up menu.
2. Open the **Action** menu in the Device Manager and choose the **Scan For Hardware Changes** option. Windows will try to reinstall the device driver.
3. If the problem continues, install a new copy of the device driver from the disk supplied with the device, or download a new driver from the manufacturer's website. See "Where to Find New Drivers" on page 70 for a list of links to device driver download sites.

Code 40

Windows cannot access this hardware because its service key information in the registry is missing or recorded incorrectly. (Code 40)

A Code 40 error appears when the service subkey for this device in the Windows registry is not valid. To fix the problem, uninstall the driver and use the Scan For Hardware Changes command in the Device Manager's Action menu to reinstall it.

Code 41

Windows successfully loaded the device driver for this hardware but cannot find the hardware device. (Code 41)

A Code 41 error occurs when Windows loads a device driver, but it is unable to find the device itself. This can only happen with non–plug-and-play devices. The device might be missing or turned off, or the device driver could be missing or damaged.

To solve this problem, follow these steps:

1. Confirm that the device is in place, that it is connected firmly to the computer, and that the power is on.
2. Right-click the name of the device in the Windows Device Manager and choose the **Uninstall** option from the pop-up menu.
3. Download a new copy of the most recent device driver for this device from the manufacturer's website.
4. Open the **Action** menu in the Device Manager and choose **Scan For Hardware Changes**.
5. When the Wizard detects the device, instruct it to use the version of the device driver that you downloaded in Step 3.
6. If Windows does not automatically detect the device, open the Windows Control Panel, choose **Printers And Other Hardware**, and click **Add Hardware** in the See Also list on the left side of the window (in Classic View, go directly to **Add Hardware**). The Add Hardware Wizard should detect the device and reinstall the driver.

Code 42

Windows cannot load the device driver for this hardware because there is a duplicate device already running in the system. (Code 42)

A Code 42 error indicates that Windows has detected two or more instances of the same device. Either the device driver has created two children with the same name, or Windows has found devices with identical serial numbers in two different locations.

To fix this problem, restart your computer.

Code 43

Windows has stopped this device because it has reported problems. (Code 43)

A Code 43 error occurs when the device relays a trouble message to Windows through the device driver. Consult the hardware manual supplied with this device, or contact the device manufacturer's technical support center for information about clearing this problem.

Code 44

An application or service has shut down this hardware device. (Code 44)

Code 44 appears when the device has been shut down by a software command. To restore this device, restart the computer.

Code 45

Currently, this hardware device is not connected to the computer. (Code 45)

This error code appears when the device (which had previously been active) is not connected to the computer, when the power on an external device is turned off, or when the power to the device is disconnected.

To fix the problem, reconnect the device to the computer. If it's an external device, check the power switch and the power cable; if it's an internal device, make sure the card is firmly inserted into the motherboard, or confirm that the data and power connectors are in place on both the device and the motherboard.

Code 46

Windows cannot gain access to this hardware device because the operating system is in the process of shutting down. (Code 46)

This error appears during Windows shutdown. Let the shutdown continue; the device should work when you start the computer again.

Code 47

Windows cannot use this hardware device because it has been prepared for safe removal, but it has not been removed from the computer. (Code 47)

A Code 47 error appears when a user has used the Safe Removal command on a removable device (such as a PCMCIA card, a docking station, or certain USB devices), or the user has pushed a physical Eject button. To clear this condition, either remove and replace the device from its socket or dock, or restart the computer.

Code 48

The software for this device has been blocked from starting because it is known to have problems with Windows. Contact the hardware vendor for a new driver. (Code 48)

A Code 48 error indicates that the device driver is not compatible with the current version of Windows. To solve the problem, contact the device manufacturer's technical support center.

Code 49

Windows cannot start new hardware devices because the system hive is too large (exceeds the Registry Size Limit). (Code 49)

This is a rare error condition that occurs when the Windows Registry contains too many entries. It's possible that the Registry still includes listings for devices that are no longer connected to the computer.

To fix the problem, expand all of the top-level entries in the Device Manager and look for hardware devices that you no longer use. Right-click the name of each of these devices, and then select the **Uninstall** option from the pop-up menu. If that doesn't clear the error condition, reinstall Windows from the distribution CD.

POST Beep Codes

These lists of beep codes are taken from the BIOS manufacturer's specification documents. For more detailed information about BIOS POST error codes, consult the documents identified as the "Source" of each list of beep codes.

Table A-1: AwardBIOS Beep Codes

Number of Beeps	Error Message	Explanation
1 long, 2 short	Video adapter error	Either the video adapter is bad or it is not seated properly, or the monitor cable is loose.

"The only AwardBIOS beep code indicates that a video error has occurred and the BIOS cannot initialize the video screen to display any additional information. This beep code consists of a single long beep followed by two short beeps. Any other beeps are probably RAM (Random Access Memory) problems."

Source: AwardBIOS Error Messages (www.phoenix.com/en/ Customer+Services/BIOS/AwardBIOS/Award+Error+Codes.htm)

Table A-2: PhoenixBIOS Beep Codes

Beeps	Description
1-2-2-3	BIOS ROM Checksum
1-3-1-1	Test DRAM refresh
1-3-1-3	Test 8742 Keyboard Controller
1-3-4-1	RAM failure
1-3-4-3	RAM failure
1-4-1-1	RAM failure
2-1-2-3	Check ROM copyright notice
2-2-3-1	Test for unexpected interrupts
1 long, 2 short	Checksum failure

Source: PhoenixBIOS 4.0 Release 6.0; POST Tasks and Beep Codes (www.phoenix.com/NR/rdonlyres/81E6C43C-93BD-4097-A9C4-62F05AAD6025/0/biospostcode.pdf)

Table A-3: AMIBIOS Beep Codes

Number of Beeps	Error Message	Troubleshooting Action
1 short	Memory refresh timer error	Reseat the memory, or replace with known good modules.
2 short	Parity error in base memory	Reseat the memory, or replace with known good modules.
3 short	Base memory read/write test error	Reseat the memory, or replace with known good modules.
4 short	Motherboard timer failure	These are all fatal error messages that indicate a serious problem with the system. Consult your system manufacturer. Before declaring the motherboard beyond all hope, eliminate the possibility of interference by a malfunctioning add-in card. Remove all expansion cards except the video adapter. • If beep codes are generated when all other expansion cards are absent, consult your system manufacturer's technical support. • If beep codes are not generated when all other expansion cards are absent, one of the add-in cards is causing the malfunction. Insert the cards back into the system one at a time until the problem happens again. This will reveal the malfunctioning card.
5 short	Processor error	
6 short	Gate A20 test failure	
7 short	General exception error	
8 short	Display memory error	If the system video adapter is an add-in card, replace or reseat the video adapter. If the video adapter is an integrated part of the system board, the board may be faulty.
9 short	ROM checksum error	See Troubleshooting Action for 4–7 short
10 short	CMOS shutdown register read/write error	
11 short	Cache memory test failed	
1 long	POST has passed all tests	n/a

Source: AMIBIOS8 Check Point and Beep Code List, Version 1.71
(www.ami.com/support/doc/AMIBIOS-codes.pdf)

B

FREE AND INEXPENSIVE SECURITY PROGRAMS FOR WINDOWS XP

This appendix contains pointers to online sources for utility programs that provide antivirus, antispyware, and other forms of protection for computers running Windows XP. At a bare minimum, every Windows user should install and use an antivirus program, an antispyware utility, and a firewall.

Antivirus Programs

These free programs are generally for private, noncommercial, single-home use only. Businesses, nonprofit organizations, and others who don't qualify for the free license may order a paid copy through the developers' websites.

For links to other antivirus programs, including many that are available as try-before-you-buy downloads, see the list of Microsoft Partners at www.microsoft.com/security/partners/antivirus.asp.

AVG Anti-Virus Free Edition
http://free.grisoft.com

avast! Home Edition
www.avast.com/eng/download-avast-home.html

AntiVir Personal Edition
www.free-av.com

ClamWin Free Antivirus
www.clamwin.com

Vcatch
www.vcatch.com

Antispyware Programs

Microsoft Windows AntiSpyware
www.microsoft.com/athome/security/spyware/software/default.mspx

Lavasoft Ad-Aware SE
www.lavasoft.de/ms/index.htm

Spybot Search & Destroy
www.safer-networking.org/microsoft.en.html

SpywareBlaster
www.javacoolsoftware.com/spywareblaster.html

Firewall Programs

For most users, the firewall software supplied with Windows XP Service Pack 2 should be enough to keep intruders out of their computers. But a second hardware or software firewall can provide added protection.

ZoneAlarm
www.zonelabs.com

KerioPersonal Firewall
www.kerio.com/kpf_download.html

INDEX

USB (Universal Serial Bus)
  drives, 182–183
  troubleshooting, 202
Usenet. *See* newsgroups
user manuals, 18–19
utility disks, 73, 240–242

V

viruses, 34, 134–135, 242
voltmeter, 10

W

websites
  links to drivers, 70–71
  spyware/adware removal
      programs, 137–138
  startup item explanation, 51–52
wide area network (WAN),
      146–147, 152–153
Windows kernel, 42
Windows Product Activation,
      171–174
Windows Recovery CD, 227–228
Windows Registry, 107–109
  cleaning up, 114–116
  organization of, 110–111
  Registry Editor, using, 109–114
Windows, reinstalling, 225–227
Windows Update, 70
worms, 135

Y

Y2K (Year 2000) problem, 106
yellow exclamation mark, 68, 69,
      73, 92
yellow question mark, 56, 167

STEAL THIS® COMPUTER BOOK 4.0
What They Won't Tell You About the Internet

by WALLACE WANG

This offbeat, nontechnical book examines what hackers do, how they do it, and how readers can protect themselves. Informative, irreverent, and entertaining, the completely revised fourth edition of *Steal This Computer Book* contains new chapters that discuss the hacker mentality, lock picking, exploiting P2P file sharing networks, and how people manipulate search engines and pop-up ads. Includes a CD with hundreds of megabytes of hacking and security-related programs that tie in to each chapter of the book.

MAY 2006, 384 PP. W/CD, $29.95 ($38.95 CDN)
ISBN 1-59327-105-0

THE eBAY SURVIVAL GUIDE
How to Make Money and Avoid Losing Your Shirt

by MICHAEL BANKS

This no-holds-barred guide to safe and successful buying and selling on eBay reveals the strategies of winning bidders and offers tips for beating competitors to get the items you want—without overpaying or becoming the victim of scams. Filled with practical advice for avoiding frauds, what to do if an item doesn't sell, how to list items effectively, choosing an auction type, how to get the best price, and much more. An excellent resource for anyone looking to steer clear of scammers, execute successful transactions, and win good stuff!

SEPTEMBER 2005, 288 PP., $19.95 ($26.95 CDN)
ISBN 1-59327-063-1

THE CULT OF iPOD

by LEANDER KAHNEY

Wired editor and former Wired News reporter Leander Kahney follows up his best-selling *The Cult of Mac* with *The Cult of iPod*, a comprehensive look at how Apple's hit iPod is changing music, culture, and listening behavior. *The Cult of iPod* includes the exclusive back story of the iPod's development; looks at the many ways iPod users pay homage to their devices; and investigates the quirkier aspects of iPod culture, such as iPod-jacking (strangers plugging into each other's iPods to discover new music) as well as the growing legions of MP3Js (regular folks who use their iPods to become DJs).

NOVEMBER 2005, 160 PP., $24.95 ($33.95 CDN)
ISBN 1-59327- 066-6

THE BOOK OF™ NERO 7
CD and DVD Burning Made Easy

by WALLACE WANG

Ahead Software's Nero program is the most popular CD and DVD burning software in the world. While it seems like it should be easy to burn CDs and DVDs, doing so can be much more complicated than it appears, and many users reach high frustration levels after burning multiple coasters that don't work. This simple, task-oriented, step-by-step book covers the entire Nero program suite, including audio CD burning, data backup, managing photos, DVD video burning, designing CD/DVD labels, editing sound, creating virtual drives and CD/DVD data disks, and playing audio and video. This update to the bestseller (nearly 20,000 copies sold) has been completely rewritten to focus on the tasks that most people perform with Nero 7.

JUNE 2006, 216 PP., $24.95 ($32.95 CDN)
ISBN 1-59327-110-7

VISUAL BASIC 2005 EXPRESS: NOW PLAYING

by WALLACE WANG

A beginner's guide to Visual Basic 2005 Express, with a twist—short movies on the CD show exactly how to write programs. *Visual Basic 2005 Express: Now Playing* provides a short primer on how programming works in general, and then, once readers understand the basic principles behind computer programming, teaches how to use the Visual Basic Express program itself and how to write programs using the Visual Basic language. One CD includes numerous short source code examples that readers can run and modify, and movies that show how to accomplish specific tasks with Visual Basic 2005 Express; the other CD contains a full version of Visual Basic 2005 Express.

MARCH 2006, 480 PP. W/2 CDS, $29.95 ($38.95 CDN)
ISBN 1-59327-059-3

PHONE:
800.420.7240 OR
415.863.9900
MONDAY THROUGH FRIDAY,
9 A.M. TO 5 P.M. (PST)

FAX:
415.863.9950
24 HOURS A DAY,
7 DAYS A WEEK

EMAIL:
SALES@NOSTARCH.COM

WEB:
WWW.NOSTARCH.COM

MAIL:
NO STARCH PRESS
555 DE HARO ST, SUITE 250
SAN FRANCISCO, CA 94107
USA

Electronic Frontier Foundation
Defending Freedom in the Digital World

Free Speech. Privacy. Innovation. Fair Use. Reverse Engineering. If you care about these rights in the digital world, then you should join the Electronic Frontier Foundation (EFF). EFF was founded in 1990 to protect the rights of users and developers of technology. EFF is the first to identify threats to basic rights online and to advocate on behalf of free expression in the digital age.

> ## The Electronic Frontier Foundation Defends Your Rights!
> ## Become a Member Today!
> ## http://www.eff.org/support/

Current EFF projects include:

Protecting your fundamental right to vote. Widely publicized security flaws in computerized voting machines show that, though filled with potential, this technology is far from perfect. EFF is defending the open discussion of e-voting problems and is coordinating a national litigation strategy addressing issues arising from use of poorly developed and tested computerized voting machines.

Ensuring that you are not traceable through your things. Libraries, schools, the government and private sector businesses are adopting radio frequency identification tags, or RFIDs – a technology capable of pinpointing the physical location of whatever item the tags are embedded in. While this may seem like a convenient way to track items, it's also a convenient way to do something less benign: track people and their activities through their belongings. EFF is working to ensure that embrace of this technology does not erode your right to privacy.

Stopping the FBI from creating surveillance backdoors on the Internet. EFF is part of a coalition opposing the FBI's expansion of the Communications Assistance for Law Enforcement Act (CALEA), which would require that the wiretap capabilities built into the phone system be extended to the Internet, forcing ISPs to build backdoors for law enforcement.

Providing you with a means by which you can contact key decision-makers on cyber-liberties issues. EFF maintains an action center that provides alerts on technology, civil liberties issues and pending legislation to more than 50,000 subscribers. EFF also generates a weekly online newsletter, EFFector, and a blog that provides up-to-the minute information and commentary.

Defending your right to listen to and copy digital music and movies. The entertainment industry has been overzealous in trying to protect its copyrights, often decimating fair use rights in the process. EFF is standing up to the movie and music industries on several fronts.

> **Check out all of the things we're working on at http://www.eff.org and join today or make a donation to support the fight to defend freedom online.**

ELECTRONIC FRONTIER FOUNDATION · 454 SHOTWELL STREET · SAN FRANCISCO, CA 94110 · 415.436.9333

COLOPHON

It's Never Done That Before was laid out in Adobe FrameMaker. The font families used are New Baskerville for body text, Futura for headings and tables, and Dogma for titles.

The book was printed and bound at Malloy Incorporated in Ann Arbor, Michigan. The paper is Glatfelter Thor 60# Antique, which is made from 50 percent recycled materials, including 30 percent postconsumer content. The book uses a RepKover binding, which allows it to lay flat when open.

UPDATES

Visit **www.nostarch.com/indtb.htm** for updates, errata, and other information.